Talent in the

How to Attra
Engage Top Talent

EDITED BY ALEX DAVIES

Commissioning editor
Alex Davies

Managing director
Sian O'Neill

Talent in the Legal Profession: How to Attract, Retain, and Engage Top Talent
is published by

Globe Law and Business Ltd
3 Mylor Close
Horsell
Woking
Surrey GU21 4DD
United Kingdom
Tel: +44 20 3745 4770
www.globelawandbusiness.com

Talent in the Legal Profession: How to Attract, Retain, and Engage Top Talent

ISBN 978-1-83723-000-6
EPUB ISBN 978-1-83723-001-3
Adobe PDF ISBN 978-1-83723-002-0

DISCLAIMER
This publication is intended as a general guide only. The information and opinions which it contains are not intended to be a comprehensive study, or to provide legal advice, and should not be treated as a substitute for legal advice concerning particular situations. Legal advice should always be sought before taking any action based on the information provided. The publisher bears no responsibility for any errors or omissions contained herein.

Contents

order to better appeal to young graduates, and what a "career in law" means to those entering the workforce. Comprised of interviews with trainee lawyers and law school graduates, this chapter contains valuable insight for employers on how to appeal to young people entering the industry, and what they can do to retain that talent.

Chapter six, by Caroline Vanovermeire, global director of talent, leadership, and organizational development at Dentsu, and Kathryn Rousin, global director of learning and development at White and Case LLP, focuses on attracting and retaining diverse talent. Who are the underrepresented talent pools we should tap into as law firms? How should we go about attracting them? Are there gender and/or generational differences? How can we increase our appeal to diverse talents? How does employer branding and the internal employee experience play a role in this? The chapter explores how, once they have been successful in attracting diverse talent, law firms and individual leaders can engage and retain them to achieve an authentic, truthful, and inclusive culture and a sustainable, profitable, and future-proofed law firm.

Loyalty, defined as a strong commitment and attachment to an organization, its goals, and its values, may seem like an outdated concept in a fast-changing and competitive world, say the authors of chapter seven. Jean-Baptiste LeBelle, head of HR, and Alice Boullier de Branche, senior HR manager at Allen & Overy look at firm culture and how loyalty can be seen as a source of competitive advantage, as loyal people tend to perform better, stay longer, and advocate for their employer even after leaving the firm. The chapter takes into account the expectations of the new generation, in terms of diversity, purpose, ESG, and values. There are many different aspects of a firm's culture that have an impact on talent retention, including competitive compensation and benefits, opportunities for learning and development, a positive and supportive work environment, and the ability to foster a sense of purpose and alignment, where employees understand and share the vision, mission, and values of the organization, and how their work makes a difference. The culture of a firm is mainly the result of a process of exchanges and role-modeling that leads to the adoption of the same values and behavior at all levels of the organization. It is a virtuous cycle – the firm can build its own culture by rewarding and showcasing role models who exhibit the desired behaviors and not hesitating to sanction inappropriate ones. The chapter looks at how to how to build a firm culture that is attractive and retentive.

In chapter eight, Chrissie Wolfe of LAB Consultancy attempts to define what talent actually is. The law is a nuanced profession that serves many different types of individuals and businesses and the roles of lawyers and legal services providers, not to mention employers, are constantly evolving. On that basis, so too should the definition of talent. What is the purpose of lawyers in the current climate? What will it be in the future? What skills and attributes are required to fulfill that purpose? And with all these questions in mind, where can this talent be found?

Interpersonal relationships are pivotal in today's legal landscape, where the dynamics of work environments are rapidly evolving. Chapter nine by Lara Selem, co-founder of Selem Bertozzi Consulting, sets the stage, emphasizing the importance of interpersonal relationships and firm loyalty in the legal sector. With the shift towards remote working, understanding its impact on interpersonal dynamics becomes crucial, as does mastering effective communication in a virtual era. Lara's chapter addresses the challenges and opportunities of fostering social connections in hybrid models, recognizing that the balance between virtual and in-person interactions is key to maintaining strong team bonds. A significant focus is placed on mental health and wellbeing, acknowledging their critical role in a healthy work environment. The cultivation of a loyal firm culture is explored, highlighting the strategies that can be employed to achieve this. Leadership's role in shaping and reinforcing this culture is examined, underscoring the influence leaders have on firm dynamics. Innovative approaches to team building and engagement are discussed, offering creative solutions to enhance team cohesion. The chapter also confronts the challenges in building firm loyalty, providing insights into overcoming common obstacles. Lara concludes with a future outlook, summarizing the key takeaways and projecting future trends in interpersonal relationships and firm loyalty in the legal profession.

Research has shown that 25 percent of law firm associates plan to leave their current firms within the year. Most law firm associates will "hop" at least once or twice during their first five years. In contrast, consultants at the Big Four consulting/accounting firms stay at their "first firm" for nine-and-a-half years on average. What can law firm leaders glean from these consulting firms? Are law firms willing to implement the proven strategies used by these firms, or will they continue to "churn and burn" associates? In chapter ten, Tea Hoffmann, managing principal at Law Strategy Corp, explores the contrasts between law firms and similar professional service firms and analyzes the long-term strategies utilized to retain talent.

As the practice of law becomes increasingly digitally-enabled, lawyers continue to feel pressure to improve their overall digital literacy and, in some cases, choose to become actual or quasi-technologists. Likewise, law firms and in-house teams have found that offering access to the latest technologies is part of providing the best work experience for their people. In a recent survey conducted in the context of a law firm's global trial of a new generative AI solution, 88 percent of respondents stated that being part of the trial of a cutting edge technology solution made them feel that they were being prepared for the future. In today's ever-evolving legal landscape, the impact of technology on attracting and retaining talent cannot be understated. Chapter 11 by Tara Waters, partner and global chief digital oficer at Ashurst LLP, explores those expectations and impacts, and highlights the opportunities being created for law firms and practitioners alike.

In chapter 12, Rebecca Holdredge and Becky Jo Morgan of Levenfeld Pearlstein, LLC look beyond the bonus, rethinking the approach to motivating legal talent. They first assess the current state of legal talent motivation, including the limitations of traditional financial incentives and the rise in salaries, before examining the shift in professional desires, and looking at how to tailor motivation strategies to individual needs. The chapter looks at the power of non-financial incentives and how people can be empowered through recognition and career growth, and the role of the working environment and business culture. The chapter delves into how emerging departments such as KM and practice operations can motivate talent and looks ahead at how the future of motivation in a law firm might look.

Chapter 13, by Catherine McGregor, independent advisor to law firms and legal departments around the world, looks at how talent and performance can be nurtured in the post-pandemic era. It examines the impact of remote working and how this has affected professional development in both a positive and negative way, before delving into the benefits of a coaching style of delivering feedback and how it can be used in a professional setting. Catherine also explores the differences in feedback that are given to minorities and how biases can be corrected so that all legal talent can be nurtured and developed.

Chapter 14, by Molly Peckman, looks at what partners can do to nurture and reward talent, and why they should care about the cost of a lost associate. Using the acronym HELP, Molly looks at honesty, empathy, listening, and professional development, and demonstrates how all partners could do with a little help from their friends.

In chapter 15, Patrick McKenna draws on his decades of experience in the industry to offer insight into how to keep your best talent engaged in the firm. Patrick maintains that whenever he has asked leaders of high-performing teams what their partners want and what is important to them, he elicits the same four responses, the most important of which is always being able to learn and grow their skills. As a general rule, firm leadership needs to help partners understand that they are in competition with millions of other professionals all over the world, capable of doing the same work that they can do. The sad news is that nobody is owed a career. To continue to be successful you must dedicate yourself to retraining your individual competitive advantage. This chapter prescribes specifically what leaders need to do with their teams and with individual partners to help them rethink how and where to invest some portion of their non-billable time into building and developing their marketable skills.

Succession plans will be impacted throughout the next decade by the retirement of senior law firm partners and a bumper crop of associates seeking new or different work styles. As Baby Boomer lawyers shift out – willingly or not – thinning ranks will be expected to service clients conditioned to have high expectations for speed and results. This is the same class of clients who, already aware of the hollowing out of legal talent, have been adding to their in-house departments. They will also be proactive in electing to send outbound work elsewhere and get it done by other means, if and when necessary. Chapter 16, by Heather Suttie, legal market strategy and management consultant, looks at the importance of succession.

About the authors

Alice Boullier de Branche is the senior HR manager of the Paris HR team at Allen & Overy. She graduated from a business school (ESSEC Global BBA) and has a Master's degree in Sociology (Paris VII). Alice has been working on HR matters at Allen & Overy for over ten years. She joined A&O to work on training and development, then later specialized in providing human resources support to the fee earners population. She is especially engaged in areas such as performance evaluation, compensation strategies, recruitment, retention, and talent development, as well as diversity and inclusion initiatives.

Serena Brent qualified as an associate in the banking and finance team at Mayer Brown in March 2024. She trained at the firm, completing her other three seats in the corporate, tax, and restructuring departments.

Victoria Cromwell is a solicitor with over 12 years' experience in practice at Addleshaw Goddard and Linklaters, and as a professional support lawyer at Freshfields Bruckhaus Deringer. After private practice, Victoria taught post-graduate law for Kaplan and BPP, and led on the development of BARBRI's SQE courses. As head of new business and account management, Victoria leads on the strategy, creation, and execution of B2B contractual covering law firms, universities, corporate entities (including ALSPs), and government and public sector. Victoria is co-chair of the International Bar Association's Academic and Professional Development Committee and sits on the City of London Law Society (CLLS) training committee. Victoria is committed to improving access to the legal profession, and in 2020 co-founded the Social Welfare Solicitors Qualification Fund with the CLLS and Young Legal Aid Lawyers to support social welfare lawyers to qualify as solicitors to help improve access to justice for the most vulnerable in society.

Having operated in various professional development organizations across the legal sector for over two decades, **Robert Dudley** joined BARBRI in 2015

...s international director, moving into his current head of employability and engagement role in January 2023. Here, he is aiding individual candidates on their journey to qualification through the Solicitors Qualifying Exam (SQE). Robert proactively supports aspiring lawyers from school age through to gaining Qualifying Work Experience (QWE) and practice-ready skills. With QWE an essential consideration for aspiring solicitors looking to qualify in England and Wales, he is creating innovative partnerships across the industry to help pave clear, accessible routes to qualification in conjunction with BARBRI's SQE Prep courses. Robert holds a BA (Hons), an LLB (Hons) and PG Dip Law from The College of Law, London along with a postgraduate certificate in career development. He is a member of the Institute of Student Employers, the International Bar Association (IBA), and a representative for the European Lawyer's Association.

Anne Harnetty is the founder and director of Jonson Beaumont, which specializes in search and selection in professional service firms for the c-suite and Jonson Beaumont Core, which is a merger integration service providing project management and planning for all aspects of integration. Anne has over 35 years' experience working in the legal sector and is a director of several CEO, COO, and CFO forums. She has a wealth of experience providing constructive advice to managing partners and boards on a range of issues within the legal sector and exchanging ideas and insights. Anne is the author of *Mergers with the Benefit of Hindsight*, published in 2022, and also works with Millbourn Ross as a merger broker.

Tea Hoffmann is the managing principal of Law Strategy Coach. Her mission is to be the change agent law firms and lawyers need to become more successful long-term. Tea practiced law for over 13 years, serving in a law firm and as the GC of a publicly traded company. Over the next 15 years, she served as a legal consultant, keynote speaker, chief business development officer for an AmLaw 100 firm, and chief strategy officer for an AmLaw 200 firm. In 2014, she founded Law Strategy Corp. Since then, she has coached over 400 partners in law firms across the United States, Canada, Mexico, and Italy. In addition, she has facilitated over 200 high-energy retreats and developed a first-of-its-kind soft skills online training program. Tea is a certified life, wellness, executive coach and a Franklin Covey™ facilitator. She is a fellow in the College of Law Practice Management, has served on the editorial board of the Law Practice magazine for the American Bar Association, and has had her work published in multiple journals and legal publications. She also serves on the Forbes Small Business Council.

Rebecca Holdredge is the director of knowledge management at Levenfeld Pearlstein, where she is able to leverage over two decades of experience as an attorney, actuary, and innovator to transform the landscape of legal services. She specializes in integrating business, law, and technology, pioneering strategies that not only enhance client value but also invigorate and motivate legal talent through innovative practices. Her approach to complex business challenges blends advanced analytics, design thinking, and modern technologies, fostering an environment that inspires legal professionals to innovate and excel. Rebecca's collaborative leadership style promotes creativity and strategic risk-taking. As a recognized thought leader, Rebecca often shares her expertise on topics like data visualization, design thinking, legal innovation and change management. Her academic credentials include a J.D. magna cum laude from Tulane University Law School, and a B.S. magna cum laude from Washington University. Her commitment extends to founding Blueprint Legal Solutions, a nonprofit aimed at improving legal operations and access to justice.

Jean-Baptiste Lebelle is the head of HR at Allen & Overy's Paris office. He holds a law degree from Paris II Assas and graduated from Sciences Po Paris. Jean-Baptiste taught at the Sorbonne and HEC on recruitment, retention, and career management in law firms. Jean-Baptiste has over 20 years of HR experience in the consulting sector and he is especially engaged in topics related to compensation policies, recruitment, talent retention, diversity and inclusion, and wellbeing applied to law firms. He switched from headhunting for law firms to HR, becoming PWC Legal's HR director for Paris before A&O.

Sophia Margetts is a trainee solicitor at Osborne Clarke's London office. She studied English at Bristol University before taking the GDL and LPC, and started her training contract in September 2023.

Suhail Mayor is a trainee solicitor at DLA Piper, currently completing his second seat in litigation and arbitration. Having previously worked across intellectual property and technology and corporate crime, he holds an LLM from King's College London.

Dr Catherine Mcgregor is an author, executive coach, and management consultant. She started her career in teaching and the performing arts and is grateful to draw on these skills and experiences in her work in the corporate world to give unique insights and perspectives. Catherine is the author of *Business Thinking in Practice for In-House Counsel: Taking Your Seat at The Table* (Globe Law and Business, 2020), which focuses on the application of human-centered business skills by legal departments and received numerous accolades. Catherine spends most of her time working with executive leadership consultancy, Chief Legal Executive, where she leads all professional and executive development and executive coaching efforts working with many Global 100 and Fortune 500 legal departments. Her work is focused on developing the skills that professionals will need to master opportunities in the exponential age in blending human work with AI and other technologies.

Patrick J. McKenna is an internationally recognized author, lecturer, strategist, and seasoned advisor to leaders of premier law firms, having the honor of working with one of the largest firms in over a dozen countries. Patrick is author/co-author of 12 books. His three decades of experience led to his being the subject of a Harvard Law School case study entitled *Innovations In Legal Consulting*. One example of that innovation was launching the first instructional program designed to address the issues that new firm leaders face in their first 100 days – graduating over 80 participants, many from AmLaw 100 and 200-sized firms. Patrick is the recipient of an Honorary Fellowship from Leaders Excellence of Harvard Square and was voted by readers of *Legal Business World* as one of only seven international thought leaders.

Becky Jo Morgan is a seasoned director of practice operations at Levenfeld Pearlstein, with over 29 years of comprehensive paralegal experience. Her journey in the legal field has seen her evolve from a hands-on role in the corporate and securities group to an influential leader in firmwide practice operations. In her current role, Becky expertly oversees the daily operations of various practices, demonstrating a profound ability to collaborate with practice group leaders in designing and executing strategic group plans. Her approach integrates crucial elements of business planning, talent development, workflow, and operations management, all aimed at fostering a productive and motivating environment for legal professionals. Becky's career is marked by a commitment to process improvement and project management, highlighted by her tenure as the firm's practice group manager and paralegal project manager. Her acumen extends to providing adept support in transactional matters across diverse areas like real estate, trusts and estates, and financial services. Becky's expertise is further endorsed by her Yellow Belt certifications in Legal Lean Sigma and project management and in change management. This blend of operational leadership and legal knowledge positions her uniquely to drive innovation and inspire growth in legal talent.

With over 30 years of law firm experience, **Molly Peckman** launched her training, development, and coaching company (Molly Peckman Training and Development) in 2017 to help organizations and professionals maximize their talent. At MPTD, Molly works with organizations on their talent management strategies including training, development, evaluation, engagement, retention, orientation, integration, respectful workplace, and business development. Molly is an engaging speaker and provides customized training programs on communications, leadership, business development, and management skills. She facilitates focus groups, conducts needs assessments, and presents at retreats. Molly also provides one-on-one coaching on career and business development and is a certified master coach. Molly served as the head of talent at a global firm and helped create that firm's culture of learning by building an integrated legal talent department, spearheading the diversity initiative, designing the competency and career path model, and creating the training curriculum. Molly is a frequent writer and lecturer on legal talent management and law firm life. She served as a trusted advisor to the Professional Development Consortium and chaired NALP's Lawyer Professional Development Section. Molly is a graduate of Temple University (J.D., BA Journalism) and practiced as a litigator in Philadelphia.

Kathryn Rousin is an advisory board member and former co-chair of the IBA's Academic and Professional Development Committee. Kathryn is the global director of learning and development at White & Case, responsible for leadership and management training and coaching worldwide. She works directly with senior business leaders on talent and learning initiatives to help deliver on organizational strategies. She has 20 years' experience in global leadership roles in talent management and learning and development in the legal sector, consulting and delivering training in EMEA, Asia Pacific, the US, and Latin America. Kathryn qualified as a solicitor in England and Wales, practicing in mergers and acquisitions at two international firms before moving into talent management and learning and development. Kathryn has a BA and MA in Modern Languages from the University of Oxford in the UK, postgraduate diplomas in Law and Legal Practice from the University of Law in the UK, and a postgraduate diploma in Organizational Leadership from Saïd Business School, University of Oxford.

Lara Selem is an attorney and professor, expert in legal management, and co-founder of Selem Bertozzi Consulting. In Brazil, she is a pioneer in disseminating the subject, having advised over 1,200 law firms since 1998. With multiple specializations, including international ones, she has become a reference in strategic planning, governance, compensation, succession, and leadership for law firms, with extensive experience in consulting and mentoring. She also serves as external board advisor for medium and large law firms, and is an active speaker and author of 19 books.

Charlotte Smith is an executive coach and management consultant supporting GCs, law firm partners, and legal tech entrepreneurs with innovative legal leadership and organizational excellence strategies. As a solicitor qualified in England and Wales, Charlotte's expertise is rooted in over 15 years of experience working in and with the profession, both in the UK and the US. Relocating to the US, she founded her consultancy Level7 with a mission to deliver critical support and drive innovation across Silicon Valley's legal landscape. Her approach addresses legal's critical challenges, from leadership development to culture, through innovative strategies that blend energy management and human performance enhancement. In 2024, Charlotte championed initiatives like pre-acquisition executive evaluations for legal tech firms and developed professional branding strategies for legal professionals with an emphasis on thought leadership. Charlotte emphasizes the irreplaceable human element in the era of AI and technology, positioning her consultancy at the forefront of equipping legal teams for the dynamic evolution of careers in today's legal landscape. Her contributions ensure legal professionals and teams are prepared to thrive amid the changing demands of the legal profession, making her an invaluable asset to those looking to excel in this new era.

Heather Suttie is an internationally recognized legal market strategy and management consultant to leaders of premier law firms and legal service digital transformation. As chief digital officer, Tara is responsible for setting and overseeing the strategy for how Ashurst develops and delivers digital capabilities that support enhanced client and employee experiences and drive new business opportunities.

Chrissie Wolfe is a clinical negligence solicitor and a strategic and operational consultant for the legal sector with a particular focus on talent and culture. Formerly a solicitor at Irwin Mitchell, Chrissie set up her own consultancy in 2021 and has since worked with some of the industry's most innovative leaders, including Richard Susskind, Mark Cohen, and Isabel Parker. She sits as director of operations at the Digital Legal Exchange as a consultant and has worked directly with the SRA to design and implement the SQE route to solicitor qualification. Aside from the day job, she has a social media following of over 120,000 in the legal space and is a frequent conference speaker and presenter on a range of topics within legal and beyond.

providers worldwide. For 25 years, she has accelerated performance within law firms and legal service businesses – global to solo, BigLaw to NewLaw – by providing consultative direction on innovative strategies pertaining to business, markets, management, and clients. Heather is an authority on Big Four Legal and one of the world's only legal market strategists with both legal MDP and client consulting expertise, which qualifies her as a conduit within and between traditional and non-traditional legal enterprises. She consults based on solid business acumen attained through corporate management, including restructurings and turnarounds. A speaker and writer, she presents at legal conferences, comments on global legal market and industry trends, and contributes to international legal publications where she writes "prescriptively" and "with a certain stark honesty about the business of law".

Caroline Vanovermeire is the global director of talent, leadership, and organizational development at dentsu and founder of Effra consult. She specializes in working with organizations and partnerships that are at a crossroads due to growth and/or disruption. Typical activities are related to culture shaping, organizational effectiveness, talent management, leadership, assessment, and development. In addition, she is an NED for Biolizard, an agile data science consulting company with expertise in scientific data analysis, data mining, machine learning, and artificial intelligence. Caroline has also mentored start-ups in the fintech industry. She is a published author and has won several awards acknowledging her expertise, experience, and thought leadership, often pioneering. In her free time, Caroline is a trustee for the Regenboogschool, a charity that offers cultural, inclusivity, and Dutch language education for four- to 18-year-olds, as well as a key supporter of Sense, a charity for deaf blind people, and has been a proud member of its corporate fundraising board for over five years. She has also volunteered for the Media Trust.

Tara Waters is a partner and global chief digital officer at Ashurst LLP in London. Having spent seven years working as a web developer prior to becoming a lawyer, Tara is known for being the rare lawyer who truly understands new technologies and the needs of technology-enabled businesses. Tara has spent the past decade working at the intersection of technology and the law, balancing advising and mentoring emerging technology companies and their advisers with pioneering the establishment of Ashurst's own technology-enablement. Her expertise and experience includes supporting a full range of corporate and finance transactions, strategic business advice, and

Executive summary

It makes good business, financial, and reputational sense to keep your best performing staff, but with the most extraordinary recruitment market in 40 years, now more than ever human capital needs nurturing if you believe that people are your greatest asset. The pandemic changed the way we work forever, and we need to reflect on what we learned during that time. What are the true causes of attrition? How do we understand what it is staff need in order to retain them in the business?

Talent in the Legal Profession: How to Attract, Retain, and Engage Top Talent aims to answer these and many more questions. Looking at the perspectives of changing attitudes to the profession, an increasingly dynamic and diverse workforce, the impact of technology, and alternative forms of compensation, and how to future-proof the talent that already exists in your organization, the book is essential reading for anyone managing a legal team.

The book's contributors offer insight and inspiration, combining experienced and leading voices alongside those only recently joining the profession, in order to provide a comprehensive overview of the state of the talent marketplace, and how it is likely to evolve.

If firms were to lose large numbers of lawyers, it would compromise morale, disrupt culture, and damage a firm's reputation. It also upsets clients. Our opening chapter by Anne Harnetty of Jonson Beaumont looks at how firms can innovate to help them differentiate via their culture rather than salary increases. Leadership style is critical to cultural norms and a shared cultural vision gives a sense of identity and belonging. How can firms stop making assumptions about culture? The legal industry is brimming with guidance on tools to increase productivity but there seem to be few tips about creating a culture that makes an organization a great place to work, where people feel valued, trusted, and respected. In this chapter, Anne sets the tone for what will follow.

The legal profession is currently in a state of flux to an extent not seen for many years. The rising use of generative AI, coupled with an increased focus on wellbeing and changes to the UK-based qualification regime mean attracting and retaining legal talent is a tough job for firms and organiza-tions. The next generation of lawyers are increasingly showing they want more from the profession, but is legal ready to adapt sufficiently to provide it? In the first of three chapters looking at changing attitudes and routes into the profession, Victoria Cromwell of BARBRI looks at what tools firms and organizations have available to attract young lawyers, particularly from diverse talent pools, and whether junior lawyers still view law as a career for life. It considers attitudes to partnership, attrition, and alternative career paths, both inside and outside of private practice, and addresses the funda-mental question – has the legal profession started to lose its shine?

In chapter three, Charlotte Smith of Level7 traces the prestige of the legal profession to its historical origins before looking at how the future is being shaped by alternative attitudes, and emerging trends in legal careers. She looks at progress towards gender equity in law and the new culture and lead-ership dynamics in legal firms. Turning her attention to attrition and talent migration, Charlotte looks at the causes for exiting traditional law and where legal talent is heading. She explores attitudes to partnership and the rise of ALSPs and legal tech ventures for those of an entrepreneurial persuasion, as well as the media and pop culture's influence on law's prestige.

In response to the persistent talent gap and lack of diversity that has plagued the legal sector for the past decade, the Solicitors Regulation Authority (SRA) in the UK introduced the Solicitors Qualifying Exam (SQE) in 2021. In chapter four, Robert Dudley, head of employability and engagement at BARBRI, delves into how the SQE is not just an assessment, but a strategic initiative addressing critical issues in recruitment, retention, diversity, acces-sibility, and inclusion within the legal profession. Set to become the main route to qualification for 2024 graduates and potentially replace the existing Legal Practice Course (LPC) route completely by 2032, the SQE enables candi-dates from both law and non-law backgrounds – and those already in the sector, such as paralegals – to qualify as solicitors. It's also driving new oppor-tunities for school leavers through legal apprenticeships, helping firms and in-house teams to grow talent from the ground up, enabling a greater diver-sity of thought and creating more robust attraction and retention strategies, all of which support the positive evolution of the legal sector and future-proofed operations. Chapter four looks at how this will influence talent in the legal profession.

Chapter five aims to shed light on what trainees and recent graduates value most when applying for jobs, what employers and firms can still do in

Chapter 1:
Why is there a talent acquisition and retention battle?

By Anne Harnetty, managing director, Jonson Beaumont Ltd

It makes good business, financial, and reputational sense to keep our best-performing staff, but with the most extraordinary recruitment market in 40 years, now more than ever human capital needs nurturing if you believe that people are your greatest asset, and have a vested interest in retaining them. The loss of lawyers in large numbers compromises morale, disrupts the firm's culture, can damage a firm's reputation, and upsets clients.

After COVID-19, the world of work changed forever. It is hard to remember that first lockdown. Many firms had to spend significant amounts of money on laptops, mobile phones, and desks to enable staff to work from home. Many railed against the cost. Many did not believe that working from home was viable or sustainable. Perhaps we were used to working in a particular way, we were rigid, a bit conservative, and certainly not agile in our thinking. How quickly did we change our thought process from how much it had cost to have staff working from home to the fact we had made a wise investment?

The Great Resignation is widespread and has persisted. It is a talking point for managing partners because it is an unprecedented situation.

In a recent survey, *Harvard Business Review* found that 41 percent of employees in the global workforce are considering resigning and 36 percent of those leaving their roles do so with no new job in place.[1] We are still seeing a sustained battle for talent, and it is an unparalleled situation that is ongoing. In the two years from 2019-2021, London-based law firms lost 44 percent more associates than they hired. According to Codex Edge, a legal market analytics firm, the average associate attrition rate for the top 100 law firms in England and Wales increased by 37 percent. In the autumn of 2021, a new pay war began with salaries being boosted by as much as 25 percent. For most, that is not sustainable.[2]

In July 2022, Thomson Reuters stated that the risk of losing associates was still elevated at 37 percent and the risk of losing partners was 25 percent. One thing is certain, retaining employees is cheaper than the cost of replacing them. Data shows that it is largely juniors – those with fewer than six years' post-qualification experience – who are choosing to move on, with many leaving law altogether. Given that associate attrition costs firms between £150,000 and £350,000 per lawyer lost, with costs including recruiting, training, and onboarding, all of which take time, this is an issue that we cannot afford to ignore.[3]

What are the true causes of attrition? Do we really understand what it is that staff want in order to retain them in the business and are we taking meaningful action to keep them? As leaders, should we be thinking differently, rather than the quick fix of giving more money to staff proposing to leave and hoping the issues will go away? Harvard Business School said, *"Leaders must go from trying to have all the answers to being comfortable with being uncomfortable".*[4] We cannot assume we know what's happening; we need to take the time to investigate the root causes of attrition. It is also time to think creatively about roles and acknowledge that, if we listen, roles can transform for the better, rather than begrudging change. There is an assumption that salary is the most important factor in attracting and retaining staff, but do we ask if it is actually what staff want? With an increase in salary comes immense hours and intense pressure. Firms need to take the time to learn why staff are leaving and act differently, so they gain the edge in attracting and retaining talent, and more can be done. Firms need to innovate in spaces that will help them differentiate via their culture, not the wage packets they're waving in front of juniors.

A 2021 FT Innovative Lawyers 2021 report[5] showed that 90 percent of lawyers said there were firms they would refuse to work for regardless of pay because they believe the working culture would impact their wellbeing. Adapting our mindset is essential and it is easier to look at a seemingly obvious solution rather than alternatives that may challenge the status quo. Law firms now need to start an innovation war, earn loyalty, and retain talent. Certainly, from a people perspective, it is time to adjust in response to changes and demands.

How do you know if or why your staff are unhappy and ready to leave? The reality is, most of us don't know how they're feeling. In a recent Managing Partners Forum survey, 69 percent of firms revealed they only found out how their staff were feeling at an exit interview.[6] Apart from the obvious that it is too little, too late, staff are usually less than honest at an exit interview. They want to leave with minimum fuss and get a decent reference, so they tell the firm what they want to hear, because once they have resigned, they have mentally left the firm and are thinking about the new opportunity they are moving to. Recruiters always hear the real reasons for the departure, and it is usually promises made that are not delivered that drive people out of the door. The promise of a four-day week that never quite happens; the promise of career progression that is deferred; the lack of genuine regard for their well-being; a poor work–life balance; and above all the feeling that they are just not appreciated or recognized. Salary does not stop burnout. If employees do not feel appreciated, they sense a transactional relationship and then believe their needs are not being met. Working from home means that, on average, lawyers work another five-and-a-half hours per week. For many, they do not know if they are working remotely or living at work.

Before working from home was the norm, work loyalty was easier because it came from being aligned to people and mentors. Those loyalties have been replaced by solitary work where people must be self-driven. Out of sight, out of mind applies for many and their concerns will include how they can learn and progress without mentors at hand.

What were people looking for pre-COVID compared to now?

Pre-COVID, job security, fair compensation, and promotion were high on people's agendas when moving role. Many wanted a structured career path to equity partner. Junior lawyers now want more autonomy, better training, more inclusive work distribution, and a better quality of life in the job. They want to feel valued and a sense of belonging among colleagues, as well as see the potential for personal growth. Their long-term aim may no longer be equity, as many do not now see it as the Holy Grail. They want the flexibility to integrate work with their personal life. To ensure that all of these are achievable, firms need to create a strong value proposition for staff that delivers on promises made. Whatever that proposition is, it needs to fuel a culture in which everyone can bring their full range of talents, feel valued, and do great work.

Staff who were used to a social environment saw it die out with COVID-19 measures and we now have a new cohort of juniors who have never been part of a social structure and have yet to learn what culture could look like. Firms lost a large number of senior associates because they rethought their life choices due to the pandemic. Those seniors did much of the pastoral team-building work. No one wants to go for coffee, drinks, or dinner with someone they find it hard to relate to, someone they might perceive as an older partner who talks shop.

What do value propositions look like?

The value proposition for staff must have a link beyond profitability and a different purpose. Staff want to see diversity, equal pay between men and women, and parity at work. The Law Gazette looked at independent research carried out for the Solicitors Regulation Authority and found that white men are nearly six times more likely to become a law firm partner than black, Asian, and minority ethnic women. Diverse organizations that attract and develop individuals from the widest pool of talent consistently perform better. You can see it in firms like Freshfields, and the pro bono work it does. Its target groups include women, children, LGBT+ people, trafficking survivors, and refugees.[7] It ensures its pro bono clients also benefit from the skills of its business services professionals (for example, from its IT, marketing, and human resources departments).

Firms must foster a culture of belonging, flexibility, and growth. It is vital that firms consider how they help people learn and grow and know how to facilitate connection and inclusion. Your value proposition therefore must be real and aspirational. As an organization you need to involve staff, so they take the opportunity to tell everyone who you are as an organization. If they recognize and promote your culture, it makes you unique. A strong employer brand indicates that employees are happy and engaged, which enhances your reputation and in turn helps you retain and attract staff.

Juniors need a better voice; firms are now recognizing that, and many have introduced a junior shadow board as part of their governance. It ensures they have internal feedback about what juniors want. It guarantees communication, feeding information bottom-up and top-down. Junior lawyers know people of their own level in other firms so discuss what is happening. Your firm should want to know what is being said, both good and bad, and respond quickly. Everyone should know about the positives because when anything is done badly the legal market knows about it – so change the narrative.

Your value proposition should be authentic to you, and it should emphasize what it is you value as an organization. What is it you stand for? It is critical to connect social causes, diversity, inclusion, and sustainability because that is what candidates are looking for. Ethical and environmental considerations are gaining momentum. As Generation Z and Millennials increase in the workforce, these issues will continue to be high on the agenda in the coming years.

Major firms including Allen & Overy, Clifford Chance, Freshfields, Herbert Smith Freehills, Linklaters, Macfarlanes, Norton Rose Fulbright, and Slaughter and May have come together to promote and amplify diversity and inclusion in the industry and jointly tackle the challenges they face in increasing representation. We saw a major step forward in 2020 with the first leadership-led, cross-firm collaborative aimed at tackling the underrepresentation of black, Asian, and minority ethnic groups in the UK's legal industry when eight law firms formed CORE (Collaboration on Race and Ethnicity)[8] and as an industry, we need to see more of this type of initiative.

Your words and actions must match the employee experience. Ensure that you balance your intentions and ambitions with what you are really doing. You cannot have a mismatch between what you say and what you do. Simon Sinek says, *"Hearing is listening to what is said. Listening is hearing what isn't said."*[9] Even if you think you have got it right and you have found a way to connect with your staff to retain them in the longer term, it is worth checking that this is reality. In 2018, Pinsent Masons came together with three of the UK's biggest banks and nine of the UK's top law firms to author and launch an unprecedented alliance to change avoidable working practices that can cause mental health and wellbeing issues for employees. All the signatories committed to a set of principles centered on improved communication, respect for rest periods, and considerate delegation of tasks – The Mindful Business Charter.[10] Take a look on social media and a different picture emerges. One post reads:

"Hilariously, the firm has signed up for The Mindful Business Charter so they make clients aware that we are on holiday and not available for work, but if a client says jump, we must ask how high?"

So, this exceptional concept has been lost because of a lack of communication. Once signed up to such an initiative, the perception is that all is well. This post was also on social media:

"I would like more focus on culture beyond words and client-focused initiatives. The firm likes to paint itself as being flexible and putting mental health first but that is just a façade. I would like to see much greater support for working parents and support for people's mental health."

Will firms have to redefine their recruitment strategy to deal with the current market conditions?
A recruitment strategy is a clear plan that explains what roles you will recruit

for, when, why, and how. It should be tied to your overall firm objectives. Your strategy must be possible to implement and easy to communicate. Whilst you can tweak your tactics, the strategy must always be clear. It is easy to say we've lost X amount of people and we need to replace them, but it might not be feasible or realistic in a short time span.

To do that you need to:

- Establish and leverage your employer brand.
- Improve job postings with compelling job descriptions.
- Prioritize diversity, equality, and inclusion practices.
- Treat candidates as customers.
- Conduct great interviews. Treated well, candidates do a fantastic PR job for you. Treated badly, the whole market hears about it. Understand the difference between probing questions and being aggressive. It happens even at senior levels, where the impression given can be so poor, no one wants to work with them.
- Lock interview times into diaries. The candidate's time is as important as yours, especially when they have taken holiday time to attend an interview and the partner cancels at the last minute.
- Ensure you have strong relationships with your recruiters and don't base everything on price.

The war for talent is continuing and of course you will have to adapt your recruitment strategy to meet your needs.

One of the most popular routes now (and to save recruitment fees) is LinkedIn.

In February 2022, LinkedIn showed nearly 2,500 roles in the top 100 UK law firms. For those roles, there were just 4,500 applicants – that's 1.64 applicants per advert. Of those 2,500 jobs, 1,195 had no applicants.

An easy assumption to make is that the platform does not work effectively. Actually, we should be questioning why it is not working and raise questions.

- Who is letting it happen in the firm?
- What is their recruitment strategy? If they can see that they have no response, why is there no collaboration between marketing and HR to get a better advert out there?
- Do they mind people quite openly seeing how poorly they are doing? This sends a message to the market that there's something wrong with this firm because they've had no applicants.

The reality of crafting an advert has changed. Lots of information about the firm can be found anywhere and it is not compelling. If a firm is advertising on LinkedIn, they are usually open about who they are. If those reading the advertisement can be bothered to plow through that puff piece then somewhere they will find relevant information, but it's lost in all the fluff.

Anyone can look up a firm and find out about them. What can you do that's different?

There are excellent examples of firms that have thought this through. Let's look at a firm recognized by The Times as one of the UK's 20 Best Law Firms to Work for and one of London's 50 Best Mid-Sized Companies to Work for. It's leading the way in employee engagement amongst law firms, with a range of innovations including widespread flexible working. Its advert included the following:

- Flexible working is not a dirty word.
- We want the very best to join the firm and we want you to stay.
- We recognize that everyone has different needs and responsibilities at different times in our lives and flexibility can be necessary.
- We are committed to ongoing professional development, not only with established providers but through our internal "lunch and learn" scheme, which offers regular legal updates as well as soft skills training.
- We believe the best organizations are those that listen to their employees from across the business. There are regular staff briefings to keep staff up to date on key developments within the firm, supported by monthly newsletters.
- More importantly, we want to hear from you. We actively respond to firmwide engagement surveys.
- We have an active junior board who meet regularly to help shape how we do business and membership is encouraged from across our teams. We also have an active social and CSR committee who put on social and charity events across the year.

Candidates will be attracted to adverts that make them want to read further. These are compelling reasons, and they would certainly want to find out more. What would those compelling reasons look like?

- How do they innovate as a firm?
- What do they instigate in terms of wellbeing?
- How do they make staff feel part of the firm, even though they work remotely for part of the week?

- Do people respect one another, including business/professional services staff?
- Are the skills that professional service or support staff bring recognized by fee earning staff? Or do you still refer to them as 'non-lawyers'?

Firms that include business service staff in events and initiatives are indicative of a firm that wants to ensure everyone at all levels is comfortable and supported.

The concept of a junior board is exciting because it ensures that staff at all levels have a voice that is being listened to and enables an exchange of ideas that might not otherwise be discussed. It shows a culture that is listening and is not afraid to be different. There are firms that have made it part of their governance structure. Headed by salaried partners, their meetings are fed to the executive committee and the COO, so communication is bottom-up and top-down. They are the voice of what makes a difference to staff at their level.

What part does culture play in the retention battle?

Chambers surveyed associates in 2020 and asked them the most important thing to them when choosing a new firm. Almost 90 percent said a positive culture and social make-up, and this is still the case.[11] Culture needs to be entrenched. It must create a sense of unity and a new sense of purpose because staff who felt they lost their way during the pandemic need that. How do you make staff feel part of the firm even when they are working remotely? In reality, many firms do not recognize their own culture because it is a soft concept. Everyone in the firm should contribute to its culture, but they can only do that if they know what values, beliefs, and behaviors you want as part of your culture. If you cannot define what it is, how can staff connect to it?

Do you listen to your staff to understand what culture they want to be part of? Do you have core values that are lived by everyone? It can be as simple as respect. Do you reward and recognize all aspects of work and achievements and give regular feedback? Many of us see the surface level of culture. Many firms have re-purposed their offices to accommodate hybrid working, incorporating breakout spaces and meeting rooms and making them look beautiful. Here we have the swan – elegant, stylish, and getting people excited to be in the office. What, however, is happening in the depths of the pond to that elegant and stylish swan? Under the surface, what are the values? Does everyone know what they are and are they really practiced, or are they lost in the mire of the pond? The culture must please multi-generational levels that are in every firm, who of course have different ways of looking at things. Younger lawyers often living away from home need to build relationships and social networks. Work might well be their social life, so it is more likely that they want to get back to the office.

Leadership style is critical to cultural norms and will ensure that staff understand that defining culture is necessary because a shared cultural vision gives a sense of identity and belonging. It ensures that staff become excited that work is a destination where they go to collaborate and learn. Company websites describe their culture in similar terms – collaborative, supportive, and thoughtful. You only have to look on social media to see that the staff in those firms use their networks to describe something very different, especially where firms have been acquired.

"Biggest does not mean best and there is no discernible direction or culture to the firm."

"The firm used to have a brilliant and supportive culture, however as we have grown, we have lost this."

One business services employee working in finance stated that their team culture was lovely but, "I do my best to avoid anyone who actually practices law". This is a clear sign that an assumption has been made that culture is aligned. Firms must live their culture, not simply make a statement and assume that it is fine. Even PII renewals now ask questions about culture.

Ed Whittington Moore Barlow, one of The Lawyer's Hot 100 Lawyers, is a man who understands culture. He says:

"Be positive, tolerant, hard-working, care about and be polite to the people around you. Step up in a crisis and help, bend over backwards for colleagues and clients, scrap the ego and muck in. Form a vision, hold that vision, manage the energy, coach rather than command, and as important as everything else, don't take life too seriously and have a laugh along the way."[12]

Mental health is something the sector is increasingly aware of but the biggest elephant in the room is the fact the billable hour is never addressed. Yet it is the measure used to gauge how lawyers are performing. We have Reginald Herber Smith to thank for it because in the 1950s he found that lawyers who tracked their time made more money. Smith, however, did not see profit as the primary motive for his method. He regarded the billable hour as a fair, logical, and transparent way to value legal services, which would promote client satisfaction because he was looking at legal aid for the poor. Seventy years on, is it time to change that concept and perhaps measure achievements in a different way? Does it in fact drive negative, outdated, and unsustainable behaviors? Lawyers feel the pressure of the billable hour to increase profits, improve productivity, and influence who gets promoted – the more hours you work, the better. The main problem with the billable hour as a performance metric is that it specifically rewards and underpins behaviors that can be to the detriment of staff because lawyers become more anxious as they fixate on the billable hour. Should we be asking how we can record time without exhausting targets? If that happened, perhaps it would encourage collaboration and affect staff at all levels. It has been well documented[13] that a partner at a leading law firm was diagnosed with burnout because he constantly billed excessive hours. He routinely had chargeable hours of up to 2,600 a year against a target of 1,400, with an additional 200-300 hours spent on business development. He won a disability discrimination claim about the way he was treated by his firm.

The American Bar Association published a study in 2016 that psychological predictors of wellbeing decreased as lawyers were required to bill more hours.[14] If people leave because of stress and feel that they are drowning in the billable hour, why do we not throw them a life belt before it gets to that stage?

What set of values drives successful behaviors and makes staff happy to stay with a firm? They could include client loyalty, business development, new relationships, and service innovation, rather than simply measuring activity-driven metrics of utilization and the billable hour. The only way new behaviors can be aligned and embedded is if partners and senior managers are aligned to new metrics.

What do staff really want?

Sometimes, money and benefits are not worth it if the culture of the firm is perceived as toxic or if there is no perception of growth or learning. Staff want a renewed and revised sense of purpose in their work. They want social and interpersonal connections with their colleagues and managers. Above all, they want to feel valued by the firm and their managers. They want meaningful interaction, not just transaction. Remote working is now the norm for most firms but for many it is a solitary way of working. Not only do they feel isolated, but they also feel anxious, so they want learning and training opportunities in person. Mentoring and coaching provide informal opportunities to speak to senior colleagues about work and personal development that many feel unable to discuss via a Teams or Zoom meeting. Buddy systems with peers can encourage collaboration. If firms fail to meet these demands for autonomy and flexibility at work, junior lawyers will become resentful of their workload and how it is allocated. Partners have to stop turning informally to their favored junior lawyer regardless of their workload. To counteract this, many firms have introduced blind work allocation to avoid bias. There must be a system in place that works because if a junior tells you that they are over capacity you cannot just say OK, but can you do it for me anyway. Monotonous assignments that offer no chance of learning are an issue for young lawyers. It is time to think outside the box as a leader. What do your staff really want and what can you change?

Many lawyers would like part-time work. Can you re-imagine that piece so that people can job share? Could you offer career sabbaticals? Some equity partners get this – could you offer it to other staff? In 2019, Clifford Chance began piloting two months' unpaid leave for eligible associates and senior associates. Broadening career sabbaticals to associates is likely to become a growing trend and is a useful way for firms to attract and retain talent, especially in high-demand, short-supply, niche legal areas. Could you offer career secondments or introduce family-friendly functions? Many firms carried out online family events during lockdown. Could you extend that in some way?

Can you help staff balance the demands of work and careers with their personal obligations and interests? A huge change during lockdown was that men and women both took on parental duties. Prior to the pandemic, many men did not feel that they could take parental leave, regardless of their rights. There has, however, been an uptake in parental leave since COVID. It is crucial that firms pay attention to gender-neutral policies to ensure that they retain and support their top talent. If we are re-imagining office space, is there room for creche facilities? Or can you make arrangements with a local nursery for the care of your staff's children? We need to explore these types of concepts rather than simply rejecting them. For many, that is a salary sacrifice worth making. We should not be looking at these issues as short-term fixes but as long-term adjustments. If we accommodate new ideas, they should be guilt-free. Pilot schemes are an ideal way of testing new ideas.

Does hybrid working require the firm's leaders to learn new skills to keep a dispersed team not only productive but happy? How can you connect to your team? To ensure that you continue to build trust, engage, listen, and relate to what they are saying. Once we have attracted them to the firm, how do we retain them?

If you are asking partners to engage in this way and invest more time in coaching, how do you now reward partners, so they know that their contribution is recognized? The best leaders stay present and are emotionally engaged, communicating openly and authentically. Leaders must actively listen, ask the right questions, and be open to showing compassion.

Leaders are going to have emotion-loaded interactions. You must ensure there is not a disconnect between your actions as a leader and the culture you say you are promoting. If you consistently send emails in the early hours of the morning, there is an expectation that the person you are sending it to should be awake and able to reply. If you continually work when you are on holiday, you set an expectation. Perhaps that expectation needs to change so that you switch off and gain a work–life balance. Your policy might state that working out of hours is not expected, but if you see your boss do it constantly, the policy becomes meaningless.

Do leaders need to change to develop and retain talent? It is not easy because as a leader you need to understand your employees and develop a real empathy for what the issues are that your staff are facing. You need to have compassion and the determination to change and act. There is no doubt that you will be challenged to reimagine how you lead. A recent Harvard survey of 1,500 executives in 90 countries showed 71 percent said that adaptability was the most important leadership quality.[15] Post-COVID law firm leaders need to be strong coaches and strong mentors and they need to create strong teams to meet the challenges ahead. We now must acknowledge that wellbeing is important and there may be family issues that impact work and living arrangements.

Your people are your law firm. Going from office-centric work to hybrid working has for most been a culture shock. As a result, there will be turbulence. People working from home may feel left out. In-office workers may suspect that their colleagues are not doing a full day's work and grow resentful. New colleagues may struggle to connect with people that they are working with and need help to facilitate interaction. Consequently, leaders must give a lot of thought to how they will create bonds between people and shape the company's culture. This will require managers to be active, involved, and creative. Employees and managers will have to continue to learn how to build trust through meeting objectives because any vestige of suspicion that people not present in the office cannot be hard at work should have been erased. As employers, we need to understand what employees expect and appreciate. We also need to address gaps in areas that staff identify as reasons they will leave. To do that, we must have mechanisms in place to understand how we can support and ensure people are happy, rewarded, and recognized in their role. Above all, we need to cultivate a culture of trust.

References

1   https://hbr.org/2021/10/5-reasons-not-to-quit-your-job-yet
2   www.artificiallawyer.com/2021/11/29/the-winners-in-laws-great-resignation-will-be-firms-that-focus-on-innovation-not-compensation/
3   www.thomsonreuters.com/en-us/posts/legal/flexibility-uk-law-associates-survey/
4   https://hbswk.hbs.edu/item/six-unexpected-traits-leaders-need-in-the-digital-era
5   www.ft.com/content/b57dbe83-65c3-4ea7-95d1-1df878c763bd
6   www.mpfglobal.com/poll-findings.aspx
7   www.lawgazette.co.uk/practice/white-men-dominate-law-firm-partnerships-sra-research/5063473.article
8   www.legalcore.co.uk/aboutus
9   https://www.linkedin.com/posts/simonsinek_hearing-is-listening-to-what-is-said-listening-activity-6741924509055504384-Adta/
10 www.mindfulbusinesscharter.com/
11 www.chambers-associate.com/law-firms/diversity/us-biglaw-diversity-inclusion-trends
12 www.thelawyer.com/hot-100-career-quiz-moore-barlow-chief-ed-whittington/
13 www.legalfutures.co.uk/latest-news/firm-discriminated-against-partner-suffering-mental-health-problems
14 www.americanbar.org/news/abanews/publications/youraba/2017/december-2017/secrecy-and-fear-of-stigma-among-the-barriers-to-lawyer-well-bei
15 https://hbswk.hbs.edu/item/six-unexpected-traits-leaders-need-in-the-digital-era

Chapter 2:
A career in law – changing attitudes to the legal profession

By Victoria Cromwell, head of new business and account management, BARBRI

The changing face of the legal profession and its effect on recruitment

In the 2013 edition of his seminal work, *Tomorrow's Lawyers*, Richard Susskind predicted that legal institutions and lawyers would change more radically in two decades than they had in the past two centuries.[1] Fast forward ten years and AI is now widely used in practice (although Susskind believes that "most of the short-term claims being made about its impact on lawyers and the courts hugely overstate its likely impact... most of the long-term claims hugely understate its impact..."),[2] and the qualification regime in England and Wales has had a complete overhaul with the introduction of the Solicitors Qualifying Examination (SQE) in 2021. On a societal level, the introduction of the Legal Aid, Sentencing and Punishment of Offenders Act 2012 (LASPO) on 1 April 2013 decimated legal aid funding, creating legal aid deserts[3] and making access to justice significantly more challenging for the most vulnerable in society.[4] This in turn introduced many challenges for those delivering legal services, be they legal advice centers/clinics[5] or criminal barristers.[6]

In 2023, the International Bar Association's Future of Legal Services Commission published a White Paper[7] and heatmap survey that identified the key issues affecting the legal profession and then assessed the likely impact of those issues and how ready the profession is to respond to them. The heatmap considered the issues across four key pillars – people, clients, business, and the rule of law. The key themes identified for the short- (one year), medium- (five years), and long-term (ten years) were, unsurprisingly, the attraction and retention of talent, technology/AI, and mental health/well-being. The survey was conducted before the impact of programs such as ChatGPT, so technology/AI was not in the top five short-term priorities, but it is reasonable to assume that this would not be the case were the survey to be re-run today. As the IBA recognizes:

"AI is a phenomenon which... is likely to transcend a number of other challenge areas across the sector; its impact on talent – both displacement and technical skillset or training changes – will be significant, as will the regulatory frameworks it may operate within and potentially its ability to fairly represent society. Critically, it's one of the few areas that respondents commonly reported as high impact, but also requiring of a proactive industry response to help preserve the rule of law – something which is arguably lacking at present."

Despite these seismic changes, there seems to be no shortage of aspiring solicitors qualifying into the profession. The Law Society of England and Wales Annual Statistics Report for 2022[8] (the most recently published) noted that, as of July 2022, the number of solicitors on the roll stood at 216,173 (a 3.3 percent increase from July 2021) and the number of practicing certificate holders also increased by two percent to a total of 156,976 solicitors. Interestingly though, the number of trainee solicitor registrations (in the year to 31 July) fell from 5,495 in 2021 to 4,952 in 2022, a drop of 9.9 percent. Rather than this indicating a lack of appetite to enter the profession, it is more likely this can be attributed to alternative career paths such as in-house roles, qualification through a paralegal role, and solicitor apprenticeships – more on these later. This is reinforced by the fact that holders of practicing certificates working in private practice dropped by nearly two percent in 2022, but the number of solicitors outside private practice reached 34,680 – an increase of 3.9 percent.

At university level, the Law Society Annual Report noted that students graduating with law degrees in England and Wales increased by five percent (it's important to note that a significant percentage of those undertaking law degrees have no intent to practice in England and Wales or indeed at all), but, as noted above, trainee solicitor registrations were down a massive 9.9 percent to 4,952. It was training contracts in the City of London that showed the largest decline, despite it being the area with the most registrations overall. It is important to note that the report did not include statistics for those starting Qualifying Work Experience (QWE) (the vocational part of the new SQE). These QWE placements would have a direct effect on the number of trainee registrations as they are a direct replacement, and it is the larger City firms that have been for the most part quicker to embrace this new path to qualification. The significance of this data should definitely be viewed through this lens. Overall, on an annual basis, new solicitors admitted to the roll were the highest in the past ten years reaching 7,160 (a 2.6 percent increase).

Generative AI – friend or foe?

One of the central challenges faced by the legal profession is the proliferation and integration of generative AI. As artificial intelligence continues to advance, there is a growing concern about its impact on traditional legal roles. The automation of routine tasks and the ability of AI to sift through vast amounts of legal data have raised questions about the necessity of certain legal positions. While some argue that AI can enhance efficiency and streamline processes, others worry about the potential displacement of human lawyers. The legal profession must grapple with adapting to these technological changes while ensuring that human skills – such as critical thinking, empathy, and ethical decision-making – remain indispensable. Disclaimer: in keeping with the title of this section, I asked ChatGPT to write the above paragraph for me. As perhaps an indicator of the strength of these tools, I think it represents a pretty good summary of the current view of generative AI in the profession.

At a junior level, the concern persists that AI will reduce jobs, as document review and discovery (typical paralegal/trainee tasks) are now being carried out by machine learning. The flip side of this is that the opportunity for more meaningful training at a junior level becomes possible without the types of repetitive tasks mentioned above. Lawyers, particularly at the senior level, are paid for their experience and ability to draw on practice/deal knowledge to provide advice and solve more complex legal issues. We have all heard the horror story of the lawyer who used ChatGPT to prepare for a court hearing and came unstuck.[9] The program cited some entirely fictitious cases as precedent, and the lawyer unsurprisingly lost his case (and came away a little red-faced and with a financial penalty in the process). This example rightly gives cause to pause and reflect on the benefits versus detriments of relying on this type of technology, particularly in the high-stakes legal world. What this case perfectly demonstrates, however, is that the emphasis should be on what time-saving benefits these kinds of programs can bring, whilst being cognizant of the point at which relying on it too heavily can lead to results such as the above example. The red-faced lawyer saved time by having his brief AI-generated, but the human review and check were still very much required.

As ChatGPT rightly states above, the balance can be struck by embracing

AI that enhances the delivery of client service in a streamlined and cost-effective way, whilst ensuring that human skills, such as critical thinking, empathy, and ethical decision-making – which clients highly value – are not lost.

Wellbeing and the legal profession

The legal profession has historically been associated with high levels of stress, and mental health challenges are becoming more widely reported, particularly at the junior level. Long working hours, intense competition, and the weight of responsibility of the billable hour contribute to a work environment that is unsurprisingly detrimental to the mental wellbeing of legal professionals. Legal mental health charity LawCare's 2021 survey[10] noted that legal professionals are at high risk of burnout, with 69 percent having experienced mental ill health, and one in five reporting being bullied, harassed, or discriminated against at work. LawCare has also reported a 24 percent increase (in October 2023) of people contacting it for support.

Recognizing the need for change, law firms are increasingly implementing wellbeing initiatives to support their lawyers. Gone, thankfully in the main, is the attitude of "I went through it – so should you" from partners and senior fee earners to those starting their careers in the profession. Wellbeing initiatives can include enhanced mental health resources, counseling services, flexible work arrangements, and stress management workshops. Firms that prioritize the mental health of their employees not only contribute to a healthier work environment but also enhance their attractiveness to prospective talent, and Gen Z are increasingly demonstrating that this is something they value in an employer.[11] However, the effectiveness of these initiatives depends on their genuine integration into the organizational culture, rather than serving as mere tokens to address this growing concern. As an example, in the International Bar Association's 2022 global report into Mental Wellbeing in the Legal Profession,[12] 82 percent of institutions surveyed reported that they take mental wellbeing seriously, but only 16 percent provide training for senior management. More concerningly, it still appears that a stigma around mental wellbeing remains. Nearly half of all legal professionals surveyed by the IBA indicated that fear of the impact on their career would put them off discussing their mental wellbeing with their firm or organization.

In England and Wales, training contracts/QWE and mental health appear to be a regulatory blind spot for the Solicitors Regulation Authority, with no guidance or support for either firms or their employees. There is a concern that this will get worse with the new QWE regime, as regulation of this vocational period of training decreases even further. For more on this, see chapter four.

New routes to qualification
One of the biggest changes to the legal profession in the UK is undoubtedly the new route to qualification. The effect this has already had for talent attraction and development and to widening access to the legal profession cannot be understated.

By way of background, the new Solicitors Qualifying Examination (SQE) replaces all previous solicitor training routes into the solicitor's profession (LPC/GDL/QLTS), and is a national centralised licensing examination that all aspiring solicitors must pass prior to practice – further detail on the SQE can be found in chapter four. One of the core aims of the SRA in introducing the new SQE route was to break down barriers to entry to the profession, but is this happening in reality and what part do employers have to play in this? The Legal Services Board in its report on Barriers to the Legal Profession[13] noted:

"The provision of legal services at the highest levels and in the most prestigious firms is dominated by white, male lawyers from the highest socio-economic groups. Our belief is that such an outcome does not occur as a result of overt discrimination but instead barriers to entry and progression occur over the lifetime of individuals seeking a career in law from initial education, to training, to gaining experience within a law firm."

This report is over ten years old, but I think it is fair to say it is still relevant to a large extent today. What the SQE is trying to do is to reduce these barriers to entry through education and training. Progression is another matter, and more on that below.

The SQE reduces barriers to entry by offering more flexibility to aspiring solicitors. For example, solicitor apprenticeships are now a popular route into the profession and appeal to those for whom university and the associated costs present an insurmountable hurdle. The apprenticeship route enables completion of a pathway to qualification with or without a degree, with individuals working in firms or organisations straightaway and therefore enabling them to earn whilst completing the academic stage alongside

– typically one day a week. The speed of this journey depends upon an individual's experience, but a school leaver would take five to six years to qualify on this route. Any reader interested in finding out more would be advised to follow on LinkedIn City Century (an initiative aiming to increase solicitor apprenticeships in City firms), Damar Training (innovative non-degree solicitor apprenticeships),[14] and Joanna Hughes (founder and director at Joanna Hughes Solicitor Apprenticeships) who is a huge apprenticeship advocate.

Attracting talent early from diverse talent pools

As the legal landscape evolves, attracting and retaining young legal talent has become a constant challenge for law firms and organizations. Recognizing the need to diversify the talent pool, firms are implementing innovative strategies to appeal to the next generation of lawyers. Flexible work arrangements harnessing the opportunities of the new SQE, and a commitment to diversity and inclusion, have become key components of recruitment efforts.

Aspiring solicitors from more diverse backgrounds have typically faced barriers such as not obtaining the requisite high grades in GCSEs/A-levels (although steps in the right direction are now being taken by many firms adopting the Rare Contextual Recruitment System[15] to identify strong candidates, irrespective of their background), the cost of undertaking professional legal qualifications, or being unable to undertake work experience due to caring responsibilities.

A commitment to D&I now forms part of most firms' values statement, and initiatives such as the Macfarlanes Training Scholarship[16] show that the profession is embracing creative ways to recruit aspiring lawyers from diverse talent pools. The scholarship is a unique program developed by the firm and delivered in partnership with Brunel University London Law School, and is designed to break down some of the socio-economic barriers that discourage talented students from joining the legal profession. The firm supports three students annually, and covers the full cost of university tuition fees, alongside paid work experience, a paid placement year at the firm, and mentoring from senior lawyers throughout. This significantly reduces the financial burden faced by many socially mobile graduates when they enter the workplace and gives participants the opportunity to develop their legal knowledge and skills while building their networks in the profession.

Law schools and universities have a part to play in this too. As an example, BARBRI supports partner firms to enable wider access to the profession through the BARBRI Bridges initiative, which offers, amongst other things, fully funded SQE1 places for clients of partner charity Breaking Barriers and Humanitarian Scholarships for those fleeing conflict. On a personal level, I am co-founder of the Social Welfare Solicitors Qualification Fund (with the City of London Law Society and Young Legal Aid Lawyers), which supports aspiring solicitors committed to working in the field of social welfare law.

As the demand for diversity has increased, organizations such as Rare Recruitment, Aspiring Solicitors, and Strive (who support Flex Legal with their Flex Trainee initiative) have flourished, with a mission to actively support candidates who wouldn't otherwise be able to access the profession.

As part of its 2023 Annual Report,[17] Lamphouse Strategy, an insights specialist for the legal sector, looked at 125 leading global law firms and the initiatives they publicly talk about having in place (on their website or any responsible business reports). Some of the most commonly discussed strategies include:

- 44 percent offer work experience / internships for students from lower socio-economic backgrounds.
- 36 percent provide scholarships and bursaries to students from an ethnic minority.
- 19 percent have legal apprenticeships (this is much higher if you look at just the Top 50 UK firms – 44 percent).

Whilst their analysis shows that firms tend to communicate more about the tools they have for attracting talent, they are less likely to talk about strategies to retain and develop talent, e.g. partner sponsorship programs and retention-specific programs.

Do aspiring solicitors still view law as a "career for life"?

The perception of law as a "career for life" is undergoing a paradigm shift. The next generation of lawyers, influenced by a dynamic job market and evolving societal expectations, are less inclined to view their legal careers as linear or permanent, and the rise of freelance and self-employed legal professionals through organizations such as Keystone Law, gunnercooke, Obelisk Support, LOD, and Flex Legal are challenging traditional career trajectories. Many young lawyers are exploring diverse career paths, including in-house counsel roles, legal consulting, entrepreneurship, and even completely unrelated fields. This trend raises important questions about the nature of commitment to the legal profession and the expectations of long-term loyalty from both employers and employees.

A 2023 survey[18] that benchmarked global legal talent, commissioned by Chambers & Partners in association with Lamphouse Strategy, found that associates (compared to partners) are less happy, less motivated, and less likely to recommend their current firm. Just 21 percent of associates say they intend to stay at their current firm for up to two more years, 30 percent for up to five more years, and 49 percent for more than five years. Similarly, Flex Legal's Future Lawyer Report 2023 (638 junior legal professionals) found that nearly two-thirds (65 percent) of respondents see themselves in their current role for between two and five years. Whilst 70 percent of respondents of Major, Lindsey & Africa's 2023 survey report, *Gen-Z: Now Influencing Today's Law Firm Culture*[19] said they plan to pursue the law firm track, only 39 percent said they would join a Big Law firm (down from 59 percent in the 2020 survey). Additionally, 53 percent of Gen-Z respondents said they were interested in eventually transitioning to an in-house, government, or non-profit role long-term, compared to 23 percent who hope to one day make partner at a law firm. The Gen-Z Survey was conducted between January and March 2023, and surveyed law students and young lawyers from around the world, with a particular focus on those attending the top 100 law schools.

The pursuit of partnership has traditionally been the hallmark of a successful legal career. However, changing attitudes among junior lawyers suggest that the allure of partnership is waning. The traditional partnership track, characterized by long hours and intense competition, may no longer align with the values and priorities of the younger generation. As a result, law firms are re-evaluating their partnership structures and exploring alternative models that provide more flexibility and work-life balance. The Chambers & Partners research found that 57 percent of associates say partnership is a realistic aspiration in their current firm. However, there are differences by demographics. Associates who identify as LGBTQ+, ethnic minority, having a disability, or neuro-divergent are less likely to aspire to partnership. The Flex Legal Future Lawyers Report reported 63.2 percent of respondents cited career development as a reason to stay in their current role. There is also a possibility that some talented juniors are moving to legal tech/start-ups etc. due to dissatisfaction with the hierarchical structure in traditional "pyramid" law firms. Firms that encourage and support entrepreneurship and seek to develop alternative models may be more successful in retaining ambitious talent.

Attrition rates within the legal profession have seen a noticeable increase, with lawyers opting to leave private practice completely. Burnout, dissatisfaction with the traditional law firm model, and the desire for a better work–life balance are among the leading causes of attrition. Firms are grappling with the challenge of retaining their talent, prompting a re-evaluation of organizational structures and policies to address the evolving needs of their workforce. Flexible working brought about by COVID-19 seemed to go some way to address this, but there has been a recent trend of firms trying to encourage lawyers back into the office, in some cases for a minimum of four days per week. In addition, KPMG's CEO Outlook survey[20] found 64 percent of leaders globally, and 63 percent of those in the UK, predicted a full return to in-office working by 2026. As is regularly discussed, there is also the question as to whether the phasing out of the billable hour would improve work–life balance and aid retention.[21]

In a move to create a workplace that attracts, retains, and promotes people from different backgrounds, with different perspectives and life experiences, firms such as Hogan Lovells and HSF have joined the Reignite Academy, which provides opportunities for lawyers who have taken a break from city careers to return to private practice. The Academy provides successful candidates with a six-month paid period of work experience and training with a view to "reigniting" their careers.

Similarly, flexible resourcing organization Obelisk Support has a specific program, the Legal Returners' Springboard,[22] for those returning to legal practice. The program provides expert advice from lawyers, GCs, expert coaches, and fellow returners to support and inspire those preparing to return to working in the law.

In-house and beyond – alternatives to private practice
For all the reasons set out above, the legal profession is witnessing a surge in interest in alternative career paths, both within and outside private practice. In-house counsel roles have become increasingly attractive to lawyers seeking a different professional experience. The opportunity to work closely with business teams, gaining industry-specific knowledge, and enjoying more stable hours and general work–life balance are enticing factors for many legal professionals. The Chambers & Partners/Lamphouse Strategy Leading Teams research supports this. In terms of where associates would think of moving to next were they to leave their current firm, 73 percent said they would move to an in-house role. The most influential factors were looking for a better work–life balance and more interesting work. The Law Society Annual Statistics Report for 2023 noted that those employed in-

house by organizations ranging from FTSE and private companies to local authorities now make up over one-quarter of the profession.

Additionally, legal consulting, legal tech, and legal ops roles are emerging as viable and exciting career options, offering lawyers the opportunity to apply their legal expertise in new and innovative ways. In 2020, professionals from the KPMG Legal Operations Transformation Services practice in member firms around the world made predictions in relation to how they believed the legal function will evolve from the present to 2025.[23] The report is specific to in-house teams, and one of the key predictions was that, by 2025, half of legal teams would not be lawyers. Whether half turns out to be the correct number, it is very clear that both in-house and private practice are heavily investing in legal tech, legal innovation, and legal ops roles. In his 2022 book, *The Legal Team of the Future*, Adam Curphey (senior manager of innovation at Mayer Brown) talks about the need for multidisciplinary teams for the provision of legal services and this by its nature opens up the possibility of new and evolving roles attracting talent with very different skillsets.

KPMG predicted that improvement and standardization of processes and increased use of technology would enable new strategies for sourcing legal services, "*...and as demands intensify to do more with less, the traditional legal function hierarchy will likely morph into a more agile and cost-effective structure*". A quick review of several well-known legal job boards at the time of writing shows this to be true. Advertised roles on offer include legal technologist and tech innovation and there are even several legal tech and legal ops graduate programs opening up in top firms including Magic Circle firms Linklaters and Allen & Overy.

KPMG further predicted that, by 2025, every organization would be able to rely on its contract lifecycle management to be the central source of truth for all contracts. Centralizing how contracts are managed (including from negotiation to execution) is likely to improve a firm or organization's ability to manage cost and risk and improve consistency of performance. Such centralization will inevitably involve legal tech, and the legal technologist and beyond roles that accompany it. More evidence of the broader roles developing in the legal profession.

Has the legal profession lost its shine?
Whilst the short answer to this is no, students and aspiring lawyers expect more from the profession and their career and employers need to adapt to provide this. Financial remuneration alone is no longer good enough, and

there is substantial evidence[24] that graduates entering the profession today would rather sacrifice some of their income if it means an improved work–life balance. Firms and organizations are now navigating a redefined legal profession marked by technological advancements, changing attitudes, and a redefinition of professional priorities. The next generation of lawyers is demanding more from the profession, prompting a re-evaluation of traditional structures and practices. Firms and organizations that recognize and evolve and adapt to these shifts are likely to thrive in the evolving legal landscape.

Societal developments, regulatory changes, and technological advancements will undoubtedly play a part in the appetite of future generations to embark upon a career in law. As we have seen, the integration of generative AI and other advanced legal technologies, a much stronger emphasis on well-being, and the changing perception of a legal career as a lifelong commitment are reshaping the dynamics of the legal profession. As legal grapples with these challenges, it is essential to strike a balance between embracing change and innovation and preserving the core values that define the practice of law. The future of the legal profession lies in its ability to evolve, responding to the needs and expectations of the next generation.

References

1   Susskind, R., *Tomorrow's Lawyers*, Third Edition 2023 (Oxford University Press).
2   www.linkedin.com/pulse/ai-law-six-thoughts-richard-susskind/
3   www.lexisnexis.co.uk/research-and-reports/legal-aid-deserts-report.html
4   www.lawsociety.org.uk/contact-or-visit-us/press-office/press-releases/a-decade-of-cuts-legal-aid-in-tatters
5   www.ljmu.ac.uk/about-us/news/features/impact-of-cuts-to-legal-aid
6   www.city.ac.uk/news-and-events/news/2022/07/barristers-on-strike-why-criminal-lawyers-are-walking-out-and-what-they-really-get-paid
7   ibanet.org/document?id=future-of-legal-services-report-23
8   www.lawsociety.org.uk/topics/research/annual-statistics-report-2022#
9   www.theguardian.com/technology/2023/jun/23/two-us-lawyers-fined-submitting-fake-court-citations-chatgpt
10 www.lawcare.org.uk/latest-news/life-in-the-law-new-research-into-lawyer-wellbeing
11 www.abodehr.com/blog/how-gen-z-is-shaking-up-big-law
12 www.ibanet.org/document?id=IBA-report-Mental-Wellbeing-in-the-Legal-Profession-A-Global-Study
13 https://legalservicesboard.org.uk/wp-content/media/2010-Diversity-literature-review.pdf
14 https://damartraining.com/employers/industries/solicitor-apprenticeships/

15 www.rarerecruitment.co.uk/products/crs
16 www.macfarlanes.com/join-us/early-legal-careers/macfarlanes-training-scholarship/
17 www.lamphouse.com/annual-report/
18 Leading Teams research by Chambers & Partners and Lamp House Strategy (2023). Data represents responses from over 3,200 associates.
19 www.mlaglobal.com/en/insights/research/genz-now-influencing-todays-law-firm-culture
20 https://kpmg.com/uk/en/home/insights/2022/09/kpmg-ceo-outlook-uk.html
21 www.lawgazette.co.uk/news/firms-moving-away-from-billable-hours/5114967.article
22 https://obelisksupport.com/be-a-consultant/return-to-legal-work/springboard/
23 https://kpmg.com/xx/en/home/insights/2020/12/future-of-legal-article-series.html
24 www.pinsentmasons.com/careers/vario/blog/redefining-work-life-balance – one article of many.

Chapter 3:
Changes to the legal profession – how a career in law could look

By Charlotte Smith, founder, Level7

In 2003, as the digital age was dawning with the advent of social media, I embarked on my journey in the legal profession, starting my LLB. As an older millennial, I began my career at a time when Facebook was spreading across our law school computers. Completing the Legal Practice Course at the College of Law in York from 2006 to 2007, followed by a training contract, made me the first in my family to enter the profession. My smooth admission to the roll of solicitors in England and Wales was set against a historical backdrop that began long before my time.

Entering the profession

Let me take you back. My grandmother was especially proud that I became a lawyer. She was born in 1923. A decade before, in 1913, Britain, the UK was on the precipice of World War I – a bloody conflict that would see many young men sent to die on the battlefields of Flanders.

In 1913, Gwyneth Bebb[1] brought a case against The Law Society. In *Bebb v. Law Society*, the Court of Appeal explored whether the gender-neutral language of the statutes meant that women could gain admission to the Bar. It settled that women were excluded under "persons" in the Solicitor's Act of 1843. Yes, you read that correctly. Women weren't people. It was further ruled unanimously that, before the passing of the 1843 Act, women were under a general disability because of their sex and were unable to become solicitors. Gwyneth Bebb did not win her case. Towards the close of the War, in 1918, the Representation of the People Act was passed, giving women over 30 the vote and men under 21 who had been fighting. Post-War represented a change in societal attitudes, with a whole generation of men dead or returning traumatized and maimed. Women had proven during the War that they could do the work of men. In the post-War years, we saw landmark legislation, the Sex Disqualification (Removal) Act 1919, making it illegal to exclude women from jobs, including the legal profession, because of their sex. In 1922, Carrie

Morrison became the first woman solicitor in England. Helena Normanton and Ivy Williams were among the first to join the Bar as barristers.

A career in the law

A lifelong career in law was a standard expectation for lawyers and still is for many. The most common pathway to becoming a solicitor in the UK was a two-year training contract, which included rotations in four distinct practice areas. My rotations covered employment law, commercial contracts, intellectual property, and civil litigation, leading to my qualification as a solicitor. The development of one's legal practice varies based on the training location, firm size, and specialization. At a boutique law firm focused on the travel industry, my experience was divided between litigation, which comprised half of my workload, and commercial matters, including employment law, contracts, and intellectual property issues.

By age 29, I had solidified my specialization and developed a successful employment law practice. My work encompassed various services, including seconding employees overseas, crafting specialized employment contracts and handbooks, and providing comprehensive advice and counsel. I handled matters from pre-litigation stages to resolving employment law disputes in court. Under the guidance of a managing partner who trusted and empowered me, I was granted the freedom to innovate. This environment nurtured my intrapreneurial spirit, allowing me to contribute significantly to our team's revenue. Our firm, characterized by its boutique size and a hands-on, "roll up your sleeves" attitude, was the perfect incubator for my ideas. Recognizing an opportunity to enhance our service offering and client support further, I pioneered an employment law subscription product, a concept now acknowledged as "alternative legal services". This initiative represented a significant shift from conventional legal practices and the billable hours model to offer our clients subscription access to employment advice and counsel. I partnered with specialist insurance underwriters to augment our service in litigious situations, integrating insurance-backed employment litigation solutions. This collaborative effort resulted in a comprehensive package of employment law services tailored specifically for travel firms and designed to meet the needs of business-focused clients. The venture seamlessly aligned with my practice area, resonating well with industry clients who valued our pragmatic, business-oriented, and value-driven approach.

The legal profession's sex and elitism

Attending junior lawyers' division events in the mid-2000s, I couldn't help but notice the number of privately educated peers, reflecting the ongoing challenges to this day in social mobility within the legal sector.

I recall a fellow junior lawyer suggesting I work on muting my Yorkshire accent and pronunciation to sound more "successful". Experiences like this encapsulated the pressure to fit a specific mold in law, highlighting the industry's biases and lack of diversity.

A survey by the Solicitors Regulation Authority in 2016[2] revealed stark educational disparities in England's legal profession. Over a quarter of lawyers were privately educated, nearly four times the national average. In higher legal ranks, the gap widens to 51 percent of solicitors and 55 percent attending Oxbridge, compared to only seven percent of the UK population in private schools and less than one percent at Oxbridge. Coming from a state school background, a female barrister, Jane Sisson-Pell, fueled my legal aspirations; I met her during a school-funded work experience program at the Crown Prosecution Service when I was 15.

In 2007, I joined a boutique firm in Leeds with three female partners and one male. This firm was the exception rather than the rule, with larger regional and London-based legal firms being rather more male-dominated. Of my class at law school in 2006, I'd estimate that about 50 percent was female. A 2022 study[3] analyzing UCAS data revealed that female applicants to law programs outnumbered males by a two-to-one ratio. We can point to many reasons for the shifting attitudes; with more women entering the profession, some have suggested a female preference for the law over STEM subjects. Working at a firm led by female partners, fresh in my early career, I had the perspective that the challenges of the generations before us had been overcome. Women's prevalence in the law had progressed significantly from a century earlier, with a notable increase in women pursuing law.

Yet, when we look at leadership roles within the legal profession, the presence of women declined drastically mid-career. To shed light on this, we should look at the traditional hierarchical structure of the legal profession, which notably falls short in accommodating the needs of working parents, especially mothers, and individuals with caregiving responsibilities.

The motherhood penalty

The demanding hours and rigid structure of many legal roles often clash with family responsibilities, disproportionately affecting women who commonly shoulder more caregiving duties. Looking at my law school peers, many who became mothers left the profession mid-career due to the impractical and unappealing prospect of life as a lawyer and mother in the legal profession. Life as a mother clashed with the traditional law firm model, the high cost of childcare, the need and desire to be there for their child, frequent illness in the early years, or wanting to be at their kids' school plays. This lack of support led to their departure.

The desire for parenting time – whether due to culture, conditioning, biology, or simply the luxury of enjoying one's children – plays a significant role in why women leave the legal profession. The joy of being present for their children and the practical need to manage childcare responsibilities are fundamental concerns.

The law firm business model, a hierarchical organization focused on billable hours, has barely changed since the 1910s. This model demands conformity to a work culture that often feels unnatural for many, especially women, who are forced to adapt to a male-dominated environment.

I remember the moment I came across a striking graph in an article from *The Economist*. It depicted a stark contrast between men and women in the workforce after the birth of their first child. While the line representing men barely dipped, the women's line plummeted dramatically, illustrating a grim reality – the motherhood penalty.

This term was defined by researchers from the London School of Economics and Princeton University, who analyzed data across 134 countries.[4] They found that, on average, 24 percent of women leave the workforce in the first year after childbirth, and even after ten years, 15 percent do not return. This visual and the accompanying research brought home the sobering impact of motherhood on women's careers worldwide, encapsulating the challenge in a single, powerful image.

Motherhood from a wider lens

Upon my move from the UK to the US, I was met with a stark contrast in maternity leave policies, mirroring the broader cultural differences in perceptions of motherhood and employment. In the UK, mothers are eligible for up to 52 weeks of maternity leave, with statutory paid leave available for up to 39 weeks, although the compensation falls below the cost of living. Meanwhile, California, despite having among the most liberal policies in the US, offers only up to 12 weeks of paid family leave. This is deemed progressive in a country where some states provide little to no maternity benefits, forcing many mothers to return to work prematurely. The absence of a national statutory paid maternity, paternity, or parental leave policy in the US highlights a significant gap in support for women and caregivers, starkly contrasting with the more generous policies of other countries.

Although the UK ranks fourth globally for its maternity leave provisions, it remains behind the more generous Scandinavian countries, with Sweden setting a high standard. Beyond the disparity in leave entitlements, the high cost of childcare represents a significant burden, particularly affecting dual-income families and working mothers, amplifying the strain on balancing work and family life. This worldwide inconsistency calls for a concerted effort from legal professionals and leaders to cultivate empathy and push for policy reforms.

There's a pressing need to recognize and address employees' challenges in juggling their careers with their family and caregiving duties, advocating for a more supportive and inclusive work environment globally.

Peak to pivot – the journey beyond

By the age of 29, I had become a partner. Despite this success, I encountered a profound internal void. The legal profession's elitism, stark lack of diversity, seeing and hearing about instances of sexual harassment for young lawyers, the unhealthy always-on, work-hard-play-hard mindsets, and significant challenges confronting working mothers – including the "motherhood penalty" – ushered me to a crossroads.

The profession's rigid demands for conformity stifled my creativity and clashed with my deepest values. Entering the legal field, I was driven by the belief that it would offer a stable and meaningful career. Yet disillusionment set in. The profession's challenges had me questioning my future within it. I observed friends launching start-ups, thriving in technology, innovating in media, and living nomadic lives as web designers. My successful "side gig" – a food blog and supper club, which regularly received media attention – became my gateway to rediscovering my passions and interests outside the legal domain. As I saw it, some of the most successful individuals, living the happiest and most fulfilled lives, had ventured beyond the conventional path. This period of deep reflection and introspection led to a decisive shift. I departed from my law career midway, embarking on a quest more closely aligned with my values and authentic self.

Redefining legal careers – adapting to new trends

My experience encapsulates a significant trend – a growing number of lawyers are transitioning away from traditional roles, driven by a desire for improved work–life balance, personal growth, and innovative applications of legal expertise.

The shift is evident across various sectors, including academia, media, public policy, and the nonprofit sector, where lawyers are finding fulfilling roles that leverage their skills in new ways. For instance, about ten percent of law graduates were pursuing roles in academia in 2022, attracted by the opportunity for continuous learning and flexible work schedules.

The American Bar Association[5] emphasizes the potential for lawyers to leverage their legal backgrounds and pivot towards new careers, highlighting the importance of identifying transferable skills and interests for career development. Alternative career paths for lawyers also include roles in digital marketing, teaching, project management, and recruitment. These paths offer the opportunity to apply high-level problem-solving abilities, strong organizational skills, and legal expertise in dynamic and engaging new contexts.

Moreover, the legal industry is evolving, with many lawyers dissatisfied with traditional career paths seeking roles that offer more flexibility, creativity, and personal fulfillment. This includes opportunities in legal sales, real estate brokerage, and even becoming authors or legal educators, leveraging their legal knowledge and skills in unique ways.

The Bureau of Labor Statistics[6] outlines the traditional roles of lawyers, including representation in legal proceedings and advising clients on legal matters. The diversity of tasks and responsibilities in the legal profession underscores lawyers' broad skill sets, which can be effectively transferred to alternative careers. Job websites and legal recruiters specialize in placing lawyers in nontraditional roles, highlighting the growing market for legal professionals seeking alternative career paths. Networking and engaging with professional communities are also vital strategies for lawyers transitioning into new fields.

This trend towards alternative legal careers reflects broader shifts in work preferences and the legal industry's adaptation to new societal and technological changes. The move towards roles outside of traditional practice areas underscores the versatility of legal training and the vast array of opportunities available to those willing to explore new career paths. This evolution towards roles that offer more autonomy and encourage creativity is a testament to the legal industry's ongoing transformation, propelled by technological advancements.

Silicon Valley as a catalyst for change

Since my move to Silicon Valley in 2014, I have worked at the intersection of human performance, legal innovation, and technology. As an executive coach, I have had the privilege of working closely with a diverse portfolio of legal professional clients, from general counsels and in-house legal teams in big tech, biotech, VC, capital markets, IP, and patent lawyers, Leaders who are leading their teams through a start-up phase of rapid growth.

These experiences have granted me a unique vantage point, coaching in-house lawyers to adopt and embody leadership mindsets, adopt practical change management approaches, and support them in growing and developing their teams as they scale operations.

I coached an associate general counsel in a pre-IPO company as they managed the professional and leadership demands during the process of taking that company public. I've worked with lawyers in-house and in private practice in the US and UK.

Soon after leaving traditional practice, I launched a podcast. It was enriching to record podcast episodes, notably with legal tech founders, such as Alistair Maiden, founder of SYKE and legal ops pioneer whose company was recently acquired by Consilio, and Mary O'Carroll as she assumed her new role of chief community officer at Ironclad, formally leading Google's legal operations function and sitting as president of CLOC. In these conversations, I saw, heard, and viewed the level of transformation and potential within the legal industry.

The notable impact for in-house teams that I have observed is the Contract Lifecycle Management (CLM) for optimizing organizational efficiency. Witnessing teams adopt CLM technologies to streamline workflows and manage commercial agreements more effectively has been revelatory. This melding of technology creates a game-changing shift towards more streamlined, efficient operations. Technological optimization includes state-of-the-art tools and technology, but it also requires effective change management and fostering adept and resilient legal teams. This nuanced and legal practice's human and technological aspects underscore the relationship between innovation and human performance enhancement. In simple terms, each drives the other forward in the ever-evolving landscape of Silicon Valley's legal sector.

Launching my consulting firm was a leap into integrating my legal expertise with my innate strengths and the innovative spirit of Silicon Valley. My consultancy became my platform for experimentation, allowing me to explore how legal services can be enhanced through technology and creative thinking. The journey of growing my business has been one of continuous learning, adaptation, and integration, reflecting the changing landscape of the legal profession. In the past decade, the legal industry has entered an era of transformation not unlike the industrial revolution or the dot-com boom. This era is revolutionizing the delivery of legal services and expanding the definition of a legal career, challenging traditional boundaries and fostering new avenues for growth and innovation.

What does the future look like? A technology-driven legal evolution

The standardization of legal technology and AI is a future in which technology is seamlessly integrated into legal work. As attitudes within the profession evolve, so do the opportunities for legal professionals to optimize their services and teams' tech-driven solutions, challenging the status quo and establishing new norms.

Technology integration in the legal sector has created new roles and companies at the intersection of law and tech innovation. This shift is redefining traditional legal career paths, enabling practitioners to explore fields such as data privacy, tech compliance, and legal software development. Legal tech firms are making waves in contract management, document automation, practice management, e-discovery, and regulatory compliance. Artificial intelligence is at the forefront of this innovation wave, attracting significant investment from courts, legal associations, and private and corporate legal departments. These technological advancements aim to enhance the efficiency and profitability of legal practices, posing a challenge to conventional law firm business models.

Over the past decade, the legal tech start-up scene has experienced a significant surge in venture capital interest, leading to a market valuation for legal technologies estimated at USD 23.45 billion, with a forecasted compound annual growth rate (CAGR) of 9.1 percent from 2023 to 2030. In Contract Lifecycle Management (CLM), vendors' increasing saturation signals a trend toward market consolidation. This shift is facilitated by technological advancements that streamline legal processes and business operations in law firms and in-house legal teams.

The legal operations function, now an increasingly capable and essential part of legal departments and firms, focuses on initiatives like process optimization and technology implementation to enhance operational efficiency. Top legal operations leaders, especially within technology firms, command competitive remuneration packages, reflecting the high value placed on their contribution to integrating business strategy with legal expertise.

Today's legal professionals are distinguished by a unique blend of legal knowledge, business acumen, and technological expertise, making them well-equipped to navigate the complexities of the modern legal landscape.

The change catalyst of 2020

The global pandemic of 2020 served as a watershed moment for the legal profession, catalyzing significant changes in workplace dynamics. The sudden necessity for remote working and the acceleration of tech-enabled teams have reshaped operational models and aligned them with the evolving values of a new generation of lawyers. This period underscored the importance of flexibility and personal wellbeing and triggered a pivotal shift toward a more balanced work–life integration. The normalization of personal life intersecting with professional settings, exemplified by people's children making appearances in video calls, marked the beginning of a transformational phase in work culture. In 2024, the world is in a different place than in 2020 – layoffs, global uncertainty, a push for more attorneys back into the office. Some of the gains of 2020 have regressed.

The focus on lawyer wellbeing has intensified over the last decade, with influential bodies like the American Bar Association (ABA) and the Solicitors Regulation Authority (SRA) spearheading discussions on mental health and work–life balance even before the pandemic. This growing concern has led to significant evolutions within the industry, aiming to create a more supportive and sustainable work environment for legal professionals.

The call for greater diversity and inclusion within the legal sector gained momentum with the social justice movements of 2020. Law firms and legal departments have been inspired to confront systemic biases more earnestly, driven by a societal demand for inclusivity. Additionally, Generation Z's expectations for their work–life – emphasizing politics and ethics – are reshaping workplace norms, signaling a shift towards environments that value diversity and ethical practice.

Despite economic uncertainties and debates over the efficacy of diversity, equity, and inclusion (DEI) programs in a tense geopolitical climate, the legal profession's dedication to social responsibility and environmental, social, and governance (ESG) principles endures. The anticipation of the 2024 US elections adds a layer of uncertainty and an opportunity for reflection and potential redirection in the profession's commitment to these principles. The interplay between demand and the necessity for change marks this era as a transformative period for the legal profession, shaped by societal changes and the evolving expectations of the new generation, a demand for a commitment to diversity, social responsibility, and ethical conduct.

The changing face of modern legal professionals

The emergence of technology and AI has catalyzed the creation of new roles within the legal landscape, particularly in areas such as compliance and data privacy. These positions necessitate a profound understanding of legal principles and regulatory intricacies, highlighting the increasingly multifaceted and dynamic trajectory of legal careers in today's tech-driven era.

The emergence of roles such as chief innovation officers, chief knowledge officers, and chief community officers within the legal sector are increasingly commonplace and reflect the industry's response to rapid advancements in technology and the increasing importance of community engagement and knowledge management.

- Chief innovation officers (CIOs) in the legal sector are tasked with steering law firms and legal departments through technological transformation. They are responsible for identifying and implementing innovative technologies that enhance the efficiency of legal services, improve client engagement, and maintain competitive advantage. CIOs play a pivotal role in integrating AI, machine learning, and legal tech tools into daily legal practices, driving both internal process improvements and client-focused solutions.
- Chief knowledge officers (CKOs) focus on optimizing the management and utilization of the organization's knowledge assets. In legal contexts, this means developing strategies to capture, share, and leverage collective knowledge and expertise within the firm or legal department. CKOs ensure that valuable insights and information are readily accessible, facilitating better decision-making and enhancing the firm's ability to deliver high-quality legal advice. Their role is crucial in precedent management, legal research, and the development of internal knowledge bases.
- Chief community officers (CCOs) represent a newer but increasingly vital role within the legal industry, emphasizing the importance of building and nurturing relationships with the broader legal and business community. CCOs' roles at legal tech companies focus on creating value through community engagement, fostering a strong brand pres-

ence, and establishing partnerships that enhance the business' reputation and reach. They work closely with marketing, business development, and legal professionals to ensure a cohesive community strategy aligning with the firm's values and objectives.

Together, these roles signify a shift towards a more interdisciplinary, innovative, and community-focused approach in the legal sector. They underscore the need for legal professionals to excel in their traditional roles and adapt to new challenges and opportunities presented by the digital age, ensuring that law firms and legal departments remain relevant, efficient, and socially engaged.

Traditional views on making partner
The journey to partnership, long regarded as the pinnacle of a legal career for some, is being reevaluated. The legal profession's traditionally conservative approach to career progression and risk management is gradually giving way to a more dynamic and flexible mindset.

While the billable hours model is not being eradicated, the hierarchical structure in big law is being changed and there's a continued and growing recognition that the traditional career path is only one of the routes to success or fulfillment.

The traditional concept of a lifelong legal career is undergoing a shift. Today, modern lawyers have unprecedented opportunities to practice law outside traditional firm structures, thanks to the rise of alternative legal service providers (ALSPs) and the gig economy. Many blend their legal expertise with entrepreneurial ventures, personal pursuits, and flexible work arrangements, reshaping the traditional career trajectory.

ALSPs offer legal services but operate outside the traditional law firm model. ALSPs are increasingly popular, especially in tech-driven areas like Silicon Valley, the Bay Area, and the UK, with a high demand for innovative, cost-effective legal solutions. General counsels are able to use these vendors, known for leveraging technology, process efficiency, and often lower cost structures to deliver legal services. They are enabling in-house legal teams to focus on core legal strategies. ALSP business models vary. Obelisk Support, one of the earliest ALSPs, was founded by Dana Denis-Smith in 2010 to keep ex-City lawyers working flexibly around their families and other commitments. Flex Legal is another flexible staffing ALSP that was acquired by Mishcon de Reya. In the US, there are Axiom, Paragon, and others.

In response to these changing dynamics, firms, teams, and organizations are deploying innovative strategies to attract and retain talent. Benefits such as sabbaticals, intrapreneurship opportunities, and modular career paths are becoming increasingly common, allowing lawyers to pursue diverse interests while maintaining a foothold in the legal profession. The transition from traditional attorney roles to "project-based" or more flexible positions – legal project managers, knowledge management specialists, and data analysts – reflects the industry's evolving needs and the diverse skill sets of modern legal professionals.

Adapting to AI and multidisciplinary expertise

In the evolving landscape of legal practice, the integration of artificial intelligence and AI technology, though yet to be widespread across traditional law firms, is gaining traction within start-ups, Fortune 500 companies, and global firms such as Baker McKenzie and Allen & Overy. These organizations are at the forefront, investing in training programs to equip lawyers with the skills, knowledge, and technology to innovate and adapt in this new era. Codex at Stanford Law[7] and other innovation labs underscore the shift towards a modernized legal education, preparing professionals to navigate the complexities of modern legal challenges.

The vision of a modern lawyer is a business-oriented professional possessing deep legal expertise, complemented by the skills and knowledge to deploy technology/technical skills, whilst maintaining high emotional intelligence (EQ). This holistic, well-rounded model will empower legal professionals to meet the demands of contemporary legal practice.

To retain top talent, law firms and legal departments must embrace innovation, transitioning from traditional hierarchical structures to collaborative, client-centric models. This shift towards valuing soft skills, such as emotional intelligence alongside legal expertise, signifies a broader change in the industry, aligning with the dynamic expectations of both legal professionals and their clients.

Culture and leadership in the law

The legal profession is transforming profoundly, propelled by technological advancements and evolving attitudes. This shift extends beyond the challenges of burnout and ineffective leadership, revealing deeper issues related to the profession's culture and mindset. The future beckons with changes such as the advent of AI and the automation of tasks traditionally performed by associates. This evolution makes it crucial for legal leaders to refocus and prioritize the development of EQ and human-centric skills among lawyers. Addressing and mitigating resistance to change is essential, which can manifest through perfectionism, competitiveness, overwork, fear, and an overly risk-averse attitude.

During a recent panel discussion in San Francisco, I highlighted the inevitable move towards a leaner staff of associates and paralegals, coupled with a stronger focus on cultivating leaders who can inspire, motivate, and engage their teams more effectively. This year has already been marked by significant layoffs in Silicon Valley, with legal departments feeling the brunt of these changes. In this environment, traditional paths to promotion may become less prevalent. However, this period also presents an opportunity for growth and development. Enlightened teams recognize the importance of fostering a motivated and positive culture to unlock new opportunities. By investing in the comprehensive development of their staff and emphasizing lateral skills, these teams are not just aiming to minimize further losses but also striving to create a more adaptable and robust legal workforce. As we reflect on the journey through the changing landscape of the legal profession, it's evident that we are witnessing a pivotal era of transformation.

The narrative that has unfolded from the early 20th century to the present day captures a continuously evolving profession – societal and cultural shifts, technological advancements, and a growing call for diversity and inclusion are shaping it. By 2025, 75 percent of all legal teams will be Millennials or Gen-Z.[8] This evolution speaks to a broader theme of resilience and adaptability among legal professionals as they navigate the complexities of modern practice while striving for a more equitable and dynamic field.

The challenges highlighted above – from the historical struggles of women entering the profession to the modern-day dilemmas of work–life balance and technology integration – underscore the legal profession's capacity for growth and reform. As we look towards the future, the emergence of new roles, the reevaluation of traditional career paths, and the increasing importance of soft skills and leadership qualities indicate a promising direction that embraces innovation, values diversity, and prioritizes wellbeing.

Advocating for change in the legal profession

At its core, the legal profession is about serving clients' needs. Yet, the traditional models often fail to address the wellbeing of those within the profession. To build a more sustainable, inclusive, and effective legal landscape, specific changes are essential. Below are some simple and implementable strategies to elevate culture and experience in legal.

- *Delegate wisely*. Empowering your team through delegation enhances efficiency and fosters a sense of ownership and satisfaction among team members. It encourages professional growth and builds a more resilient organization.
- *Prioritize self-care*. Recognizing the importance of mental and physical health is crucial. A profession known for its long hours and high stress must embrace self-care as a necessity, not a luxury, to prevent burnout and maintain high performance.
- *Build support systems*. Strengthening internal networks within the profession and external support systems can provide a valuable exchange of ideas, mentorship, and emotional support, which is crucial for navigating the challenges of the legal field.
- *Redefine work culture*. Shifting the focus from hours worked to results achieved can lead to more productive and satisfied legal professionals. This approach encourages efficiency and creativity, allowing lawyers to find work–life harmony.
- *Manage urgency*. Not every issue needs to be addressed immediately. Cultivating the ability to discern true urgencies from routine tasks can reduce stress and improve prioritization skills within legal teams.
- *Leverage technology*. Automating routine and time-consuming tasks frees legal professionals to focus on higher-level, strategic work. This increases job satisfaction and allows firms to serve their clients more effectively.
- *Aid caregivers*. Offering flexible working arrangements and support for caregivers is crucial in retaining talent and ensuring that the legal profession is accessible to all, regardless of their personal responsibilities.
- *Expand thoughtfully*. Growth should be strategic and considerate of the team's capacity and the firm's long-term goals. This ensures sustainable development that benefits both the organization and its clients.
- *Encourage learning*. Valuing and promoting the development of soft skills alongside technical legal expertise can lead to more effective communication, leadership, and client service.
- *Promote transparency*. Open discussions about challenges, failures, and successes can cultivate a culture of trust and continuous improvement within the legal profession.

Individuals can contribute to this evolution by:

- Embracing lifelong learning and being open to developing both their technical, legal, and soft skills.
- Recognizing the pushes and pulls of legal life. Legal is a high-performance environment, and to perform at our best, it requires harnessing our energy. It also requires discipline and hard work.
- Practicing self-care and advocating for a healthy work–life balance within their organizations.
- Being mentors and allies to others in the profession, sharing knowledge and support to foster a collaborative and inclusive culture.

Organizations can play a role by:

- Implementing policies and technologies that support flexibility, efficiency, and wellbeing.
- Investing in training and development programs, emphasizing a broad range of skills, including emotional intelligence, communication, and leadership.
- Creating a culture that values diversity and inclusion at all levels of the organization.

By embracing these changes, individuals and organizations within the legal profession can contribute to a more dynamic, sustainable, and fulfilling future for all its members. The cost of inaction is high, not only in terms of personal wellbeing but also in the profession's ability to attract and retain talent and serve society effectively. Proactive steps toward evolution are essential for the legal profession's continued relevance and success.

References

1   Gwyneth Bebb: The Past Explaining the Present. *Law Gazette.* www.lawgazette.co.uk/gwyneth-bebb-the-past-explaining-the-present/5070047.article
2   SRA Survey: Quarter of Lawyers Privately Educated. Legal Futures. www.legalfutures.co.uk/latest-news/sra-survey-quarter-lawyers-privately-educated
3   Women Outnumber Men Two to One in Law Studies. Law Gazette. www.lawgazette.co.uk/women-outnumber-men-two-to-one-in-law-studies/5115053.article
4   www.linkedin.com/feed/update/urn:li:activity:7159216443752947712/
5   Job Opportunities for Law Grads. American Bar Association News. www.americanbar.org/news/abanews/aba-news-archives/2023/05/job-opportunities-law-grads/

6   Lawyers: Occupational Outlook Handbook. US Bureau of Labor Statistics. www.bls.gov/ooh/legal/lawyers.htm

7   Codex – The Stanford Center for Legal Informatics. Stanford Law School. https://law.stanford.edu/codex-the-stanford-center-for-legal-informatics/

8   Desperate for Next Generation of Lawyers, Legal Departments Must Offer Meaningful Impact. Corporate Counsel. www.law.com/corpcounsel/2023/04/04/desperate-for-next-generation-of-lawyers-legal-departments-must-offer-meaningful-impact/

Chapter 4:
The SQE and QWE – building a talent network for the future

By Robert Dudley, head of employability and engagement, BARBRI

To say the past decade has been one of constant change for the legal industry would be putting it mildly, with geo-political instability and an unprecedented global pandemic just some of the issues at play.

During this time, the talent gap has continued to cause the sector a huge challenge, with many struggling to fill roles and recover from the Great Resignation, not to mention compete with other firms to attract talent. A lack of diversity also remains a thorn in the side of the legal sector, with seemingly little having improved in recent years.

Paving the way for change, the Solicitors Regulation Authority (SRA) in the UK took a bold step in 2021 with the introduction of the Solicitors Qualifying Exam (SQE). Although perhaps not the support some quarters of the legal sector would prefer, the SQE was introduced – in part – as a long-term, robust solution to the industry's issues around recruitment and diversity. Rather than a short-term "quick fix", the SRA recognized that a major intervention was needed to right-foot the legal industry and futureproof it for the long-term.

Of course, upholding high standards and consistency in qualification was also at the core of introducing the SQE, but it brought a number of additional benefits in terms of addressing critical issues within the legal profession – namely around recruitment, retention, futureproofing skills, diversity, accessibility, and inclusion.

It is set to become the main route to qualification in the UK and eventually replace the existing Legal Practice Course (LPC) route completely by 2032. As a centralized exam that promises to create a level playing field for all candidates to ensure consistency across the profession, it enables candidates from both law and non-law backgrounds – and those already in the sector, such as paralegals – to qualify as solicitors. This is a major shift in comparison to the existing route, which presented challenges for candidates such as additional study requirements through the conversion course, the Graduate

Diploma in Law (GDL) for non-law candidates – which is no longer required for the SQE – as well as the need to secure an elusive two-year training contract.

Instead, the two-year Qualifying Work Experience (QWE) element stream-lines the process, acknowledging and building upon existing industry experience. Moving away from the traditional model, which previously served as a bottleneck for talent, QWE can be secured before, during, or after the SQE assessments, helping legal teams build valuable connections with future talent and nurture individuals from the outset. It is also a useful resource at a time when talent acquisition and retention remain issues industry-wide as employers may now be able to offer shorter QWE opportu-nities in contrast to the fixed two-year training contract. It will also appeal to legal employers who previously could not offer training contracts, seeing them miss out on upcoming talent.

The SQE is also creating new opportunities for school leavers through legal apprenticeships, helping firms and in-house teams to grow talent from the ground up, acting as a catalyst for greater diversity of thought, while creating more robust attraction and retention strategies. The sum of all this supports the positive evolution of a more diverse legal sector and future-proofed oper-ations.

Another groundbreaking aspect of the SQE is its flexibility in allowing candi-dates to pursue part-time study over an extended period. This accommodates a broader range of individuals, enabling them to earn while they learn and tailor their schedules to align with personal and professional commitments.

The introduction of the SQE and its supporting QWE requirement pres-ents a prime opportunity for the legal sector to take a fresh look at its approach to developing and building the future workforce by reconsidering attitudes towards ideal candidate pools and broadening minds in terms of the benefits of doing so commercially and from a diversity perspective. With the countdown already on to make the full "switch" to the SQE, those who embrace it now will remain one step ahead of the competition and will be able to realize the return on their investment sooner.

Upskilling and building commercial teams
Despite industry attitudes to routes to qualification gradually changing, the link between the impact of embracing the SQE and solving one of the industry's biggest challenges is yet to be made by many.

According to research carried out by BARBRI in 2023, 81 percent of SME law firms said their top challenge was recruitment, with 48 percent also struggling with retention. This "revolving door" is creating further issues in itself with the cost of recruitment a considerable issue for 43 percent of the firms we spoke to. With this in mind, wouldn't exploring alternative routes to finding quality candidates to fill these gaps be an obvious way forward? Yet just over a quarter (27 percent) of firms are still to embrace the SQE.

Not only does this mean firms are missing out on talent from a much broader, more diverse group of candidates (more on this later), but it also means they miss out on taking full advantage of the QWE element of the SQE, which can be gained before, during, or after the SQE assessments. For firms looking to upskill existing team members such as paralegals into solicitors, the route to qualification is much more efficient. Of course, there are many other benefits to the QWE too.

Trainees, including paralegals, apprentices, and graduates can make up their experience in up to four settings, including their current firm. This gives employers a chance to understand what motivates each candidate and how best their skills and aptitude might fit within their organization.

By upskilling current team members, not only are recruitment costs reduced, but the benefit of their existing knowledge of the firm can be fully realized. In fact, in our research, 40 percent of SME firms cited employee knowledge being up to date as crucial to their ability to remain competitive. This in itself builds a strong case for developing the potential of existing employees who know your business inside out.

The practical nature of the QWE means it also builds valuable skills such as commercial awareness and relationship management, creating a workforce with a good understanding of the business world and how law can best support this. According to our research, QWE provides a timely opportunity for firms to build these skills in their future employees, with 58 percent of firms citing business and financial acumen as their biggest skills gap. This was closely followed by strategic thinking and innovation (42 percent).

In terms of the other skills most sought after, 60 percent of firms said client relationship management know-how and good communications skills (58 percent) were two of the biggest factors adding value to their client service, quality, and reputation. People who were good team players (58 percent) and acted in line with the firm's values were also most sought after (31 percent). Again, people within the business who already display a good working attitude and match the values of the firm are extremely valuable if they are keen to progress and the firm shares their ambitions.

Paralegals and the QWE "bank"

One of the first groups to benefit from the SQE and forward-thinking firms taking a "grow your own" approach are paralegals. With many already satisfying the QWE two-year work experience requirement through existing experience, qualification for those who want to become solicitors can be highly efficient and cost-effective for both parties.

Harnessing their existing investment in promising paralegals is center stage in many law firms' future plans. According to our research, for almost two-thirds (63 percent) of SME law firms, paralegals will increasingly replace the traditional trainee role as a path to qualification. Firms are embracing the opportunity to develop promising individuals already amongst their ranks and upskilling them to become qualified solicitors.

Already laying the foundations for this approach, 52 percent of firms said their paralegals will take on more complex tasks in the next three years. With client-facing and relationship-building skills at the fore of development, 43 percent of firms are seeking more and more opportunities for their paralegals to interact with clients. Paralegals with a particular interest in specific areas of the business or strong capabilities in a certain department will also be able to specialize, with 44 percent of firms welcoming the chance for paralegals to become more specialized.

Fortunately, the drive to acquire these skills is also shared by paralegals themselves. Recent BARBRI research among paralegals[1] found that almost three-quarters (72 percent) thought developing relationship management skills was very important for their career development, alongside deeper commercial understanding. A further 56 percent also said developing business acumen and knowledge of the latest legal tech and tools were key areas of their progression they would like to invest in.

The SQE, in particular the QWE element, creates the perfect storm for both firms and ambitious paralegals to meet their objectives, in terms of overcoming recruitment challenges (not to mention costs) and securing workforce planning goals with a robust, "tried and trusted" future team of high performing solicitors. In turn, paralegals can fulfil career ambitions, rather than missing out on reaching their full potential due to constraints that may have existed due to the inflexibility of previous routes to qualification such as the LPC.

This embodies the purpose of the introduction of the SQE – to create a level playing field upon which people from all backgrounds and socio-economic circumstances can enter the legal profession, ultimately reflecting the diversity of the client base that the industry seeks to represent.

Growing talent from the ground up through apprenticeships

Another largely untapped route to "grow your own" for firms looking to futureproof their workforce and recruit a diverse team is apprenticeships. A highly cost-effective route to qualification due to the Government-backed support available, there are currently 1,300 solicitor apprentices undertaking the SQE qualification pathway in England. Accessible at a number of career points, from school leavers through to existing employees, apprenticeships are being favored by many in the legal sector due to their flexibility.

Apprenticeships help to ensure that legal teams are shoring up and retaining talent while enabling team members to reach their full potential. Through our collaboration with Damar Training, we're seeing legal teams supporting employees through part-time study for the SQE while helping them gain appropriate work experience towards the QWE requirement. This means they're able to access legal talent while individuals work towards qualification, making it the best of both worlds for both parties.

With an increasing number of well-known industry names leading the way when it comes to embracing the apprenticeship route to qualification, the tide is turning in the sector with our research finding over a third of SME firms (35 percent) are using apprenticeships to both attract and upskill talent.

While this is promising, almost half (46 percent) are still not using the apprenticeship route. Reasons for this slow uptake vary in nature but collectively highlight the fact there is still work to be done around how newer routes to qualification are perceived in the legal sector, particularly by traditionalists. A third (36 percent) of SME firms that took part in the research said they weren't using apprenticeships because they "prefer more traditional routes".

Fortunately, the statistics are beginning to build the case for apprenticeships, countering the skepticism held by some in the industry. According to the latest SRA data, apprentices who have undertaken the SQE to date achieved marks that were eight percent higher on average than other candidates. This makes the outlook for the 1,300 candidates currently going through the SQE route in England extremely promising, not to mention the huge opportunity for forward-thinking firms and legal sector organizations to support and recruit apprenticeship candidates.

Another sector-wide benefit of apprenticeships that links back to one of the fundamental reasons for the introduction of the SQE in the first place is its role in increasing diversity in the legal industry. This is especially true when it comes to enabling candidates from lower socio-economic backgrounds to gain entry to the profession and progress to a higher level. The latest SRA diversity stats mirror this need, highlighting a reduction from 21 percent of qualified lawyers in 2015 coming from a lower socio-economic background to 18 percent in 2023. However, from a DE&I perspective, apprenticeships are helping to create new opportunities for those who may have previously been unable – or unwilling, for whatever reason – to pursue the university route, which may have excluded talented candidates.

The introduction of the SQE in 2021 may have seemed a bold move by the SRA to some, but with statistics like these in mind, the need to shake up the industry and rethink routes to qualification was much needed.

Creating a new and improved workforce with improved diversity and inclusion

While there is encouraging anecdotal industry evidence that a much broader, more diverse candidate pool is currently undertaking (and considering) the SQE, SRA data shows that the full impact of its introduction is yet to be felt. Its latest industry data from July 2023 recorded a pass rate for the first portion of the SQE exam (SQE1) that was significantly higher for white candidates, which sits at 66 percent, compared with 49 percent for Asian candidates and 34 percent for black students.

When it comes to diversity around the wider spectrum of inclusivity, including gender, heritage, and ability, the latest SRA statistics showed some improvement. The proportion of women in law firms has risen from 48 percent in 2015 to 53 percent in 2023, and an increase in Asian and mixed/multiple backgrounds was recorded. There is still room for improvement, however. Only 32 percent of partners in UK firms identify as women, while only three percent of lawyers identified as black, and six percent considered themselves to have a disability (compared to the 16 percent national average).

Building a fairer, more inclusive legal sector is much wider than considering diversity across individual gender, heritage, and ability elements of course. Representation across a multitude of socio-economic backgrounds is a considerable challenge for the legal sector, for example. In fact, according to the 2019 Sutton Trust "Elitist Britain" report,[2] many of the UK's barristers, solicitors, and judges hail from private schools and the same few universities. Echoing this, the SRA's 2023 data[3] reported that 21 percent of lawyers attended a fee-paying school in contrast to seven-and-a-half percent nationally. In addition to this, only 18 percent of lawyers came from a lower socio-economic background.

However, attitudes are beginning to change and the need to recruit from wider talent pools to ensure inclusion is being recognized. An example of this is the City Century initiative launched in late 2022. A collaboration between the City of London Law Society (CLLS) and over 50 city law firms, including Linklaters, Allen & Overy, and Eversheds Sutherland, the initiative aims to increase the number of apprentices entering the profession. Designed to help broaden access to the sector and build a more diverse pipeline of emerging talent, the program's objective is to create 100 new partners by 2040 via the solicitor apprenticeship route.

While initiatives like this are encouraging, BARBRI's recent research shows the sector still has some work to do in understanding the full extent of the sector's inequality. With 44 percent of the SME firms we surveyed describing themselves as diverse, and 46 percent saying they only have "some" or "little" improvement to make, firms and wider legal sector organizations need to ensure they are fully inclusive across all aspects of what constitutes "diversity". This is a finding that could also reflect the ambiguity of the word "diversity", however, rather than a lack of genuine intention to try and become more inclusive on firms' parts.

Of course, no one organization or industry leader has the answer, and the solution isn't about finger-pointing. Rather, the legal sector needs to continue the conversation and keep the dialogue open. Diversity and inclusion need to be brought to the forefront of discussions about the industry's future, collectively creating a step change to make a tangible difference in the future.

More than just being "the right thing to do" and plugging the talent gap, there are a number of compelling commercial reasons to build a diverse and inclusive workforce. According to a YouGov poll,[4] joining an organization that is diverse and inclusive is important to 66 percent (two-thirds) of people when looking for a new employer. This figure increases to 78 percent for Gen Z (18-24-year-olds).

Other advantages of developing a diverse and inclusive workforce include the benefits of diversity of thought. People from a diversity of backgrounds, circumstances, ages, cultures, and life experiences not only best represent those they serve, but the difference in their thinking means a much wider perspective on possible outcomes when it comes to decision-making.

For example, one study[5] found that diversity of thought in a team made up of people from different backgrounds and demographics led to better quality decision-making, with the effectiveness of the quality of team decision-making rising from 66 percent to 87 percent where this involves a more diverse group of individuals. Interestingly, the difference rose incrementally based on the number of diversity factors within the team.

Mirroring this, a study by Deloitte[6] found diverse teams were eight times more likely to achieve better business outcomes when making decisions. On top of this, they were also three times as likely as non-diverse teams to be high-performing and 17 percent more productive on average.

Studies such as those from Harvard Business Review[7] link this increased productivity to tangible financial gain. Reviewing the fortunes of 1,700 companies across seven countries, Harvard researchers found organizations with above-average diversity achieved 19 percent higher revenues on average and nine percent higher EBIT.

While there is mounting evidence around the benefits of a diverse workforce, when it comes to translating this into action, the legal sector is still at the start of its journey. However, introducing the SQE is a significant step on that journey and, if fully embraced by the legal sector, could go some way in bridging the talent gap and creating a truly diverse, inclusive workforce.

Summary

Firms should review the organizational approach to recruitment and retention and the role that the SQE could play in attracting new talent. As part of this, they should consider exploring the alternative pathways available such as apprenticeships, as well as showcasing developing roles outside of the traditional trainee/associate model.

Check that your organization is fully exploiting all pathways open via SQE. For example, investing in your existing team members through the SQE is not only more efficient and cost-effective thanks to the QWE element, but it can boost team morale, support, and motivation and positively impact team retention.

Remove barriers to apprenticeships and paralegal development where possible. This starts by changing the narrative internally, particularly if members of your organization are holding onto the traditionalist model. If you can pilot a program with just one individual, you can demonstrate success and showcase the true possibilities.

Review your organization's approach to D&I, taking steps to become fully inclusive. It may be that you wish to explore and support industry-wide DE&I initiatives such as City Century to open doors to young talent or connect with organizations like STRIVE, which works to create accessible opportunities for candidates from diverse backgrounds, for example. Or perhaps you may look to shape a more bespoke initiative internally. Change cannot happen overnight, but it does take the full support of the industry.

Review training opportunities for those needing to satisfy the two-year QWE requirement. This is a more accessible model and experience can be gained in up to four placements across the two-year-period. It may be that you wish to explore internal and external opportunities with partner organizations to enhance the breadth of experience for your team members.

Those who embrace SQE now will be one step ahead of the competition come 2032. Ultimately, now is the time to make this shift away from the traditional LPC route rather than wait until the official deadline if you wish to futureproof operations and best support your teams.

References

1   The SME Law Firm Report 2024, BARBRI, www.barbri.com/sqe/barbri-sme-report-2024/
2   www.law.com/international-edition/2023/06/15/legal-remains-one-of-the-least-socioeconomically-diverse-sectors-in-the-uk/
3   www.sra.org.uk/sra/equality-diversity/diversity-profession/diverse-legal-profession/
4   www.peoplemanagement.co.uk/article/1831387/two-thirds-british-workers-say-workplace-edi-important-when-job-hunting-survey-finds
5   www.cloverpop.com/hacking-diversity-with-inclusive-decision-making-white-paper
6   www2.deloitte.com/content/dam/insights/us/articles/4209_Diversity-and-inclusion-revolution/DI_Diversity-and-inclusion-revolution.pdf
7   https://hbr.org/2018/01/how-and-where-diversity-drives-financial-performance

Chapter 5:
What do recent graduates and junior lawyers really want from firms?

By Serena Brent at Mayer Brown, Sophia Margetts at Osborne Clarke, Suhail Mayor at DLA Piper, and Chrissie Wolfe, LAB Consultancy

Young people entering the legal industry today are doing so at a time of great change. Unprecedented advancements in technology and artificial intelligence, atypical post-pandemic working habits, and greater demand than ever before for the legal industry to diversify its workforce are all factors, covered throughout this book, which make today a unique time to be starting a career in law. This chapter aims to shed light on what trainees and recent graduates value most when applying for jobs, what employers and firms can still do to better appeal to young graduates, and what a "career in law" means to those entering the workforce today.

Globe Law and Business spoke to young lawyers at three UK firms – Serena Brent at Mayer Brown, Sophia Margetts at Osborne Clarke, and Suhail Mayor at DLA Piper – as well as solicitor and talent specialist Chrissie Wolfe, to shed some light on these subjects. Our interviewees look beyond traditional markers of success such as salary and discuss flexible working hours, the value of mentoring, and the importance of a holistic firm culture. They also look at how AI has impacted their working lives, how firms can embrace cultural and technological changes, and what can be done to curb retention issues.

Please note that the views and opinions expressed by the contributors to this chapter do not necessarily represent the views and opinions of their company or firm.

Serena Brent
Associate, Mayer Brown

In an era of rapid change and evolving expectations, the legal industry finds itself at a pivotal crossroads, especially concerning talent acquisition and retention. Many have noted that recent graduates and junior lawyers are looking beyond traditional markers like prestige and salary and are increasingly drawn to a holistic work culture that aligns with their values. What kinds of things do you look for from a firm, and is there any one factor that stands out above the others?

When choosing a firm, I sought the opportunity to engage in work that was both intellectually stimulating and of a high caliber. Mayer Brown has exceeded my expectations in this regard. I work on the most cutting-edge deals and am always given a high level of responsibility, which forces me to learn quickly and use my initiative, while keeping me engaged in the transaction. Guidance is always there when I need it, as I work in small teams alongside some of the best lawyers in their fields, who are always on hand to answer any questions.

Flexibility as to the types of transactions that I work on is another priority for me. I (hopefully!) have a long legal career ahead of me. Therefore, I want to be able to identify my strengths and interests before choosing a specialism. One reason I chose to qualify at Mayer Brown is that junior finance lawyers are encouraged to work across at least three of the nine sub-teams within the group. This is giving me a well-rounded understanding of the practice area and enabling me to take my career into my own hands.

Above all, I look for a culture that allows me to bring my authentic self to work. At Mayer Brown, it feels like everyone is not only accepted but truly appreciated for who they are. The firm's reputation for fostering a culture of inclusivity is well-deserved – I feel no pressure to conform to any mold nor to have a "work personality". I choose to work in the office rather than at home as a result of the collaborative, friendly environment where I am surrounded by such great teachers and friends.

Some firms are redefining their work environments to cater to new preferences, focusing on creating a more inclusive and balanced professional experience. Are you aware of any changes that have been made to this effect, and what do you think can still be done?

We have very active networks that celebrate and spread awareness globally, internally and externally, about difference. They also connect lawyers with shared characteristics from our various offices. For example, I am part of the Women's, Fusion (diversity) and Enable (disability) Committees and, as part of the latter, we are writing a firmwide blog that considers the advantages and disadvantages faced by neurodivergent lawyers.

Mayer Brown ensures each employee's voice matters. Forums are held at trainee and associate level, and I have found that points raised are always actioned. On a more informal level, partners are extremely approachable. I can always raise an issue directly with them and know that they will listen and offer a fair and helpful solution. Simply put, my voice matters at Mayer Brown. Whether it's sharing ideas, raising concerns, or contributing to discussions, I've always felt heard and valued.

Coaching and mentorship initiatives are a valuable part of a junior lawyer's training. What, in your opinion, should someone in a mentorship role focus on?
A mentor should focus on developing an open relationship with their mentee, rooted in understanding and trust, so that the mentee feels comfortable asking any question, no matter how small, and can work through any challenge, no matter how daunting. A good mentor will try their hardest to make time for their mentee and put in the effort to support them in the way that they need. Mentors can offer invaluable advice with the benefit of hindsight, helping junior lawyers to navigate difficult situations and a range of challenges.

At Mayer Brown, the importance of mentorship isn't just acknowledged – it's actively cultivated. I've been fortunate to receive mentoring from lawyers at different levels and I have really appreciated my mentors investing time in getting to know me, enabling them to understand the unique challenges that I face. I've come to them with a range of challenges, from professional to personal, and have consistently received advice specific to my personality, strengths, and weaknesses. They have approached situations with an alternative perspective to mine, often with the benefit of hindsight.

The biggest change in the legal industry currently is the incorporation of generative AI models into day-to-day life. AI and technology are not just incremental changes, but paradigm shifts in legal practices, and there have been concerns raised about AI replacing entry-level jobs. Has AI influenced your working life so far, and what's been your experience of working with it?
Generative AI has brought about positive changes in my professional life. Its biggest current advantage is that it avoids the need to start with a blank page. Particularly for summarizing existing content or presenting it in a different format, it's a quick and efficient method that gives you a workable starting point.

It's been exciting getting more familiar with the technology in my work.

Mayer Brown has really embraced generative AI tools and we have several options for using it. This includes a legal-specific generative AI tool that aids in tasks such as drafting and comparing documents as well as existing tools like those from Microsoft for more general queries. We of course always bear in mind client confidentiality and data privacy, which is the right way to go about it.

Lastly, is there anything else that you think partners, recruitment specialists, and people in management roles should know about what recent graduates and junior lawyers value from an employer?
I think there's a common misconception that prestigious city law firms must necessarily be rigid and overly hierarchical. However, Mayer Brown operates a true open-door policy that enhances my working life in every way. I feel at ease in the office and my learning and development has been accelerated by more experienced lawyers always being available to offer support and guidance, which ensures that I do a better job on each deal.

As alluded to earlier, the culture here was one of the key attractors that drew me to the firm at the outset and led me to choose to stay on qualification. At Mayer Brown, there's a real sense of camaraderie that goes against stereotypical hierarchy. I will have the same type of conversation with whoever is making a cup of tea in the kitchen with me – partner, intern, or non-lawyer. I doubt there are many other firms of this size in the City where, starting at trainee level, I would have benefitted from the senior leader mentorship that I have been given.

Sophia Margetts
Trainee solicitor, Osborne Clarke

What kinds of things do you look for from a firm, and is there any one factor that stands out above the others?
The main factors I look for are job satisfaction and quality of clients. I think it's so important to be at a firm that ranks highly for job satisfaction and acts on internal surveys to do with wellbeing and CSR initiatives. I also look out for the firm's approach to office working – how do they encourage people to go in and what perks or events do they offer to make the office environment more comfortable. I also look out for opportunities to work for a range of clients in different industries (i.e., media, fashion, PE) and wouldn't want to be at a firm that solely focuses on one type of client.

Some firms are redefining their work environments to cater to these new preferences, focusing on creating a more inclusive and balanced professional experience. Are you aware of any changes that have been made to this effect, and what do you think can still be done?
I like working in the office and therefore pay attention to how firms incentivize their staff to work in there. I'm aware of firms that have fully subsidized their canteens (including free breakfast and dinner service) and invested in items, such as standing desks and ergonomic mousepads, to make the office more comfortable. I also think the rollout of open plan seating has, generally, made firms less hierarchal. My current firm has been open plan since 2011 and tables often contain a mix of partners and juniors. I have also noticed an intention to redefine the office environment so that it's more inclusive through holding events that focus on D&I issues such as female leadership and having more "non-alcohol" socials. I believe more could be done to make the work environment more inclusive – for example, allowing employees to substitute Christmas and Easter for other religious or cultural holidays.

What, in your opinion, should someone in a mentorship role focus on?
I think mentorship is the most important part of a junior lawyer's training and someone in a mentorship role should focus on regularly checking in with their mentee (to the same extent that they would check in on a client). I appreciate it's incredibly difficult in a service-led industry for mentors to find the time to mentor, but I think firms should actively encourage fee earners (at all levels) to put themselves forward for mentoring roles and have a range of mentorship programs. I know my current firm has programs targeted at both juniors and those looking towards partnership, including a program focused on female senior associates. I also think that individuals in a mentorship role should receive mandatory training and expectations should be set at the start of the mentorship relationship by both the mentee and mentor. For example, an expectation about what will happen if one of you needs to reschedule and the core topics you'll discuss together. It's always noticeable when someone has a proactive mentor. Being able to talk through your work or the stages of a legal career with someone on a regular basis is invaluable.

Many now entering the legal industry are doing so with the intention of using their experience as a lawyer to pivot into a different career. Why do you think firms are struggling with retention, and what could they do to combat this issue? Or should they lean into this change?
It's difficult to pinpoint one reason why firms are struggling with retention. I imagine work–life balance is still a main reason, but I have also heard about juniors from different firms that leave because they find the work repetitive, or they've been shoehorned into one area of work that's different to what they signed up for. I think a way to combat this issue would be to ensure that NQs receive exposure to the full breadth of their practice area in the first years of their career. In terms of engaging with career changers, I think that firms should actively stay in touch with leavers. I know that some firms have strong alumni networks, and this seems to be a good way to build client and industry relationships.

Has AI influenced your working life so far, and what's been your experience of working with it?
I have mainly worked with AI on contentious matters where we use e-disclosure software. We've still had to review the documents and check for relevancy, but the software has been very useful in editing out completely irrelevant documents and generating automated indices and bundles. We still often have to go back and make manual changes to the index or bundle, but the process takes a lot less time than it would have done without AI. This seems to be the approach with AI in general, wherein AI is seen as a way to improve human efficiency, rather than to replace it.

Lastly, is there anything else that you think partners, recruitment specialists, and people in management roles should know about what recent graduates and junior lawyers value from an employer?
I think it is the small things – partners and senior lawyers taking the time to check in with juniors and build a sense of comradery in teams, employers recognizing hard work, and, of course, a variation of work.

Suhail Mayor
Trainee solicitor, DLA Piper

What kinds of things do you look for from a firm, and is there any one factor that stands out above the others?
Simply put, it comes down to two key aspects – opportunity for professional advancement/exposure and cultural integration. Graduates are often drawn to firms that prioritize their growth and development. Opportunities for mentorship, training programs, continuing education, and challenging assignments are good indicators for people looking to advance their careers and develop new skills.

Furthermore, while everyone wants to jab with the best, the manner in how culture is fostered is another important factor in determining retention. Often, many people talk about diversity but forget about inclusion. I look at things such as:

- Rate of lateral hires.
- Legacy employees.
- Partner track timeline.
- Affinity group availability.

Most importantly, many can be motivated by a firm's mission and impact on society. They may seek opportunities to work on meaningful projects, contribute to causes they care about, or engage in pro bono work. Firms that demonstrate a commitment to social justice, environmental sustainability, or other important issues may be particularly appealing.

Some firms are redefining their work environments to cater to these new preferences, focusing on creating a more inclusive and balanced professional experience. Are you aware of any changes that have been made to this effect, and what do you think can still be done?
Many firms are placing a focus on contextualized graduate recruitment and workplace awareness through affinity groups.

Contextualized recruitment involves processes that take into account various contextual factors such as socioeconomic background, educational attainment, personal experiences, and extracurricular activities, alongside traditional metrics like academic qualifications and work experience.

Affinity groups provide a supportive space for employees who share common backgrounds, experiences, or identities to connect, share resources, and build networks within the organization. This can be particularly important for underrepresented or marginalized groups who may face unique challenges in the workplace.

What, in your opinion, should someone in a mentorship role focus on?
Access to information and opening the right doors are what come to mind. An effective mentor helps keep track of the professional focus of their mentee. The most influential people in my career so far have always sought to feed into my ambition and never stopped me from trying. I believe part of what makes a strong mentor comes down to the chemistry shared between individuals and being able to have real, open, and human conversations about circumstances.

Why do you think firms are struggling with retention, and what could they do to combat this issue? Or should they lean into this change?
It goes without saying that firms that prioritize employee wellbeing, professional growth, and cultural alignment are better positioned to retain top talent and thrive in a rapidly evolving legal landscape. From my personal experience, the promise of working fewer or more flexible hours and still getting paid the same is the biggest reason most people leave their firms. In the new age of hybrid working, people have come to value their private time more. Salary scales directly to expected billables and those on the higher end – particularly within American firms – commonly experience burnout after three years.

Do I foresee this as a long-term issue? Honestly, no. The industry is cyclical and demand will always be there for legal jobs regardless of length served. Exposure to C-suite clients, multi-faceted industry interaction, and lateral mobility are a few of the many reasons why people may choose to stay long-term.

Has AI influenced your working life so far, and what's been your experience of working with it?
AI has slowly started being implemented in my day-to-day in the form of contractual review mechanisms, language models capable of drafting basic emails, and automated document review. Personally, I do not view AI as a threat. I welcome it with open arms while keeping a conscious prudency about its application. For legal professionals, working with AI often means adapting to new workflows and incorporating technology into their practices. While there is a fear for automation of more menial tasks, we are now

shifting into a society where an "input" based person will thrive. It is no longer just about output. There exists a world where everyone can be a programmer. Understanding how to take these learning language models and adapt our legal approach for optimal efficiency will only increase productivity. In practice, it holds true that while AI can handle repetitive tasks more proficiently, on the bright side it also frees up time for lawyers to focus on more strategic and value-added aspects of their work, such as client counselling, negotiation, and case strategy.

Lastly, is there anything else that you think partners, recruitment specialists, and people in management roles should know about what recent graduates and junior lawyers value from an employer?
While there is an extensive list of natural expectations that I believe every graduate looks for in an employer, to me, the most important trait would be mentorship. The prospect for any new graduate in an industry is the chance to develop new skills while also being acknowledged for taking an initiative. I personally appreciate when I am in an environment that supports a flat hierarchy structure where anyone is approachable. As a trainee, to be able to sit down with partners and associates alike, and have open communication about social/professional objectives makes a big difference. This directly ties into feeling valued, motivation to work, and having ambition to contribute more. What promotes people to stay, more than the work, is the sense of culture attributed to the firm. I have learnt that in the long-term this plays a fundamental role in driving growth at a commercial level. Within the bounds of mentorship, reverse mentorship is also an interesting novelty I have seen being adopted more in the market. The idea of bottom-up inquiry further facilitates the opportunity for "mentors" to truly understand the impact of their mindset on juniors holistically.

Chrissie Wolfe
Solicitor and talent specialist, LAB Consultancy

What have you observed that young people look for from a firm, and is there any one factor that stands out above the others?
There is no question that the new wave of aspiring and junior lawyers has a very different outlook and set of priorities than the generations that have gone before.

The sheer volume of information, choice, and influence that young people have at their fingertips owing to a life immersed in the internet and social media makes for a much more informed, empowered, and discerning candidate who is alive to the array of opportunities the world has to offer and the variety of ways to earn a living.

With that in mind, those who choose the law do so because they are passionate, dedicated, and inspired by a unique set of factors that have driven them to select a legal career over limitless other potential options. For that, they expect a meaningful, rewarding, and purposeful job. Pay is, of course, important but it's less about money for money's sake and more about being rewarded fairly for the value they add. Work–life balance is another key criteria for many aspiring lawyers. The profession is renowned for its poor mental health, with data from Lawcare[1] making for pretty grim reading. The next generation has no desire to follow this one in that respect and will prioritize, making sure that their wellbeing is protected. Tied in with that, a recent survey by Legal Cheek[2] of 2,000 aspiring lawyers revealed that the most important factor to them when choosing a firm was "friendliness", followed by quality of work and pay. Perhaps an unexpected, but revealing stat.

Why do you think that firms are struggling with retention, and what could they do to combat this issue? Or should they lean into this change?
There is no doubt that the employment landscape has changed in recent years. Historically, it was not uncommon for law firm partners to have trained at the firm and plan to retire from there without having worked anywhere else. Now, attrition rates,[3] particularly at the junior end, have risen considerably, with many leaving the law entirely to embark on a totally different career.

The reasons for this vary between individuals but certainly the high-pressure environment, coupled with long hours and lack of transparency around progression, has been enough to drive many out of practice and into a more mental-health friendly career. There is also a huge expectation vs reality gap for many junior lawyers who have enjoyed the academic side of law but found the often laborious and costs-focused nature of fee-earning to be quite different to what they imagined. In some cases, those candidates haven't left the law, but opted for a career in legal tech or operations where they have found their creative skillset and solution-focused mindset are better suited. This has come at a time where recruitment practices have also changed to a more skills-based approach[4] so it is even easier now to pivot into another area or career given the plethora of competencies that can be gleaned from a legal career.

As well as those who are pivoting completely, law firms are losing people to alternative structures such as ALSPs and those offering a form of consultancy model. For many, particularly those who are more entrepreneurial, this offers a more favorable balance where they have autonomy over the number and type of clients that they take on and keep a significantly higher proportion of the fees. It is predicted[5] that up to a third of lawyers could be working as consultants by 2026, which is a pretty serious threat to retention.

We have seen many law firms react to the talent crisis by engaging in "salary wars"[6] in an attempt to maintain interest and engagement. In reality, that's a quick fix to a much deeper issue with culture that must be addressed before any substantial improvement in retention will be seen. If law firms are unwilling to make that change, the alternative is to accept a higher turnover and adapt the business model to endure the financial strain that it brings.

Lastly, is there anything else that you think partners, recruitment specialists, and people in management roles should know about what recent graduates and junior lawyers value from an employer?
Every business is different and there can be no one-size-fits-all approach to addressing issues with employee retention. It goes without saying that any successful, and sustainable, change process must start with looking inward at the company's own data and implementing tailored solutions that deal specifically with those pain points.

With that in mind, Flex Legal[7] has commissioned a very thorough report shedding some light on how the legal profession is seen generally by the next generation, including the key factors that would encourage them to stay in a role.

One of the most significant statistics is the significant rise in the importance of alignment with company values, with the percentage of respondents identifying this as a key factor rising from just three percent in 2022 to 45 percent in 2023. The other most important factors included the potential for career development (65 percent), competitive salary (39.5 percent), personal belief in the organization's ESG strategy (30.4 percent), good wellbeing benefits (28.5 percent), and good financial benefits (18.2 percent). A further interesting statistic is the number of respondents willing to work 50+ hours per week dropping from 18 percent in 2022 to just nine percent in 2023.

These statistics paint the picture of a generation taking a much more holistic view on work and prioritizing a career that not only gives them the financial stability they need, but also a feeling of purpose and alignment with their employer. With the level of choice that the market now provides, in law and beyond, it is unsurprising that employees have higher demands. Law firms must adapt if they want to stay relevant, or risk losing their best people to more innovative and flexible businesses.

References

1   www.lawcare.org.uk/latest-news/life-in-the-law-new-research-into-lawyer-wellbeing/
2   www.legalcheek.com/2023/05/exclusive-research-gen-z-aspiring-lawyers-seek-friendly-firms-with-good-pay-and-top-quality-work/
3   https://capacity.law/blog/the-winners-in-law's-great-resignation-will-be-firms-that-focus-on-innovation-not-compensation/
4   https://ukrecruiter.co.uk/2023/09/25/how-skills-based-hiring-is-changing-the-way-we-recruit/
5   www.lexisnexis.co.uk/research-and-reports/platform-law-report.html
6   https://careerinlaw.net/uk/latest-in-nq-salaries-nearly-170000-a-year-at-a-city-law-firm
7   https://flex.legal/future-lawyers-report-2023-24

Chapter 6:
Attracting and retaining diverse talent

By Caroline Vanovermeire, global director of talent, leadership, and organizational development, Dentsu and Kathryn Rousin, global director of learning and development, White and Case LLP

Introduction
In the rapidly-evolving legal landscape, diversity and inclusion stand out as critical drivers of success for law firms. Recognizing the transformative power of diverse experiences and backgrounds, this chapter embarks on an exploration of the intricate process of attracting and retaining diverse talent within the legal profession whilst providing practical recommendations.

Understanding underrepresented talent pools in law firms – navigating diversity and inclusion
Diversity and inclusion have become key indicators for current and prospective employees and clients. As we embark on an exploration of attracting and retaining diverse talent in law firms, the first step is to unravel the layers of underrepresented talent pools. In this section, we scrutinize typical diversity lenses, delve into the often-overlooked realms of disability and social mobility, and examine the increasing focus on social and generational diversity. Along the way, we address potential biases in decision-making and ponder the question of whether applying a diverse lens truly results in an inclusive workplace.

There are complexities in identifying metrics and obtaining diversity data in different jurisdictions due to local regulations around what and how data is obtained, stored, and safeguarded, and how confident employees feel in sharing their data. Collecting data enables firms to monitor and analyze their structures and systems, including hiring processes, work allocation, and development opportunities for underrepresented groups. As firms strive for global consistency and local relevance, it is important to acknowledge that different jurisdictions view metrics very differently, and care should be taken to ensure that metrics make sense for the relevant market and lead to the outcomes firms are working towards.

Law firms participate in several client and industry surveys that serve as important benchmarks, including regular diversity surveys conducted by the American Bar Association, Vault, Minority Corporate Counsel Association (MCCA), the Solicitors Regulation Authority, and *The American Lawyer* magazine, to name a few.

Typical diversity lenses – gender, LGBTQIA, and parenthood

Law firms often employ typical diversity lenses that focus on gender, LGBTQIA+,[1] and parental responsibilities. Recognizing and addressing the unique challenges faced by women in the legal profession is a critical aspect of building an inclusive workplace. Gender disparities in law firms often extend beyond entry level, impacting career progression and representation in leadership roles. The American Bar Association (ABA) notes a *"palpable gap in the number of women in senior law firm positions".*[2] Whilst not specifically about the legal industry, Deloitte's report, Women @ Work 2023, says, *"Our 2023 research shows that despite some improvements over the past year, many women are still not getting what they want or need from their employers".*[3] Acknowledging and actively addressing these disparities is essential to fostering true gender parity.

The LGBTQIA+ community also brings a valuable perspective to law firms through different lived experiences. Creating an environment that supports and embraces LGBTQIA+ individuals helps to ensure that diverse voices are heard and valued. Implementing inclusive policies and practices, such as diversity training and policies, mentoring, coaching, sponsorship, and affinity networks together with visible role models and allies can contribute to a more welcoming and supportive environment for LGBTQIA+ professionals.

Parenthood, including for same-sex couples, poses distinct challenges. The demands of legal practice often clash with traditional expectations of parenting roles. Law firms must actively work to eliminate biases related to parenthood, offering flexible work arrangements, parental leave policies, targeted coaching, including return-to-work support following parental leave, and support networks to ensure that parenthood, irrespective of gender or sexual orientation, does not hinder career opportunities or advancement.

Disability and social mobility – breaking barriers

Often underexplored facets of diversity in law firms are the inclusion of individuals with disabilities and those from diverse socio-economic backgrounds. Recognizing the perspectives and talents that individuals with disabilities – whether physical or mental, visible or invisible – bring to the legal profession is not only a matter of equity but also a strategic advantage. Creating an environment that enables and celebrates diverse abilities can significantly enhance creativity and problem-solving capabilities within a law firm. People with disabilities want to experience an environment in which they are not hindered by processes, practices, policies, services, or products that have not taken accessibility into account in their conception, design, or implementation. Firms can consider engaging external expert support to audit their current practices and identify easily implementable solutions to increase accessibility. Firms might also support people leaders in recognizing how they can evolve their leadership style to tap into the potential of a more diverse group of team members.

Creating an inclusive environment involves making reasonable adjustments to accommodate different needs. Whether this means addressing the needs of individuals with disabilities or providing support for those from different socio-economic backgrounds, law firms are increasingly recognizing the importance of flexibility in their policies and practices.

Similarly, addressing social mobility is pivotal to fostering greater inclusion. Breaking down barriers that hinder individuals from lower socio-economic backgrounds from entering and thriving in law firms is crucial. This involves re-evaluating recruitment processes and creating new channels such as apprenticeships, offering mentorship programs, and providing opportunities for professional development that can bridge the gap and create a more diverse and representative workforce.

We are encouraged by the growing number of legal apprenticeships being launched by law firms. Of particular note in the UK is City Century,[4] launched by the City of London Law Society, which seeks to identify, attract, recruit, onboard, educate, network, develop, and qualify significant numbers of talented and committed solicitor apprentices. At the time of writing, over 50 City of London law firms were participating, annually recruiting well over 100 apprentices from across England and Wales, many from communities underrepresented in the legal profession. By offering an additional career entry route that does not involve incurring the level of debt typically associated with more traditional, full-time university pathways, City Century makes a solicitor's career achievable and attractive, which was hitherto unimaginable or unknown to many.

Emerging focus – generational diversity

As the legal landscape evolves, so too does the focus on generational diversity. Generational diversity is an emerging focus as younger generations – particularly Generation Z, born between 1995 and 2009 – enter the legal workforce, with Generation Alpha, born after 2010, ready to start applying in a few years. Understanding the expectations, values, and work preferences of these generations, whilst having an eye to their specific needs and perspectives and being mindful not to "label" them, is crucial for attracting and retaining future talent. This involves adapting recruitment strategies (see later), embracing technological advances, and fostering a workplace culture that aligns with their values.

Removing bias from hiring and promotion processes

Implicit biases, whether based on gender, race, or other factors, can impact hiring decisions, career progression, and overall workplace culture. Addressing biases requires a multifaceted approach, including awareness training for leaders, personal coaching to act on implicit bias, implementing anonymous recruitment processes, and leveraging artificial intelligence solutions in the marketplace to mitigate subjective decision-making.

Law firms must actively work to eliminate systemic biases within their structures, fostering an environment where talent is recognized and promoted based on performance and potential rather than preconceived notions of what it takes to succeed in their environment. The further professionalization of currently used assessment and selection tools and techniques could prove a win-win for partners under time pressure. One example could be where the assessment of skills, both legal and professional, is automated through AI and/or conducted where possible with the support of HR and DEI professionals.

Are we inclusive if we apply a diverse lens?

Applying a lens of diversity is a crucial step towards fostering inclusivity in law firms, but it is not the sole solution. True inclusivity involves creating a culture where diverse voices are not only present but actively heard, valued, and belong. It means that people can speak out without the fear of retaliation and can easily find the channels for doing so. It requires mindset change and structural investment. Inclusive leadership, transparent policies, and a commitment to addressing systemic barriers are essential components of building a truly inclusive workplace. Giving employees a voice in the direction and leadership of their firms, for example, through advisory and steering committee roles and shadow boards, shows that firms are listening.

Whilst on the surface there has been improvement in the achievement of diversity metrics and targets in the world's major legal markets such as the US and the UK,[5] we still see a lack of investment in inclusivity initiatives and specialist expertise (e.g., HR and DEI professionals) to support them. Achieving targets is only part of the equation – the real aim should be to create a truly inclusive culture that ensures there is belonging, equity, inclusion, and diversity. An organization that achieves its published diversity and inclusion targets, but still witnesses behavior such as drinking games at its social functions and people not feeling able to speak up during or following such events, cannot be said to be truly inclusive or to be acting in a manner that is congruent with its values.

In a high-performance culture, billable hours and business development targets are often the main key performance indicators (KPIs) by which employee performance is measured. High billable hours, lack of work–life balance, stress, and unrealistic expectations are often cited by employees (particularly women or the main carer) as reasons for leaving their firms.[6] As AI further opens up the possibility of business process optimization, the legal sector will need to shift mindsets, performance targets, evaluation criteria, and reward structures and fully embrace new ways of working to create more sustainable firms adapted to a new world context and paradigm explained as the doughnut economy.[7] Firms will only truly create value from inclusion when it reflects the DNA of a firm and is experienced by all stakeholders in the moments that matter.[8]

Understanding underrepresented talent pools in law firms involves a multifaceted exploration of both typical diversity lenses and emerging focuses. Tackling biases in leadership and decision-making and contemplating the true meaning of inclusivity are pivotal steps in creating a legal profession that is not only diverse but authentically inclusive.

Progress and strategies for attraction and inclusion

This section explores attracting diverse talent in law firms, highlighting the progress that has been made and the strategies employed to ensure a more diverse workforce and inclusive environment where all can thrive.

The changing landscape – progress in attracting diverse talent

The legal industry has witnessed a paradigm shift in recent years, with a growing acknowledgment of the need for diversity and inclusion. Law firms, once criticized for their lack of representation, have made significant strides in recognizing the value that diverse talent brings to the profession. This progress is evident not only in the increased visibility of underrepresented groups[9] within law firms but also in the development of inclusive policies and practices that actively attract diverse talent.

In response to societal and industry changes, law firms are now actively engaging in efforts to create a more welcoming environment for individuals of various ethnicities, genders, sexual orientations, beliefs, and socio-economic backgrounds. This shift is not merely about meeting diversity targets – it reflects a genuine commitment by most to fostering a legal work-force that reflects the diversity of the clients it serves and the communities it operates within. As a result, firms have widened the channels through which they hire. There is a recent trend to offer apprenticeships or to go and speak in schools to much younger students to ensure they are not ruling out a career in law too early on. Having role models engaging directly with poten-tial future hires is critical in this regard. Law firms that have partners who are more reflective of society also tend to have a greater chance of attracting diverse talent. Clients are increasingly expecting to partner with a law firm that more closely reflects their own organization and the wider community. It could still be argued that this constitutes a bias towards visible diversity rather than true diversity. The latter would also take non-apparent types of diversity, e.g., neurodiversity, into account.

Gender differences – strategies for attraction and progress made

Addressing gender disparity has been a focal point in the legal profession's journey towards diversity. Historically, women have been underrepresented in leadership roles within law firms, prompting a collective call for change. Law firms are increasingly adopting strategies to attract and retain female talent, recognizing the perspectives and skills they bring.

Flexible working arrangements, coaching, mentorship, and sponsorship programs, and transparent career progression paths are some of the strate-gies being employed to attract and advance women in law firms. An increasing number of young lawyers are expressing much sooner in their career that they prefer the counsel or other alternative career path as opposed to the partner career. The in-house counsel role is increasing in attractiveness compared to private practice. According to Deloitte's 2023 report,[10] working women still bear primary responsibility for caring and domestic tasks, which can hinder career progression and earning potential.[11] Therefore, initiatives that facilitate work–life balance, such as parental leave policies and family-friendly practices such as caregiving leave offered to all employees, can contribute to a more inclusive workplace for women.

The progress made in this area is visible, with an increasing number of women breaking through the glass ceiling in law firms. The rise of female partners and leaders in traditionally male-dominated fields of law is a testament to the positive impact of these strategies. Most firms are now hitting 30 percent representation at partner level and some explicitly state that they are aspiring to a minimum of 40 percent women, a minimum of 40 percent men, and 20 percent flexibility to be truly inclusive, including those who are non-binary.[12] These targets are important not just for partner roles, but also candidate pools for senior roles and representation on firm committees.

Generational differences – appealing to the values of Generation Alpha to Baby Boomers

As the legal profession grapples with an increasingly multi-generational workforce, the attraction and retention of younger talent, particularly Generation Z, has become a priority. This generation, known for its tech-savvy nature and strong values, requires a different approach in recruitment and retention strategies. They will expect their recruiters and interviewers to know about their firm's ESG credentials and what specific initiatives their firm is pursuing. They will ask about flexible working arrangements. They have done their homework and are negotiating their contractual terms well on entering the firm and asking for pay rises more frequently than the firm's standard reward policies are prepared for. TikTok videos are legendary with Generation Z people saying, "You can have me but for a price".

Generation Z tends to welcome flexibility to work from home more often and volunteer in a local school or charity mid-week as well as being able to care for a pet, bringing their children to nursery, or spending time on a new hobby or project that provides meaning and fulfilment. This is not to say that previous generations do not value flexibility, but we have seen that Generation Z is more likely to set boundaries around their availability for work. This has caused intergenerational tensions in some law firms with senior lawyers often having to stay late to deal with unexpected client needs at short notice and doing the work they would have been expected to do when they were in their direct reports' positions. It is recommended that:

"Legal employers begin building the bridge by recognizing the varying needs and values of lawyers across different generations. Legal employers should consider the origin of those values rather than chalking them up to character flaws. Generational fluency paves the way for greater collaboration and understanding."[13]

Law firms are adapting to the expectations of Generation Z by offering hybrid working and flexible working arrangements and emphasizing their commitment to social and environmental causes. These strategies not only make law firms more appealing to future talent but also align with the values that Generation Z prioritize in their professional lives.

Progress in this area is evident as law firms witness an influx of new talent contributing fresh perspectives and innovative approaches to legal practice. Recognizing also the value of social and generational diversity has meant that more and more firms are introducing apprenticeships on top of their graduate schemes, as previously mentioned. This is not only crucial for the sustainability of law firms but also for ensuring a vibrant and adaptive legal profession.

Avivah Wittenberg-Cox, a thought leader in creating gender balanced organizations, highlights the importance of dealing with ageism. As an example, we should not assume that all people over a certain age are less digital-savvy than digital natives or would have lower levels of energy. We should also not assume that all colleagues will work to a certain age or would like to retire by a certain age. Since life expectancy has increased considerably, we might need to rethink policies that require partners/employees to retire by a certain age. Instead, workshops organized for employees proactively preparing for the "third quarter" of their lives[14] might result in a stronger psychological contract and higher engagement levels. These workshops might result in employees staying longer with the firm, in the same or in a different role or working pattern. It might equally enable people to move on in a more fulfilling manner, pursuing other interests or passions that they might have abandoned in their busy "second quarter" of life.

Role of the hiring manager

Hiring managers play a pivotal role in this process. Training programs that sensitize hiring managers to potential biases, provide insights into diverse perspectives, and encourage inclusive hiring practices, including automation and professionalization through the use of technology in some parts of the process,[15] as well as bespoke onboarding and mentoring programs, contribute significantly to attracting talent from underrepresented groups. By aiming for more diverse candidate pools at the recruitment stage, law firms lay the foundation for an inclusive and diverse workforce.

The ongoing journey towards inclusivity

The progress made in attracting diverse talent in law firms reflects a broader commitment to fostering inclusivity in the legal profession. While significant strides have been made, the journey is ongoing, and law firms must continue to adapt and evolve their strategies to meet the needs of an increasingly diverse workforce.

Law firms that actively embrace diversity not only enrich their organizational culture but also position themselves as leaders in an increasingly global market for talent. The progress made is a testament to the resilience of the legal profession in recognizing and adapting to the changing expectations of the workforce, ensuring a brighter and more inclusive future for the practice of law. As law firms continue on this trajectory, the real impact will be seen not only in statistics but in the flourishing of a legal profession that reflects the richness of human experiences and perspectives.

The role of employer branding and employee value proposition in law firms – strategies for success

In an era where talent is not only a valuable resource but acknowledged to be a driving force behind organizational success, the role of employer branding and employee value propositions (EVPs) has become paramount. This section explores the significance of these elements in law firms, their impact on attracting diverse talent, and suggests practical actions that can be taken by law firms to make meaningful progress.

Understanding employer branding and employee value proposition

Employer branding refers to the way an organization is perceived by both current and potential employees. It encompasses the organization's reputation as an employer, its values, culture, and the overall employee experience. The EVP, on the other hand, is the unique set of offerings and benefits that an organization promises to its employees in exchange for their skills, expertise, and commitment.

This is not just a set of tangible benefits – it is a psychological contract between the employer and the employee. Law firms need to carefully articulate their EVP to create a compelling case for why potential employees should choose and stay with them. It needs to be simple so that all employees can articulate it.

A strong employer brand and compelling EVP can serve as powerful tools for differentiation. They not only attract high-caliber professionals but also contribute to employee satisfaction, engagement, and retention.

Employees mirror consumer behaviors – quick, efficient, and qualitative
In the digital age, where information is easily accessible, potential employees approach job searches much like consumers evaluating a product or service. They seek quick, efficient, and qualitative information about potential employers. Fewer words and shorter videos that showcase authentic stories resonate better with this audience. Law firms must recognize this shift in behavior and tailor their employer branding strategies to align with the expectations of the modern workforce.

A user-friendly and informative careers website, active and engaging social media presence, and transparent communication about the firm's values, culture, and opportunities are essential components of an effective employer branding strategy. Law firms that embrace this approach not only attract more candidates but also convey a commitment to transparency and openness.

Leveraging artificial intelligence for enhanced employer branding
Artificial Intelligence (AI) is increasingly playing a pivotal role in shaping modern employer branding strategies. From chatbots on career websites to AI-driven recruitment processes, technology is streamlining and enhancing the candidate experience. For law firms, incorporating AI in the recruitment process can lead to more efficient and unbiased candidate assessments, ensuring that the hiring process is both inclusive and effective.

AI can also be utilized to personalize the employer branding experience. Tailoring content and communication based on individual preferences and behaviors ensures that potential employees receive relevant and engaging information, enhancing the overall perception of the law firm as an employer of choice.

Authenticity backed up with real use cases and experiences

One of the critical elements of successful employer branding is authenticity. Authenticity builds trust, and trust is a cornerstone of a strong employer brand.

Law firms must not only communicate their values and commitments but also back up these messages with real use cases and employee experiences. This involves showcasing success stories, testimonials, and a genuine representation of the firm's culture. Prospective hires need to see people who look like them at all levels in the organization, especially senior roles.

Practical actions for law firms to achieve this authenticity include creating a platform for employee stories, implementing regular employee spotlights on social media or the firm's website that resonate across geographies, cultures, and demographics, and actively seeking and responding to prospective and current employee feedback.

Practical actions for law firms to enhance their EVP include conducting regular employee surveys to understand expectations and preferences, offering a competitive and transparent compensation package, providing opportunities for professional development and advancement, and emphasizing the firm's commitment to its values and work–life balance. By consistently referring to and delivering on the promises outlined in the EVP, a law firm can build a reputation as an employer that values and invests in its people.

Employer branding through storytelling and various channels

Storytelling is a powerful tool in employer branding. Crafting compelling narratives about the firm's history, values, and the individual journeys of its employees humanizes the organization. Law firms can utilize various channels to bring these stories to life, including written content, video testimonials, podcasts, and social media.

Strategic partnerships with legal publications, industry events, and participation in community initiatives can also amplify the reach of the firm's stories. By leveraging a multi-channel approach, law firms can ensure that their employer brand resonates with a diverse audience and reaches potential talent through platforms where they are most active.

Progress through purposeful actions

Law firms that invest in purposeful employer branding and a compelling EVP will not only attract diverse and high-caliber professionals but will also establish themselves as leaders in creating a workplace that values and nurtures its most valuable asset – its people. By aligning organizational values with employee expectations, law firms can forge a path towards sustainable success in an ever-competitive legal industry.

Engaging and retaining diverse talents in law firms – nurturing a culture of inclusivity

Attracting diverse talent is just the first step. The true challenge lies in engaging and retaining these individuals to foster an authentic, truthful, and inclusive culture within law firms. This section explores the importance of engagement and retention, particularly in the context of diversity, and suggests practical recommendations for law firms to create an environment where diverse talent thrives.

The imperative of engaging and retaining diverse talent

A diverse and inclusive workplace not only attracts top talent but also enhances creativity, innovation, and overall organizational performance.[16] Engaged talent contributes to a positive work culture, better client service, and differentiates the firm in the industry. Notable surveys such as the Law.com international "A-List"[17] give clients, competitors, and graduates an insight into which law firms are managing to succeed across the multiple fronts of financial success, diversity, and social efforts.

Onboarding for accelerated integration

Effective onboarding plays a crucial role in accelerating the integration of diverse talent within a law firm. Tailoring the onboarding process to the specific needs and backgrounds of diverse hires ensures a smooth transition and helps them feel a sense of belonging from the outset.

Practical recommendations for law firms include assigning buddies and mentors to new hires, providing comprehensive orientation programs that highlight the firm's culture and values, and offering networking opportunities with colleagues, for example through affinity groups. An inclusive onboarding process sets the tone for a positive employee experience, laying the foundation for long-term engagement.

Evolving working patterns in law firms

The legal profession is witnessing a transformation in working patterns, particularly concerning issues such as childbirth, childcare, and overall work–

life balance. Law firms that adapt to these changing patterns demonstrate a commitment to the wellbeing and satisfaction of their employees.

Flexibility in working patterns has become a key consideration for retaining diverse talent in law firms. This flexibility extends beyond traditional notions of working hours and encompasses remote work, job sharing, and other arrangements that accommodate the needs of employees.

Practical recommendations include implementing technology that supports remote collaboration, establishing clear guidelines for flexible working arrangements, offering parental and other leave policies that accommodate different family structures, and actively promoting a culture that values outcomes over rigid working hours. By adapting to flexible working patterns, law firms not only retain their employees but also demonstrate a commitment to creating a modern and adaptable workplace. The new generation expects flexibility. Unlike previous generations, many do not aspire to be a partner in future.[18] If law firms do not offer flexibility, many younger lawyers and business services professionals will leave. Those firms that can balance flexibility with the obvious benefits of working together are likely to achieve a sustainable competitive advantage by positioning themselves as progressive and employee-centric organizations.

Purpose as a retention driver

For diverse talent, a sense of purpose in their work is a powerful retention driver. Law firms that align their organizational goals with a broader societal impact create an environment in which employees find meaning and fulfilment in their roles.

Practical recommendations include highlighting the firm's commitment to social responsibility, providing opportunities for pro bono work, and integrating diversity and inclusion initiatives into the firm's broader mission. By emphasizing purpose as a retention driver, law firms not only engage diverse talent but also contribute to a positive and meaningful workplace culture.

In our recent interactions with a group of graduates we learned that the socio-economic reality also plays a role in whether they can attach more weight and importance to societal impact in making their decision to join organizations and stay. The financial reality of debt makes that they at times need to compromise on their values and beliefs and the causes they would like to support.

Cultural leadership and inclusivity

Leadership and culture within a law firm play a pivotal role in retaining talent. A culture that fosters inclusivity, values diversity, and provides opportunities for everyone to contribute and advance is essential for long-term retention.

Practical recommendations include leadership training that emphasizes inclusive practices, creating affinity groups or networks for diverse employees, establishing clear pathways for career progression, over-representing the underrepresented employee categories in learning opportunities, and monitoring trends in the readiness category in succession planning through diversity lenses. Law firms with culturally inclusive leadership practices not only retain diverse talent but also cultivate an environment in which individuals feel valued and motivated to contribute their best.

Creating a future-proofed and inclusive law firm

In conclusion, engaging and retaining diverse talent in law firms is a multi-faceted endeavor that requires ongoing commitment and active, visible leadership and sponsorship from senior leaders. By implementing practical recommendations such as inclusive onboarding, adapting to evolving working patterns, leveraging purpose as a retention driver, embracing flexible working arrangements, and fostering inclusive leadership, law firms can create an environment where diverse talent not only thrives but contributes to the firm's sustained success.

We have explored the pivotal role diversity plays in shaping the future success of the profession. By understanding underrepresented talent pools, acknowledging gender and generational differences, prioritizing effective employer branding and employee value propositions, and implementing strategies for engagement and retention, law firms can pave the way for a more inclusive, sustainable, and prosperous future. The legal profession, like any other, thrives on diversity, and embracing it fully ensures a dynamic and resilient industry ready to face the challenges of the future. The journey towards an inclusive and future-proofed law firm requires continuous adaptation and innovation.

The authors generated an initial outline of this chapter in part with ChatGPT, then edited and expanded the draft with the results of their desk research and interviews. The views and opinions expressed in this chapter are those of the authors and do not reflect the official policy or position of any entities they represent or are affiliated with.

References

1   LGBTQIA+: Abbreviation for Lesbian, Gay, Bisexual, Transgender, Queer, Intersex, and Asexual. The additional "+" stands for all the other identities not encompassed in the short acronym. This is an umbrella term that is often used to refer to the community as a whole. www.merriam-webster.com.

2   ABA Profile of the Legal Profession Report 2023, www.abalegalprofile.com.

3   Women@Work 2023 – A Global Outlook, Michele Parmelee and Emma Codd, Deloitte Global, www.deloitte.com/global/en/issues/work/content/women-at-work-global-outlook.html.

4   https://citycentury.co.uk/.

5   See, for example, the 2023 ABA Report referred to above and the SRA website, www.sra.org.uk/sra/equality-diversity/diversity-profession/diverse-legal-profession/.

6   See, for example, reports such as Walking out the door, 2019 ABA and ALM Intelligence, www.americanbar.org/content/dam/aba/administrative/women/walkoutdoor_online_042320.pdf.

7   https://en.wikipedia.org/wiki/Doughnut_(economic_model).

8   "Moments that matter" are the moments that impact an employee's organizational experience most significantly throughout their day, year, and career. www.gartner.com/smarterwithgartner/focus-on-moments-that-really-matter-to-employees.

9   See, for example, NALP's 2023 Report on Diversity in US Law Firms, which found that, for the first time in history, women became the majority of associates. It also charts the largest year-on-year increase in the percentage of associates of color. According to the Report, LGBTQ lawyers continue to see growth in their representation at the summer associate and associate levels. www.nalp.org/reportondiversity.

10 Women@Work 2023, supra.

11 Women@Work 2023: nearly half of respondents have primary responsibility for domestic tasks such as cleaning or caring for dependents, and nearly four in ten say they feel they need to prioritize their partner's career over their own. See also Walking out the door, 2019 ABA and ALM Intelligence, which cites caregiving responsibilities as a major reason why women leave their jobs in law firms.

12 One example is the Baker McKenzie, Inclusion, Diversity and Equity Annual Report, 2022, p.8 www.bakermckenzie.com/en/insight/publications/resources/inclusion-diversity-and-equity-annual-report-2024.

13 Brittany Johnson, Bloomberg Law column, 6 September 2023.

14 See Thriving to 100 – Through Life's 4 Quarters, Avivah Wittenberg-Cox, 21-First Publishers (2022).

15 There are growing levels of comfort among employees and prospective employees with the use of AI in recruitment and selection, although it varies according to generations and geographies. See, for example, Gillespie, N. et al. (2023), Trust in Artificial Intelligence: A Global Study, University of Queensland and KPMG Australia. https://kpmg.com/xx/en/home/insights/2023/09/trust-in-artificial-intelligence.html.

16 See, for example, *Delivering Through Diversity*, McKinsey & Company, January 2018. www.mckinsey.com/capabilities/people-and-organizational-performance/our-insights/delivering-through-diversity.

17 See, for example, The Law.com International "A-List", 28 November 2023. www.law.com/international-edition/2023/11/28/the-top-law-firms-to-work-for-the-uk-a-list-2023/.

18 See for example reports such as www.legal500.com/special-reports/all-restless-souls-city-firms-braced-as-partnership-goes-millennial/.

Chapter 7:
Firm culture and the importance of trust

By Jean-Baptiste Lebelle, head of HR, and Alice Boullier de Branche, senior HR manager, Allen & Overy

Is loyalty an old-fashioned notion?

Loyalty, defined as a strong commitment, a sense of belonging, satisfaction, motivation, and attachment to an organization, its goals, and its values, may seem like an outdated concept in a fast-changing and competitive world. Even if loyalty is a concept that is based on values and principles that are essential to the practice of lawyers, the question deserves to be asked – is the notion of loyalty still important in the legal sector as it is marked by a war for talent, high pressure, a high turnover of teams, and especially a profession where changing firms (some of which are extremely similar) does not disrupt the content of one's position and career, making this change relatively easy? A lawyer can quite easily develop loyalty towards her clients rather than toward the firm that employs her and switch smoothly from one firm to another without endangering her reputation. Many studies and research papers underline that the new generation does not have the same approach to the legal profession, its ambitions, and aspirations, and that the loyalty that could exist at a time when one made one's entire career in the same law firm is long gone...

Is loyalty an old-fashioned notion that one cannot really cultivate, and one should better focus on other priorities?

There are some firms that continue to create a very strong culture of loyalty among their teams – they stand out by a low turnover rate, a powerful alumni network, an ability to rehire former collaborators, and a particularly good work atmosphere that is seen externally. This loyalty has multiple benefits, both for the individual lawyers and for the firm. For the lawyers, loyalty can enhance their reputation, their credibility, their career prospects, and their sense of belonging and satisfaction as it demonstrates commitment, integrity, and reliability. For the firm, loyalty can reduce the costs of recruitment, training, and turnover, increase the quality and consistency of service, and strengthen communication and brand. As long as people feel valued, respected, and engaged by their organization, loyalty can also foster a collaborative, innovative, and supportive culture. In fact, loyalty can be enhanced by offering lawyers the opportunity to work on diverse and challenging projects, to develop their skills and expertise, and to have a voice and a role in the firm's strategy and direction. Loyalty can also be nurtured by providing lawyers with feedback, recognition, and rewards that reflect their contributions and potential. Loyalty can also be influenced by the leadership style and role models within the firm, as well as by the alignment of the firm's values and goals with those of the lawyers. Loyalty can be boosted by meeting employees' needs in terms of wellbeing, meaning, balance, and social engagement.

A strong culture can help to build that loyalty (along with interpersonal relations) and have a huge impact on talent retention. A strong culture is one that is clear, consistent, and communicated, that creates a sense of identity and purpose, and that fosters trust and loyalty among the members. A strong culture can also help to cope with the challenges and changes that the legal profession faces, such as globalization, digitalization, regulation, and competition. A strong culture can also differentiate a firm from its rivals and create a loyal client base.

What characterizes the culture of a law firm? The culture of a law firm is not only defined by the clear and specific standards of performance that the firm sets for its lawyers and staff, but also by the subtle and unwritten rules of conduct that shape how people behave in the firm – what kinds of actions and achievements are recognized and rewarded, what kinds of behavior and mistakes are tolerated or ignored, and what kinds of violations and failures are sanctioned and penalized. The culture of a firm is the way staff greet each other when they meet, it is the way a partner reacts to an employee who needs to take time off for personal reasons, it is the way of supporting staff or implementing initiatives in response to social events, it is the way all the members of the firm (lawyers and support functions) interact without hierarchy or cumbersome formalities. To understand the true nature of a firm's culture, it is important to look at the cumulative effect of all these explicit and implicit signals that the firm sends to its members every day.

Therefore, loyalty is not an old-fashioned notion, but rather a strategic asset that can give a competitive edge to international law firms in a global and dynamic market. Loyalty can be cultivated and sustained by creating a strong and distinctive culture that fosters a sense of belonging and identity.

Loyalty to the firm is not limited to its membership but extends over time and across networks. This notion takes on its full meaning in business terms when alumni join clients and become in turn decision-makers who show a form of loyalty by trusting and recommending their former firm. For that reason, it is important to maintain good relations with leavers and never treat them as traitors, but rather as potential ambassadors and allies.

Taking into account the expectation of the new generation

The new generation of workers, encompassing Millennials and Gen Z, has different values and expectations from its employers than previous generations. The gap between the generations that manage them and the new generation can be quite large and lead to significant misunderstandings. It is therefore particularly important to understand the drivers of motivation of this new generation well and to adapt to them rather than to resist them and to apply an unsuitable framework of analysis. The values and expectations of this new generation have implications for the sector of international business law firms, a sector that has traditionally been characterized by a competitive, hierarchical, and profit-driven culture, and by a lack of diversity and inclusion policies.

One of the best ways to grasp this generational gap and to enable management to better understand their teams is to organize reverse mentoring in the firm.

Reverse mentoring is a practice where junior or less experienced lawyers share their knowledge, skills, and perspectives with senior or more experienced lawyers, who can benefit from their fresh insights, familiarity with new technologies, trends, and challenges. Reverse mentoring can foster mutual learning and collaboration, as well as bridge the generational divide and reduce stereotypes and biases. By establishing a relationship of mutual trust and respect among the different generations, reverse mentoring could be a game changer. Furthermore, it raises the awareness of management on those expectations and makes easier the necessary changes of mindset.

Other different approaches such as performance evaluations, surveys, focus groups, or one-on-one meetings can also help to better understand the new generation by seeking regular feedback on their work engagement, professional growth, career objectives, challenges, and concerns, and acting on the feedback to address any issues or gaps.

Law firms must include millennials' preoccupations in their culture. The top priority is diversity, equity, and inclusion. A Glassdoor (2019) study[1] that surveyed over 5,000 adults in four countries (US, UK, France, and Germany) showed that diversity and inclusion are key factors for attracting and retaining talent, and that Gen Z workers are the most likely to consider diversity as an important criterion in their job search. A diverse and inclusive company culture boosts the happiness, drive, and career outlook of its employees. Hence, companies need to cultivate and advance diversity, equity, and inclusion in their policies and practices for hiring, retaining, and promoting employees, and for communicating and engaging with their internal and external audiences. For example, some firms have set goals and quotas to increase the representation of women, ethnic minorities, and LGBTQ+ people in their leadership and partner positions, and have put in place mentoring, sponsorship, and networking programs to support their career development. Some firms have also created affinity groups, committees, and networks to raise awareness and address issues related to diversity, equity, and inclusion, and to offer a safe and supportive space to their members. Those policies have of course an important impact externally and towards clients, but it also provides a strong way to embrace the aspirations of the younger generations.

Firms must also align and articulate their purpose and values with the expectations and aspirations of the new generation of workers and highlight their positive impact and contribution to society and the environment. For example, some firms have developed and communicated their corporate social responsibility (CSR) or sustainability strategies, which define their goals and actions on ESG issues, such as reducing their carbon footprint, supporting human rights, and promoting access to justice. Some firms have also increased their involvement and investment in pro bono work, which allows them to provide legal services to disadvantaged or marginalized individuals or groups, or to support non-profit or public interest organizations that work for social or environmental causes.

The challenge for firms is to create and offer a flexible, collaborative, and empowering work environment and culture, which respects and responds to the preferences and needs of the new generation of workers, and cultivates their learning and development. For example, some firms have adopted or expanded their flexible work policies and practices, which enable their employees to choose when, where, and how they work, and to balance their professional and personal lives. Some firms have also implemented or improved their collaboration and communication tools and platforms, which facilitate their employees to work as a team across borders, disciplines, and sectors, and to share their knowledge and feedback. Moreover, some firms have provided or increased their learning and development opportunities and resources, which support their employees to acquire new skills, abilities, and qualifications, and to pursue their career goals and interests.

To align with the shifting expectations of the new generation of talented individuals, law firms need to change their organizational culture. If they do not, their culture may be out of touch or in conflict with what the new generation values, which can lead to disengagement, turnover, stress, conflicts, and loss of performance.

The different leverages of a firm's culture that have an impact on talent retention

Talent retention in the legal sector is a strategic challenge that requires a coherent response at multiple levels. Business law firms face fierce competition for talent, high expectations, and often significant turnover. A survey by the NALP Foundation and ALM Intelligence (2024) asked 1,200 former associates why they left their law firms.[2] The main reasons were dissatisfaction with the work environment or culture (49 percent), work–life balance issues (46 percent), and career advancement or development opportunities (38 percent). This finding is noteworthy – the top source of dissatisfaction was poor firm culture, often embodied by their manager. Therefore, to retain their best talent, law firms need to cultivate their culture in various ways and ensure that everyone in a management position adheres to or promotes that culture. Good leadership is essential for the culture of the law firm.

It is important to act on the different leverages of a firm's culture. Offering competitive compensation and benefits, aligned with the market and the expectations of the people is a prerequisite. The right behavior that nurtures the culture should be considered in the compensation rather than just the pure financial aspects of a lawyer's performance. However, it is not enough to retain the best talent. New generations require more. Compensation and benefits are not always perceived as fair and transparent by employees, which can lead to frustration and resentment. It is essential to have a clear, consistent, and transparent remuneration policy. Indeed, employees need to have information that allows them to understand the components of their remuneration. This will limit frustrations and misunderstandings or, if there are any, it will facilitate exchanges with their manager. The absence of transparency can create a sense of inequality and distrust among associates. Therefore, law firms need to offer compensation and benefits that are not only competitive, but also develop a remuneration policy that is consistent, equitable, and clear, which reflects the performance, potential, and value of each person. If the remuneration policy is consistent, then it is easy to share rewards information with staff.

Law firms should provide opportunities for learning and development, both formal and informal, to help their people grow their skills, knowledge, and career prospects. Learning and development is essential for the professional and personal growth of employees, and for the competitiveness and innovation of the organization. According to a survey by Deloitte, 94 percent of employees said they would stay longer at a company that invests in their learning and development. However, many law firms struggle to provide adequate and relevant learning and development opportunities for their people, especially for their associates. According to a survey by Above the Law,[3] 42 percent of associates reported inadequate training and mentoring, and 36 percent no feedback or evaluation at all, at their firms. This can result in a lack of confidence, competence, and motivation among associates, and a loss of talent for firms. Therefore, law firms need to provide learning and development opportunities that are not only formal, such as training programs, workshops, and courses, but also informal, such as mentoring, coaching, and peer learning. They also need to provide feedback and evaluation that is not only periodic, such as annual reviews, but also continuous, such as real-time, constructive, and recognition-based feedback. This means that the firm cares for its employees, believes in their growth potential, and invests in them. They need to recognize and celebrate a culture of performance, excellence, and impact, where employees are held accountable for their results, and where their contributions, achievements, and successes are acknowledged and appreciated. These opportunities should be aligned with the needs, interests, and goals of the people, and with the strategy, values, and culture of the organization.

A positive and supportive work environment enables people to feel safe, trusted, and empowered to do their best work. The working environment is the physical, social, and psychological context in which people perform their work, and it has a significant impact on their wellbeing, engagement, and productivity. According to a survey by Gallup (2023),[4] 76 percent of employees said that they would leave their current employer for a company that has a great culture and reputation. However, many law firms have a work environment that is characterized by high pressure, long hours, demanding clients, and competitive colleagues, which can lead to stress, burnout, isolation, and conflict among employees. These issues can affect not only the health and happiness of the employees, but also the quality and ethics of their work. Therefore, law firms need to create a work environment that is not only challenging, but also supportive, where people feel safe expressing their opinions, ideas, and emotions, trusted to make decisions and take risks, and are empowered to work autonomously and collaboratively. They also need to balance and integrate a culture of work–life balance, where employees have flexibility, autonomy, and support to manage their work and personal responsibilities, and where their wellbeing, health, and happiness are prioritized and promoted. This can help to create a culture of harmony and resilience, whilst fostering a culture of respect, trust, and empowerment among employees, leading to a culture of excellence, integrity, and client service for the organization.

How to build a firm culture that is attractive

The culture of a firm is mainly the result of a process of exchanges and role-modeling that leads to the adoption of the same values and behaviors at all levels of the organization. It is a virtuous cycle – the firm can build its own culture by rewarding and highlighting role models who exhibit the preferred behaviors and by not hesitating to sanction inappropriate ones.

Building a firm culture that is attractive is a strategic challenge for international business law firms, especially in a competitive and demanding environment. The culture of a firm can be a source of differentiation, reputation, and loyalty, both for clients and for talent. It can also influence the performance, innovation, and wellbeing of employees. Therefore, it is important to understand how to create and maintain a firm culture that reflects the vision, mission, and values of the organization, and that aligns with the expectations and needs of the stakeholders.

One of the main drivers of workplace culture is the process of socialization, which means that people learn and adopt the values and behaviors that are considered appropriate and desirable in the firm. This process can be fostered by rewarding and promoting role models who exemplify the desired culture, and by sanctioning those who deviate from it. It happens through various interactions and influences between the members of the organization, such as communication, feedback, mentoring, training, and collaboration. For example, some firms have implemented awards or recognition programs to celebrate the achievements and contributions of their lawyers and staff who embody excellence, integrity, teamwork, diversity, or pro bono work. These programs can motivate and inspire their peers to emulate the behaviors and attitudes that are valued and rewarded by the firm, and to align their goals and actions with the firm's vision and mission. On the other end of the scale, some firms have taken disciplinary actions or dismissed those who have violated the ethical standards or the code of conduct of the firm.

Another key element of firm culture is the hiring and promotion process, which determines who gets to join and advance within the organization. Those processes should be based not only on technical skills and results, but also on cultural fit and values. This means that candidates should be assessed and selected according to their alignment with the firm's culture, and should receive clear and consistent messages about what is expected and rewarded in terms of behaviors and attitudes. For instance, some firms have adopted competency frameworks or assessment tools to evaluate the potential and performance of their lawyers and staff, and to identify areas of development and improvement. Many firms have also implemented diversity and inclusion policies or initiatives to ensure that the promotion process is fair and transparent, and reflects the diversity of clients and markets.

A third aspect of firm culture is the set of practices and policies that support and reinforce the culture on a daily basis. These include, among others, onboarding and integration programs, performance management and feedback systems, learning and development initiatives, and social activities.

Onboarding and integration programs are essential for facilitating a smooth and successful transition for new hires into the firm and helping them understand the atmosphere and culture of their workplace. These programs are therefore extremely important to equip new joiners with the knowledge, skills, and tools that they need to perform their roles effectively and efficiently, and to adapt to the firm's dynamic and challenging environment.

Performance management and feedback systems are meant to align and monitor the goals, behaviors, and results of employees, and to provide them with regular and constructive feedback, recognition, and support. As highlighted, the feedback process helps to cultivate and spread the culture of a firm through behaviors that are valued and rewarded.

Learning and development initiatives are aimed at offering and facilitating various learning and development opportunities. Social activities are intended to celebrate and reinforce culture and values, through events, rituals, symbols, stories, and more, and to foster a sense of belonging and pride among employees. For example, some firms organize induction programs, town hall meetings, webinars, newsletters, or podcasts to communicate and engage with their employees on the culture and strategy of the firm. Some firms arrange social events, such as parties, retreats, sports, or charity activities, to foster team spirit and camaraderie among the workforce.

The importance of designing and delivering an authentic people's promise

To keep culture alive, there is nothing better than to formulate a people's promise that allows a company to structure its values internally and communicate them externally. A people's promise is a statement that summarizes the employer's value proposition and the expectations of an organization to its workforce, and vice versa. It is a way of articulating and communicating the culture, benefits, and responsibilities of working for the firm, and creating a mutual commitment and trust between the employer and its workforce.

Designing and delivering an authentic people's promise is important, because:

- It helps to differentiate the organization from its competitors and appeals to the needs and aspirations of the workforce.
- It helps to align and engage talent, by clarifying the vision, mission, and values of the organization, and showing how people can contribute and benefit from them.
- It helps to develop and empower talent, by setting clear and realistic expectations, and by providing the resources and support needed for people to succeed and grow.

The people's promise should not simply be defined as the managers would like, but should be lived by all employees, and embodied by management.

The experience that everyone experiences is the basis and the essence of this promise to the firm's people. It must be authentic and aligned with the reality and value of what the firm delivers, rather than a false or exaggerated portrayal of what the culture aspires to be. This promise to the people is more than a statement – it is a conviction and a demonstration.

One way to create a people's promise that reflects the authentic values and identity of the firm is to involve various stakeholders from different levels and functions of the organization in a collaborative process that allows them to share their perspectives and insights.

Law firm management must grasp the importance of culture as a key driver of success and ultimately profitability. Rather than focusing primarily on the bottom line, they should first cultivate a strong and positive culture that will then translate into financial results.

A unique and positive work environment is not only a desirable goal for law firms, but also a strategic asset that can set them apart from their competitors and give them a decisive edge in the market. By creating a strong and distinctive culture that makes their people feel valued, engaged, motivated, and loyal, law firms can enhance their reputation, performance, and profitability. They can also attract and retain the best lawyers and staff, who are looking for more than just a pay check, but also a sense of purpose, belonging, and growth. Building such a culture is a continuous achievement that involves a solid and sincere commitment from law firms. It is a dynamic and ongoing process that requires constant attention, adaptation, and improvement. All partners and managers must play their role and bring this culture to life daily, with the support of competent HR professionals. Given the evolution of the legal sector and the expectations of the workforce, this is a key element for the success and sustainability of law firms.

References

1   www.glassdoor.com/blog/glassdoors-diversity-and-inclusion-workplace-survey/
2   www.nalpfoundation.org/news/the-nalp-foundation-releases-newest-study-exploring-key-factors-driving-law-firm-associate-retention
3   https://abovethelaw.com/
4   www.gallup.com/workplace/349484/state-of-the-global-workplace.aspx

Chapter 8:
Redefining legal talent – a question of purpose

By Chrissie Wolfe, solicitor and founder, LAB Consultancy

Introduction
"[Talent is] the sum of a person's abilities – his or her intrinsic gifts, skills, knowledge, experience, intelligence, judgment, attitude, character and drive. It also includes his or her ability to learn and grow."
McKinsey, 2001[1]

"Talent equals competence [able to do the job] times commitment [willing to do the job] times contribution [finding meaning and purpose in their work]."
Ulrich, 2007[2]

"In some cases, 'the talent' might refer to the entire employee population."
Silzer & Dowell, 2010[3]

"[Talent is] A person who has the aptitude or skill to do something well. In the business context, a talent would be an employee who possesses the potential to drive organizational growth."
Workforce Group, 2023[4]

There are countless published interpretations of talent in the context of work and you need only look at the diversity of approach to appreciate that, much like beauty, it's in the eye of the beholder. It follows, therefore, that a logical and necessary first step in developing an effective strategy around acquisition, retention, development, and management is to define what talent means to the business in question at any given time.

That is not a straightforward process. The law is a nuanced profession that serves many different types of individuals and businesses and the roles of lawyers and legal services providers, not to mention employers, are constantly evolving. On that basis, so too should the definition of talent.

With this is mind, there are three key questions that a business should ask itself in order to understand and identify what talent looks like:

- What is the expected talent lifespan?
- What is the primary purpose of our business during this time?
- What skills and attributes do we need to align with that purpose?

This chapter will address each of these in turn.

What is the expected talent lifespan?

We are experiencing a time of unprecedented change in the employment landscape, from which legal is not immune. The pandemic sparked what the media dubbed as "The Great Resignation", which caused millions of workers across the globe to call into question their current career choice and what they wanted for their futures.[5]

Whilst we have seen a slight plateau[6] in the numbers of people quitting, what we have also seen is an increase in the number of people who see themselves in a role for a shorter time period than previously imagined, particularly at the junior end of the market (see Figure 1).

Historically, there has been somewhat of a stigma attached to having a CV that features several job entries in a short space of time. It was seen as a "red flag" to employers if an employee had jumped between multiple roles as they could potentially be seen as non-committal or a "flight risk". The reality is, employers now no longer have the luxury of being able to turn down candidates on that basis. With talent being a top priority for businesses across the board,[7] the best candidates have their pick of quality employers and know that they are likely to be remunerated more favorably,[8] progress more quickly, and achieve better job security if they move regularly. The notion that the quickest route to the top is staying put and climbing the ladder is fast dissipating with employees looking at more holistic factors around definitions of success and how long they are willing to wait to achieve it.

The above data is taken from the *Future Lawyers Report 2023* compiled by Flex Legal in association with O-Shaped Lawyer and Wealthbrite.[9] This was a survey of over 600 junior legal professionals in England and Wales in various roles from apprentices and paralegals to 0-3 years PQE solicitors who were asked a variety of questions about their career aspirations and motivations, and predictions for their employment trajectories.

One of the key take-aways from the report is the overwhelming number

Up to 1 year
11.1%

2-5 years
11.1%

5-10 years
11.1%

10+ years
11.1%

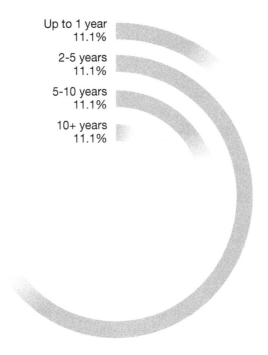

Figure 1: How long junior legal professionals see themselves staying in one particular role. Source: Flex Legal.

of respondents (65.2 percent) who see themselves in a role for just two to five years. The narrative alongside the data reads:

> *"When you delve a little deeper into why, the responses are interesting. They reveal that many of the respondents see law as a useful stepping stone to other careers. Next-step careers cited include politics, business and enterprise, HR and risk and compliance."*

This indicates that it is not just a role change that juniors are looking for after a few years, but potentially an entirely new career.

On the basis that junior employees may no longer be a long-term investment, it makes sense to re-evaluate whether traditional recruitment methods remain the best approach.

In England and Wales, the most common route to solicitor qualification has for many years been via a training contract. Large firms spend millions each year on recruiting and training a cohort of trainees for a two-year tenure who are often dubbed as "the partners of the future" and their education and development attracts a significant cost outlay. Of course, it has always been the case that only a fraction of those actually went on to become partners but many typically stayed for four to five years post-qualification. That picture is now quite different if those trainees plan to leave on qualification or shortly after, and it is therefore questionable whether that kind of financial investment will continue to prove worthwhile for all firms.

This change in attitude at the junior end of the market comes at a timely moment in England and Wales where the process of solicitor qualification has recently changed. In September 2021, the Solicitors Qualification Examination was introduced, which shifts the test of solicitor competence to a set of examinations rather than performance during a period of recognized training (a training contract), thus allowing aspiring lawyers to take control of when they qualify and the type of training that they would like to complete to satisfy the criteria. The criteria now being two years of "qualifying work experience" (QWE), which can take a wide range of forms including paralegal work, legal secretarial work, some volunteer roles, or indeed a training contract. This gives employers much greater choice as to how to support junior lawyers with their qualification journey and much greater flexibility around levels of training and investment. It also allows for other entrants to the training market – in-house legal teams and ALSPs for example – to take advantage of the option to support and develop their workforce from an earlier stage.

Although traditionally undesirable for law firms, having a high turnover of staff is not necessarily a bad thing if it is properly factored in to the business model. The top sports teams have for years operated on the basis that key players will "loan" their talents to a particular team for a few seasons before moving on to a rival. It is accepted practice and does not mean that the players are any less valuable or effective during their tenure and the team does not collapse when they leave. It can be quite the opposite in fact if the right people are brought on at the right time into a team that is open to sustainable change and growth. Richard Branson[10] has pioneered this attitude in business for decades, but the legal profession has been slow to adopt with some firms believing that borderline indoctrination to their ways and values is the solution to stop people from leaving. Based on the data above, that method appears to be wearing thin and a different approach is now required. This may even include novel contractual and remuneration structures if it is clear from the outset that short-term stay is envisaged.

In one way, the principle of "loaning" is already being embraced by way of secondments. In many cases, law firms will look to second their people to clients where the client has expressed a desire for support and the individual has expressed or implied a desire for change. This can work very well as a method of re-distributing talent rather than losing it and has the added benefit of strengthening relationships with clients by providing an effective solution.

There is, of course, the other option. Firms need to focus on dissecting the issues at the root of their high attrition rates in order to increase retention. Those factors are nuanced and will, in most cases, require a cultural, financial, and strategic overhaul to properly address but if your goal remains to have employees with your business for the long-term, the investment is wholly worthwhile.

One of those issues that has been frequently cited is purpose.[11] This is another word with a variety of interpretations and which, to a large extent, is subjective. Whilst, at its core, purpose is synonymous with function, employees are seeking it in the wider sense of doing "meaningful" work, which incorporates elements of ethics, morality, and societal good, as well as a sense of feeling valued and seen on an individual level.

It follows therefore that any business seeking to inspire and unite a workforce must first decide its own purpose, before it can hope to attract and motivate the right people to achieve it.

What is the primary purpose of the business during that time?

What the purpose of a legal services business is may seem like a straightforward question on the face of it and, perhaps, not so long ago it would have been, but we now cannot ignore the rate at which technological advancement is transforming the legal landscape. As Richard Susskind contends, *"Clients don't want lawyers, they want the outcomes you bring"*[12] and there are increasingly novel ways of achieving those outcomes, potentially without the need for traditional legal expertise.

It follows then that a focus on the ever-evolving needs of clients and a consistently agile perspective on how to meet those needs is more important than ever and must be central to the purpose of any business seeking to provide legal advice. The question is how to establish the broader mission that transcends the rudimentary objective of servicing clients and acts to both unify the workforce in a common goal and set the business apart from its competitors. At this point, the approach must become more nuanced, depending on the nature of the business and the specific work it undertakes. A few examples of how this has played out in practice are outlined below.

Shunning the F word

The pursuit of purpose is not an endeavor that takes place in a vacuum. In a bid to stand out from historic notions, once traditional law firms have shunned the word "firm" and chosen to identify themselves as a "legal business" or a "legal solutions business".[13] This is more than simply semantics and is driven by increasingly discerning clients who expect more from their legal representatives than ever before. In a feverish clamor to service this array of needs and diversify revenue streams, some law firms have looked to redefine their purpose by offering themselves as a "one stop shop". This is achieved by adding a range of "bolt on" professional services not offered before – from advocacy and (forensic) accounting to consulting, costs, managed services, and even tech solutions. In part, this has been driven by competing with the big four accounting firms, whose well documented move into the legal space has left bigger firms recognizing the need to compete.[14] This is a benefit to clients and a positive step towards a more client-centric model but it can be to the detriment of purpose.

A change in physiology without a change in mentality leads to a crisis of identity. The "F" word is easy to drop in name but it must also be dropped in substance and culture if true transformation is sought. Otherwise, the result is a business that acts like it sells solutions but thinks like it sells time and those are fundamentally distinct. Inevitably, this leads to misalignment, even if it comes hand in hand with an uptick in revenue. This is why transformation roles are now increasingly part of law firm structures – as boards recognize the need to define once again who they are and the purpose they represent to themselves, their clients, their workforce, and the wider market.

Enter the B word

The concept of a boutique law firm is not new. However, boutiques are increasingly springing up and, by their nature, they have a clear purpose. Often separating themselves from big legal businesses, they concentrate on fulfilling and delivering a niche practice for clients seeking one service. These firms do not seek to offer anything other than their chosen expertise. The marketing writes itself, as these firms assert themselves as dedicated experts in their specific area. Purpose, then, is much clearer and easily recognized. It is little surprise that these firms boast happier and more fulfilled employees who understand their role, their function, and with it their individual purpose in the organization.[15] Sometimes less really is more and boutique firms stand testament to the power of a clear purpose, both with clients and employees.

Size isn't everything

Of course, away from big law, in towns, regions and provinces, there are law firms that span a range of services – particularly private client and business advisory / representation services – and continue to thrive. These businesses benefit from their locality and often act for SME clients who are reluctant to instruct the bigger players, either fearing the price or just convenience. In contrast to bigger law firms, as mentioned above, smaller firms can actually have a very clear purpose as trusted advisors and lawyers for their client base, whilst offering a full suite of services. These firms are not small businesses though, frequently boasting revenues of £15 million plus and employing hundreds of people. Again, staff can often find themselves very settled in these organizations and enjoy a clarity of purpose.

Goodbye to silos

In-house teams have long battled with their perceived nature as "blockers" and costs centers for the businesses that they serve. An intrinsic struggle with purpose is inevitable if your unit's function is effectively rendered as an obstacle to, rather than a facilitator of, the company's goals. It alienates the legal department, or legal function, from the business and demotivates the workforce, which has historically led to the legal team becoming siloed and detached.

That approach has changed significantly since the pandemic, in line with a considerable acceleration in the speed of digital transformation in a strategic drive to increase value to customers.[16] The Digital Legal Exchange has the sole mission of accelerating digital transformation of the legal function with its community of general counsel and diverse leaders across business, technology, law and beyond, having extensive experience of successful projects across the globe. The results of effective transformation speak for themselves.[17] The impact of streamlining business units and aligning the legal function with the company's digital journey has the effect of transforming the role of the legal function from a cost center to a value creator, uniting its purpose with the company's.

Rise of the consultants

It is estimated that a third of the profession could be working as consultants by 2026.[18] The rise in popularity of fee-share models since the pandemic has been significant and it is easy to see why. What they provide is freedom and control for lawyers in respect of the hours they work, the location they can work from, and the nature and number of clients they take on, all whilst offering a considerably higher earning potential than many would have in private practice.

There is an intrinsic sense of purpose to be found in having complete choice and control over your career and setting your own goals based on your individual needs, rather than having to reverse engineer them around a set of defined values and criteria dictated by a firm. Much like those who set up boutique firms, the drive to leave private practice for consultancy can often be borne out of frustration with a meandering culture and lack of clear purpose within firms that are trying to be all things to all people. Those who have a clear sense of purpose in their own work and have confidence in their abilities to bring in clients are understandably drawn to the benefits of the consulting model. In the age of social media, the latter is increasingly easier to satisfy and the potential downsides of the model, therefore, are increasingly less.

What next?

There is little doubt that we will see a significant reshuffling of the market in the next decade. As technology continues to streamline services and create novel solutions for clients, we are likely to see "a great consolidation" of legal services offerings with those who have mastered the delicate balance of client and employee centricity coming out on top.

At a time of such volatility, the question of purpose needs to be consistently reviewed and adapted proactively as needed. Accordingly, a variety of diverse team members are going to be required at different stages of the business journey and there is a benefit in separating out what are immediate needs vs long-term objectives. For that reason, along with attrition rates, recruiting the partners of the future is a very different proposition from recruiting the associates of the present and the purpose of their respective roles needs to be carefully defined.

What skills and attributes do we need to align with that purpose?

Regardless of how you come to define the purpose of your business, it is essential that you have a workforce that is united, inspired, motivated, and has the capability to fulfill that purpose. Technical ability and commercial acumen are, at this point, baseline criteria and there is a far broader suite of skills that are necessary to move the needle in an increasingly digital world.

That is not to say that all of these skills need to be encompassed within one person, or even within a team of practicing lawyers. Adam Curphey in his book *The Legal team of The Future: Law+ Skills*[19] identifies that, as a profession, we have too long expected qualified lawyers to have it all. That is at least partly driven by the traditional law firm model of fee earners + support staff where the latter's primary function is to take some of the administrative burden away from the lawyers, rather than add value of their own. The reality is, that serves no one. It creates a hierarchy between lawyers and "non-lawyers", which has resulting impacts on culture and morale and restricts the breadth of expertise and the value that can be encompassed within the advice provided to clients. As Curphey rightly states, "We need to stop talking about the lawyer of the future and start talking about the legal team of the future".

With that in mind, it is necessary to take a more holistic view of what you are trying to achieve, i.e. your purpose, and work backwards to the skills, attributes, and behaviors that are needed to embody and fulfill the same. On that construction, most businesses will find that they almost certainly require a collaborative, multidisciplinary team.

There will of course be nuances depending on the nature of the business and the clients it serves but these nuances are, in effect, tailored "bolt-ons" to a set of core qualities that are indicative of capability to deliver legal services effectively in the current climate. Table 1 illustrates a toolkit that encompasses not only skills but the attributes and behaviors that complement them in order to achieve a truly holistic approach.

I have taken inspiration here from my own experience but also from a combination of sources, including Adam Curphey's book referenced above and the writings of Mark Cohen, renowned global legal market expert, who has canvassed the topic of talent in the legal profession extensively in Forbes.[20]

Table 1: The toolkit for effective delivery of legal services.

Attributes	Skills	Behaviors
Resilient	Problem solving	Empathetic
Curious	Critical thinking	Collaborative
Adaptive	Tech savvy	Communicative
Agile	Data literacy	Enthusiastic
Creative	Interpersonal	Motivated
Self-Aware	Design thinking	Efficient
Emotionally intelligent	Team work	Client-focused

The qualities outlined in this table transcend the essential components of being a lawyer and go to the heart of fulfilling what is the central purpose of providing legal advice, which is to be a trusted advisor to clients in pursuit of solving their problems. Whilst historically lawyers have had a narrow remit to operate within, the increasingly digital landscape, combined with ever-rising competition from rival businesses and business models warrants a revised approach and a broadening of horizons when it comes to the value that can be delivered. There is a need now to collaborate as a team to deliver data-backed, novel solutions with efficiency in a human way. The qualities above speak for themselves in that regard. A workforce that comprises these elements, who are united in pursuit of a common goal, are an unstoppable force for the good of clients and wider society.

Where do we find this talent?
Historically, there has been a hazy divide between law schools and employers in respect of delegation of responsibility for educating and training the next generation of lawyers. Broadly, it has been the role of the academic institutions to teach the black letter law and the role of employers to develop the practical skills – much like a driving test, with universities taking charge of

the theory element and employers actually teaching candidates how to drive. This is problematic for at least two reasons.

It results in a serious expectation vs reality gap

As any legal professional knows, although the essence of legal services is fundamentally problem solving, the day-to-day role of a lawyer encompasses drastically more than that. So much so that the application of the law to a set of facts is often completely overshadowed by the pressures of being commercially astute, managing client and colleague expectations, time recording, costs targets, billing, long hours, compliance, urgent deadlines, prioritizing caseloads of hundreds of files, imposter syndrome, office dynamics... the list goes on. This is the reality of becoming a lawyer for a significant number of hopefuls that law school simply does not prepare them for, nor do the glossy box sets suitably highlight. It is therefore little surprise that so many leave traditional practice, either for an alternative legal role that minimizes some of those pressures or a different career altogether.

It results in a serious skills gap

In line with their expectations, the skills graduates develop for successfully navigating a career in law are often lacking upon graduation. A traditional law degree places heavy focus on memory, analytical skills, and regurgitation of precedents but offers little to encourage design thinking and the creation of novel solutions and processes that would help students develop the toolkit above. That is not an oversight. Universities duly prioritize students passing their exams with good marks and the wider skills now valuable to succeed in the legal workplace are, for the most part, not examined as part of the curriculum. That is, in part, justified on the basis that many law students do not actually go on to become lawyers and universities must therefore cater to those students who are studying law primarily for the subject matter. The content of the law degree will inevitably evolve over time and may ultimately extend to teaching the full spectrum of skills required. In the meantime, there are a variety of options for how to find and train the next generation:

- *Non-law graduates.* The new route to solicitor qualification (the SQE) no longer prescribes that a law degree or a qualifying law degree is necessary to qualify as a solicitor. This allows for students to study a completely different subject at undergraduate level, learning an entirely separate skillset, before completing their legal knowledge component through the SQE. Graduates in subjects such as technology, design, and computing are much more likely to have developed the wider skills in the toolkit that will set them up well for success in the modern workplace.

- *Law degree + upskilling.* Fortunately, the next generation are savvy and resourceful[21] when it comes to their futures and many will choose to voluntarily upskill themselves using online resources such as Coursera, which should not be overlooked as a valuable source of transferable skills.
- *Training + upskilling.* Many firms have teamed up with SQE providers[22] to design bespoke training programs that fulfill the needs of the individual business.
- *Apprenticeships.* In England and Wales the Government-funded solicitor apprenticeship program has gained significant support from firms across the country with more than 2,000 currently completing the six-year program that is available to those who have completed five GCSEs and three A levels (or equivalent).[23]
- *Access schemes.* There are a range of schemes available that offer opportunities to diverse and under-represented groups of students seeking careers in law.[24] The value of a diverse workforce cannot be underestimated and these schemes act as both sources of unique talent and drivers of social mobility in the profession, which remains heavily geared towards the most privileged students.
- *Career changers.* The law is an increasingly popular choice as a second career for a variety of professionals. Those who have come from alternative corporate careers, technology, or subject matter experts are clearly an attractive choice for niche roles where tailored knowledge and experience is valuable.

This is, of course, a non-exhaustive list and as the skills and attributes required of a successful legal professional continue to expand, so too should employer horizons on sources of talent. People evolve faster than business and savvy, upskilled professionals may well be found thriving outside of the traditional frameworks.

Conclusion

Talent in the legal profession has long been characterized by a narrow set of criteria. Technical skills, commercial awareness, and attention to detail are now only the canvas on which a much more intricate picture must be painted. Data literacy and agility are paramount to navigating the increasingly digital landscape and creativity and curiosity beyond simply doing things better, but doing things differently, are now required to meet the ever-evolving needs of clients.

As businesses look down the lens of unprecedented changes in technological advancement and employee behaviors, a novel approach is needed to define both the purpose of the business and the talent needed to serve it. Those who were once the partners of the future may now be your "key players" for only a season or two, metaphorically speaking. That is a very different ball game, which potentially warrants a very different strategy. Alternatively, you can tackle the stats to foster a culture of loyalty and progression. Either way, change is inevitable. Resisting will come at a cost, to your people and your profits.

References

1   Michaels, E., Handfield-Jones, H., and Axelrod, B. (2001). *The war for talent*. Boston: Harvard Business School Press.

2   Ulrich, D. (2007). *The talent trifecta*. Workforce Management, 86(15).

3   Silzer, R., and Dowell, B. E. (Eds.) (2010). *Strategy-driven talent management: A leadership imperative*. San Francisco: John Wiley & Sons.

4   Workforce Group (2023) https://workforcegroup.com/who-is-a-talent/

5   www.edsmart.org/features/the-great-resignation-statistics/

6   www.mgmt.ucl.ac.uk/news/driving-factors-behind-slowing-down-great-resignation

7   www.gartner.com/en/articles/what-matters-to-ceos-and-cfos-right-now

8   www.linkedin.com/pulse/does-loyalty-company-pay-ramesh-ranjan/

9   Future Lawyers Report 2023, compiled by Flex Legal in association with O-Shaped Lawyer and Wealthbrite.

10 "Train people well enough so they can leave, treat them well enough so they don't want to." Sir Richard Branson (2014), Twitter.

11 www.mckinsey.com/capabilities/people-and-organizational-performance/our-insights/great-attrition-or-great-attraction-the-choice-is-yours

12 www.legalfutures.co.uk/latest-news/susskind-lawyers-wrong-to-think-technology-cannot-replace-them

13 https://dwfgroup.com

14 www.lawgazette.co.uk/practice/big-four-increasing-share-of-legal-market/5115164.article

15 www.mlaglobal.com/en-gb/insights/articles/from-biglaw-to-boutique-why-are-associates-making-the-move?byconsultantorauthor=jason-keller

16 www.microsoft.com/en-us/microsoft-365/blog/2020/04/30/2-years-digital-transformation-2-months/

17 https://financialpost.com/pmn/press-releases-pmn/business-wire-news-releases-

pmn/financial-times-honors-dxc-technology-and-unitedlex-for-innovation-in-legal-operations

18 www.legalfutures.co.uk/latest-news/quarter-of-lawyers-could-work-at-fee-share-firms-within-three-years

19 *The Legal Team of the Future: Law+ Skills* (2022), Adam J. Curphey.

20 www.legalmosaic.com/what-is-digital-legal-talent/

21 www.forbes.com/sites/forbesbusinesscouncil/2024/01/23/gen-z-in-the-workforce-challenging-or-change-makers/#

22 www.legalcheek.com/2021/12/baker-mckenzie-picks-barbri-to-put-trainees-through-sqe/

23 www.linklaters.com/en/about-us/news-and-deals/news/2023/june/linklaters-proud-to-back-city-century

24 www.lawcareers.net/MoreLaw/DiversityAccessSchemes

Chapter 9:
Interpersonal relationships and (re)building a culture of firm loyalty

By Lara Selem, co-founder, Selem Bertozzi Consulting

Introduction

In the current legal landscape, interpersonal relationships and loyalty to the firm are essential for organizations' success. They influence organizational culture and operational effectiveness and are crucial to building trust networks and client satisfaction. Loyalty goes beyond talent retention, reflecting commitment to the firm. With remote work, adapting communication and maintaining team cohesion are challenges that require engagement strategies and professional development.

In Brazil, the legal culture values interpersonal and personal relationships, with an emphasis on building networks and lasting bonds, reflecting a culture of belonging. Internationally, the approach is more formal, focusing on efficiency and productivity, with more structured management systems. However, globally, technology and remote work impact the dynamics of relationships and loyalty, challenging the maintenance of cohesion and organizational culture.

Both in Brazil and globally, law firms face common challenges in the digital era, needing to adapt management practices to maintain cohesion and loyalty. This chapter analyzes these aspects, offering insights for law firms to thrive in the current legal market, highlighting the importance of enhancing interpersonal relationships and cultivating genuine loyalty to the firm.

The impact of remote work on interpersonal dynamics in law firms

The COVID-19 pandemic accelerated the transition to remote work in law firms, significantly altering interpersonal dynamics and challenging traditional practices of organizational culture, collaboration, and team management.

Remote work replaced face-to-face interaction with digital communication, raising questions about the effectiveness of virtual communication and its impact on building trust relationships and professional support networks.

Leaders and managers face the challenge of maintaining team cohesion and organizational culture from a distance, requiring the adoption of technological tools and the reevaluation of leadership skills and management strategies. Additionally, remote work affects the balance between professional and personal life for lawyers, with implications for wellbeing and productivity.

It is crucial to understand how remote work is reshaping professional relationships in the legal industry and what strategies can optimize operational efficiency and employee satisfaction. Addressing these challenges in the remote work environment requires attention and adaptation by law firms, reflecting the need to maintain operational efficiency and service quality in a changed environment.

Challenges include maintaining effective communication and collaboration, preserving organizational culture, managing performance and engagement, balancing professional and personal life, information security and compliance, professional development and mentoring, and adapting to new technologies.

Addressing these challenges requires a multifaceted approach that combines technology, people management, and cultural adaptation. Law firms that successfully navigate these changes will be better positioned to thrive in the current and future legal landscape.

To mitigate the impacts of remote work on the dynamics of relationships in law firms, it is essential to implement practical actions aimed at maintaining effective communication, team cohesion, and employee wellbeing. Here are some key strategies:

- Regular team meetings.
- Efficient communication tools.
- Flexible schedules and respect for work–life balance.
- Mental health and wellbeing programs.
- Mentoring and professional development sessions.
- Virtual team building events.
- Transparent and open communication.
- Clear remote work policies.
- Virtual spaces for informal interaction.
- Continuous assessment and feedback.

By implementing these actions, law firms can not only reduce the negative impacts of remote work but also seize the opportunities it offers to improve efficiency, job satisfaction, and team cohesion.

The transition to remote work in law firms, driven by the COVID-19 pandemic, has brought a series of significant challenges and opportunities. The dynamics of interpersonal relationships and team cohesion have been deeply impacted, requiring a reevaluation of communication, management, and organizational culture strategies.

Remote work has transformed the way law firms operate, presenting unique challenges but also valuable opportunities. By embracing these changes and implementing adaptive strategies, law firms can not only survive but thrive in this new work environment.

Strategies for effective communication in the virtual era
In the current digital era, enhanced by the transition to remote work, effective communication is vital for the success of organizations, especially in the legal industry.

It is essential to explore strategies, tools, and techniques to optimize communication in virtual environments, focusing on maintaining strong connections with colleagues and clients at a distance. Adapting communication practices to the digital realm is a response to the pandemic and a natural evolution in the face of technological advancement.

Effective communication in the virtual era involves more than just the use of technology – it requires understanding how the nuances of face-to-face communication are transformed in the digital environment, including adaptations in body language for videoconferences and effectiveness in writing emails and instant messages.

Selecting appropriate tools, such as videoconferencing platforms and collaboration tools, is crucial, as is their correct use and user training. Communication strategies must be adapted to different audiences, considering the limitations of visual and contextual cues in the virtual environment.

We also present practical techniques to improve virtual communication, such as establishing clear rules, practicing active listening, and maintaining clarity in messages. The goal is to provide insights for professionals to enhance their communication skills in the digital era, strengthening virtual connections.

Addressing the challenges of effective communication in law firms is crucial to maintaining efficiency and effectiveness in a digitalized environment. Among these challenges, we highlight adaptation to technology, maintaining confidentiality and security, clear and effective communication, managing relationships at a distance, balancing formality and accessibility, managing efficient virtual meetings, communication overload, and continuous training and development.

Overcoming these challenges requires a strategic and adaptive approach, focused on continuous training, implementing robust security policies, practicing effective communication, and maintaining a healthy balance between technology and human interaction. By successfully addressing these challenges, law firms can significantly improve the efficiency and effectiveness of their communications in the virtual era.

To address the challenges associated with effective communication in the virtual era in law firms, it is essential to adopt a range of practical strategies. These suggestions aim to improve communication, information security, and relationships with clients and colleagues in the digital environment:

- Training in digital tools.
- Cybersecurity policies.
- Clear and structured communication.
- Building virtual relationships.
- Balance between formality and accessibility.
- Efficient management of virtual meetings.
- Controlling communication overload.
- Spaces for informal interaction.
- Regular feedback and evaluation.
- Focus on mental health and wellbeing.

By implementing these suggestions, law firms can not only reduce the challenges of remote work but also seize the opportunities that digital communication offers to improve efficiency, job satisfaction, and strengthen professional relationships in the virtual environment.

The transition to the virtual era has brought significant challenges to communication in law firms, but also unique opportunities to enhance the efficiency and quality of professional interactions. The key to overcoming these challenges lies in adopting a holistic approach that combines efficient use of technology, adapted communication practices, and a strong focus on the human aspect of interactions.

As the virtual era continues to evolve, law firms that adapt and adopt effective communication strategies will be better positioned to face future challenges and seize the opportunities that technology and digital communication offer.

Fostering social connections in hybrid work models

In the current business landscape, hybrid work models have become essential, combining the flexibility of remote work with the benefits of in-person interactions.

It is crucial to explore how to foster effective social connections in these models, balancing virtual and in-person interactions to strengthen team bonds. With technology reshaping work, cultivating meaningful relationships among team members is vital for organizational success.

The transition to hybrid work meets changing worker expectations, valuing flexibility and autonomy. However, challenges such as isolation and maintaining organizational culture arise with the lack of in-person interaction. Conversely, in-person work favors interpersonal relationships but can impact work–life balance.

The challenge is to create a hybrid environment that promotes efficiency and wellbeing, implementing policies and technologies that support both work modes and promote social connections. Maintaining effective communication and a sense of belonging is crucial for cohesive and engaged teams.

We need practical strategies to balance virtual and in-person interactions in order to strengthen team bonds. Leaders and managers face the challenge of keeping teams connected and productive in a hybrid work environment. In law firms, implementing hybrid models and fostering effective social connections present specific challenges, essential for adapting to a flexible and diverse work environment.

Challenges observed include maintaining organizational culture, efficient communication and team cohesion, balancing flexibility and availability, managing performance and productivity, integrating new team members, information security, professional development and mentoring, and managing client expectations.

To overcome these challenges, law firms need a strategic approach involving the adaptation of internal policies, investment in technology and training, and effective internal and external communication. By doing so, they can leverage the advantages of a hybrid work model, maintaining service excellence and satisfaction for both employees and clients.

To address the challenges associated with implementing hybrid work models in law firms, it is essential to adopt practical strategies that promote efficiency, team cohesion, and the maintenance of organizational culture. Here are some suggestions:

- Establishment of clear guidelines.
- Adequate technology and training.
- Regular team meetings.
- Virtual spaces for socialization.
- Mentoring and professional development programs.
- Flexibility with structure.
- Information security.
- Efficient onboarding processes.
- Continuous feedback and evaluation.
- Managing client expectations.

By implementing these strategies, law firms can reduce the challenges of hybrid work, promoting a more flexible, productive, and cohesive work environment that benefits both employees and clients.

In conclusion, the adoption of hybrid work models in law firms represents a significant evolution in the modern work environment. While it brings unique challenges such as maintaining organizational culture, communication effectiveness, balancing flexibility and availability, and information security, these challenges are surmountable with well-planned strategies and practices.

As law firms continue to navigate the post-pandemic era, those that effectively implement and manage hybrid work models will be better positioned to face future challenges while maintaining a cohesive team, a strong organizational culture, and a high level of client service.

Prioritizing mental health and wellbeing

Mental health and wellbeing at work, especially in high-pressure professions like law, are receiving increasing attention.

There is no overstating the importance of prioritizing the mental health and wellbeing of professionals, highlighting the crucial role of interpersonal relationships in supporting mental health and balancing work and personal life. With the rise in occupational stress and professional burnout, addressing these issues is vital for both individual health and organizational success.

Interpersonal relationships at work significantly impact mental health, offering support or contributing to stress. The quality of these interactions affects job satisfaction, productivity, and professional effectiveness. Moreover, in professions like law, balancing work and personal life is crucial but challenging, with long working hours and high expectations potentially harming mental health.

Organizations and leaders must recognize the importance of mental health and take proactive steps to promote it, creating a work environment that supports healthy interpersonal relationships and policies that encourage a healthy work–life balance.

Firms need strategies to strengthen mental health support at work, focusing on interpersonal relationships and work–life balance. The goal is to improve individual wellbeing and contribute to healthier and more productive work environments.

Addressing mental health and wellbeing in the context of law firms presents specific challenges, reflecting the unique aspects and pressures of the legal profession, including high-pressure culture, stigma around mental health, early identification and intervention, access to mental health support resources, balancing professional and personal responsibilities, promoting healthy work environments, developing leadership sensitive to mental health, and integrating wellness practices into daily life.

Tackling these challenges requires a multifaceted approach involving cultural changes, organizational support, adequate resources, and leadership committed to the wellbeing of lawyers. By doing so, law firms can not only improve the mental health and wellbeing of their professionals but also increase productivity, job satisfaction, and talent retention.

To address the challenges related to mental health and wellbeing in law firms, it is crucial to implement practical and effective strategies. Here are some suggestions:

- Promote a culture of openness.
- Mental health support programs.
- Training for leadership sensitive to mental health.
- Flexibility in work.
- Monitoring workload.
- Decompression spaces.
- Wellness activities.
- Constant feedback and communication.
- Recognition and appreciation.
- Partnerships with mental health professionals.

By implementing these strategies, law firms can create a healthier and more sustainable environment where mental health and wellbeing are prioritized, contributing to overall effectiveness and job satisfaction.

The importance of prioritizing mental health and wellbeing in law firms cannot be underestimated. Given the unique challenges faced by the legal profession, including high pressure, long working hours, and stigma around mental health, it is imperative to adopt a proactive and integrated approach. The strategies to address these challenges must be multifaceted, ranging from promoting a culture of openness and support to implementing wellness programs and work flexibility.

Cultivating a culture of loyalty in law firms

Loyalty is essential for the success and sustainability of organizations, especially in law firms. It is important to develop a culture of loyalty in a competitive and constantly evolving sector, strengthening internal relations and contributing to the firm's reputation and stability.

Loyalty in law firms involves lawyers' dedication to the firm's goals, commitment to the team and clients, and is crucial where trust and confidentiality are fundamental. Cultivating this culture leads to greater job satisfaction, lower employee turnover, and lasting relationships with clients.

Developing and maintaining a culture of loyalty requires strategies that include effective communication, recognition of collaborators, career development, and inspiring leadership. Here we explore key strategies for cultivating loyalty, highlighting the role of leadership and practices that encourage employee loyalty, aiming to create a cohesive and committed work environment, improving the internal environment and the firm's market position.

Addressing the challenges in building a culture of loyalty in law firms is crucial for establishing a lasting and effective culture. Challenges include balancing competitiveness with collaboration, managing expectations and recognition, transparent and consistent communication, career development and growth opportunities, organizational culture and shared values, talent retention, adapting to changes in the legal market, and inspiring and reliable leadership.

Overcoming these challenges requires a strategic approach, focused on building a strong organizational culture, developing effective leadership, transparent communication, and fair recognition and rewards. By addressing these aspects, law firms can cultivate a culture of loyalty that benefits both the organization and its collaborators.

To overcome the challenges of cultivating a culture of loyalty in law firms, it is important to adopt practical and effective strategies. Here are some suggestions:

- Promote collaboration and recognize contributions.
- Open and transparent communication.
- Professional development and career planning.
- Positive organizational culture.
- Flexibility and work–life balance.
- Inspiring and accessible leadership.
- Fair recognition and rewards.
- Adaptation to changes.
- Continuous feedback and evaluation.
- Promoting mental health and wellbeing.

By implementing these strategies, law firms can create an environment in which loyalty is naturally cultivated and sustained, benefiting both the firm and its employees.

Building and sustaining a culture of loyalty in law firms is a complex but extremely valuable process. The challenges, ranging from balancing competitiveness with collaboration to developing inspiring leadership, require a careful and strategic approach. Strategies to overcome these challenges include promoting collaboration, maintaining open and transparent communication, offering professional development opportunities, creating a positive organizational culture, providing flexibility, developing accessible leadership, implementing fair recognition systems, adapting to market changes, providing continuous feedback, and promoting mental health and wellbeing.

The role of leadership in shaping the firm's culture

Leadership is crucial in shaping and strengthening organizational culture in law firms, emphasizing loyalty and interpersonal relationships. In a competitive environment, the positive influence of leaders is essential for team success and cohesion. Leaders shape the work environment with their attitudes and decisions, creating a space that promotes trust, mutual respect, and collaboration, essential for a culture of loyalty and strong interpersonal relationships.

Effective leadership inspires and motivates employees, fostering a sense of belonging and commitment to the firm. However, maintaining this culture requires communicative, transparent, accessible, and empathetic leaders, capable of balancing business demands with employee wellbeing.

It is important to explore how leaders can influence and reinforce a culture of loyalty and strong interpersonal relationships, addressing leadership qualities and behaviors that contribute to a positive culture, strategies to engage and motivate teams, and how leaders can be agents of change, improving the internal environment and contributing to the firm's success and reputation.

Significant challenges stand out in leadership to shape the culture of loyalty and interpersonal relationships in law firms. These include balancing authority with empathy, maintaining consistency in organizational culture, adapting to changes in the legal market, developing future leaders, conflict management and communication, promoting diversity and inclusion, aligning personal and organizational goals, and measuring the impact of culture on performance.

Overcoming these challenges requires leaders who are not only efficient strategists and decision-makers but also skilled communicators, mentors, and positive change agents. They must be able to inspire trust, promote a collaborative work environment, and support the continuous development of their employees.

To address the challenges associated with the role of leadership in shaping the culture of a law firm, particularly in terms of promoting loyalty and strong interpersonal relationships, several practical strategies can be adopted:

- Leadership skills development.
- Open and regular communication.
- Recognition and appreciation.
- Mentoring and career development.
- Promotion of diversity and inclusion.
- Efficient conflict management.
- Balancing professional and personal life.
- Modeling behavior.
- Continuous assessment of organizational culture.
- Adaptation and flexibility.

By implementing these strategies, leaders in law firms can effectively form a culture of loyalty and strong interpersonal relationships, creating a more cohesive, motivating, and productive work environment.

The role of leadership in shaping and reinforcing a culture of loyalty and strong interpersonal relationships in law firms is fundamental and multifaceted. Effective leaders are those who can balance authority with empathy, promote open communication, recognize and value their team's contributions, and create a work environment that supports the professional and personal development of their employees.

Innovative approaches to team building and engagement

In today's dynamic work environment, building a cohesive team and engaging employees is crucial for organizational success. Innovative approaches to team building and engagement can be utilized, using creative methods that promote unity and a sense of belonging. With high employee turnover and job satisfaction being key to productivity, effective strategies are essential.

Building a team and engaging employees involves more than just team-building activities or meetings – it's about creating a culture that values each individual and promotes a collaborative and inclusive environment. This includes understanding employee motivations, recognizing their contributions, and encouraging active participation in the organization.

With the increase in remote work and the diversification of teams, challenges arise in keeping employees engaged and connected. Therefore, it is necessary to explore innovative and creative methods adapted to these new realities, keeping team members motivated and committed.

There are many innovative approaches to team building and engagement. Creative techniques and the use of technology can strengthen interpersonal relationships, improve communication, and increase team cohesion, even in dispersed environments. By adopting these approaches, organizations can improve efficiency, productivity, and create a more satisfying work environment.

Specific challenges arise when implementing these innovative approaches in law firms, reflecting the unique characteristics of the legal environment. These include diversity of professional profiles, balance between professionalism and creativity, remote work and decentralized teams, workload and availability, measuring impact and ROI, integration of new members, changing organizational culture, and sustainability of initiatives.

To overcome these challenges, law firms need a strategic and adaptive approach that considers the peculiarities of the legal environment and the individual needs of employees. Here are some practical strategies that can be adopted:

- Diverse team building activities.
- Use of technology for remote engagement.
- Flexible timing for engagement activities.
- Mentoring and coaching programs.
- Impact measurement.
- Effective integration of new members.
- Open communication and feedback.
- Participative leadership.
- Promotion of diversity and inclusion.
- Sustainability of initiatives.

By adopting these strategies, law firms can effectively face the challenges associated with team building and engagement, creating a more cohesive, motivating, and productive work environment.

Adopting innovative approaches to team building and engagement in law firms is essential to create a dynamic, cohesive, and motivating work environment. Addressing the challenges associated with these initiatives, such as the diversity of professional profiles, the need to balance professionalism with creativity, managing remote teams, and the sustainability of activities, requires a strategic and adaptive approach. Practical strategies are fundamental to overcoming these challenges.

Facing challenges in building loyalty to the firm

Building loyalty to the firm and developing strong interpersonal ties are essential for the success and stability of organizations, particularly in law firms.

Attention should be called to the importance of overcoming common challenges in cultivating loyalty and strengthening interpersonal relationships. In a competitive and dynamic professional environment, employee loyalty and strong interpersonal relationships are crucial for cohesion, efficiency, and resilience of the organization.

Loyalty to the firm involves a deep commitment to the organization's values and goals, while strong interpersonal ties contribute to a collaborative work environment and effective communication. However, challenges such as changes in the legal market, diversity of employee expectations, and communication in hybrid or remote environments can hinder this process.

Here we address the obstacles faced in building loyalty and strengthening interpersonal ties in law firms, and discuss strategies to overcome them. We emphasize the importance of effective leadership, innovative people management policies, transparent communication, and initiatives that promote employee engagement and wellbeing. By focusing on these aspects, law firms can improve the work environment and strengthen their position in the legal market.

Addressing the creation of loyalty to the firm and strengthening interpersonal ties in law firms presents several significant challenges, including diversity of expectations and values, changes in the legal market, balancing autonomy and integration, communication in hybrid or remote environments, conflict management and interpersonal differences, talent retention, development of aligned leadership, and measuring the success of loyalty initiatives.

Overcoming these challenges requires a multifaceted approach that considers the nuances of the legal environment and the individual needs of employees, aligning them with the strategic objectives of the firm.

Here are some practical strategies to be implemented:

- Transparent and regular communication.
- Development and mentoring programs.
- Recognition and reward.
- Promotion of diversity and inclusion.
- Flexibility in work.
- Team building activities.
- Efficient conflict management.
- Inspiring and aligned leadership.
- Continuous assessment.
- Promotion of wellbeing.

By adopting these strategies, law firms can create an environment more conducive to loyalty and strengthening interpersonal ties, which in turn contributes to employee satisfaction, talent retention, and the overall success of the firm.

Building loyalty into the firm and strengthening interpersonal ties in law firms are fundamental to creating a cohesive, productive, and motivating work environment. Addressing the challenges associated with these goals, such as diversity of expectations, changes in the legal market, balancing autonomy and integration, and effective conflict management, requires a strategic and adaptive approach.

Future outlook

In concluding our analysis of interpersonal relationships and loyalty to the firm in the legal profession, it is evident that these are fundamental pillars for the success and resilience of law firms. The challenges and strategies discussed reflect a common reality – the need to adapt to a constantly evolving work environment while maintaining a strong and cohesive organizational culture.

In Brazil, where the legal culture is deeply rooted in traditions but simultaneously faces the need for modernization and adaptation to new market realities, the emphasis on building interpersonal relationships and loyalty to the firm is particularly relevant. This approach, often characterized by valuation of personal relationships and a strong sense of community, can offer valuable insights for building a more humane and engaged organizational culture.

Comparatively, on the international scene, especially in legal markets like the US and Europe, there is a tendency to value efficiency, innovation, and rapid adaptation to market changes. However, even in these environments, the importance of interpersonal relationships and loyalty cannot be underestimated. Combining a more formal approach with the valuation of human relations can lead to a balanced and dynamic organizational culture.

Looking to the future, it is likely that the legal profession will continue to face challenges related to technological adaptation, management of remote and hybrid teams, and the need to balance efficiency with employee well-being. Brazil's experience, with its emphasis on personal relationships, along with the more formalized practices observed in other countries, can provide a hybrid model for building strong and adaptable organizational cultures in law firms around the world.

In summary, the ability to cultivate solid interpersonal relationships and promote a culture of loyalty will increasingly be seen as a competitive differentiator and a key factor for success in the dynamic global legal market. Law firms that manage to harmonize efficiency, innovation, and humanization in their practices will be better positioned to thrive in the future.

Chapter 10:
What legal can learn from other industries

By Tea Hoffmann, managing principal, Law Strategy Corp

Over the last ten years, I have been fortunate to coach over 400 lawyers, train more than 50 firms, and lead retreats for countless others. I have also helped numerous firms design well-thought-out and well-intended strategic plans. In that time, the same issues have bubbled to the top as "critical". If you have been a law firm leader for some time, you can probably name these without reading ahead. So, before you get too excited about new issues, you can relax. For many firms, not much has changed in the last 50 years.

Why? The mindset of most law firm leaders has not changed. Most law firm leaders have little experience running a business, managing people, or planning budgets. While some have hired non-lawyer staff, many firms remain resistant to this idea, and if they do hire them, they are not as well respected as the lawyers within the firm. In addition, how most law schools train lawyers has not changed, and how many lawyers practice law – using the number of hours billed (not collected) or the amount of business they have (even if it is not profitable) – has not changed. Most firms still do not operate like traditional businesses, although most should. In this chapter, I aim to provide some exciting ideas from other professional service firms, in order to address one of the most cited issues facing law firms. That issue is attorney retention.

The American Bar Association reported equity partner turnover remained steady from 2014 to 2021. However, for associate attorneys, attrition rates rose by just over six percent during the same period.[1] Unsurprisingly, many firms suffer from constant associate retention issues and general dissatisfaction among their ranks. According to Thomson Reuters, there are several reasons for these issues. These include long hours, high stress, lack of autonomy, pressure to bill time, toxic culture, lack of mentoring, and, of course, compensation issues.[2] According to an analysis by Decipher Investigative Intelligence, the average turnover for AmLaw 200 firms is 26.3 percent – to be blunt, for every four lawyers at your firm, you will lose one each year.[3] The cost of losing an associate can average $200,000 to $500,000, considering recruiting and training costs, the price of a resource shortage, administrative and human resource man hours, and other factors.[4] In addition to the "hard" cost of losing an associate or lawyer, firms with high turnover become known for their inability to retain talent, resulting in an uphill climb to attract new people.

Retention rates are much better at other professional services firms.[5] For example, accountants report a turnover rate of less than five percent and an average tenure exceeding five years.[6] Architects average a 12 percent turnover rate.[7] So, what are law firms doing wrong?

Before I outline solutions, below is a list of additional reasons that lawyers have listed on various surveys as reasons they left their prior firm:

- Feeling underappreciated.
- Unhappy with firm leadership.
- Job did not align with communicated expectations.
- Lawyer perceives they are having little or no impact.
- High stress.
- No communicated path for advancement.
- Absence of flexibility in the workplace.
- Lack of diversity.

Hire based on need, not on tradition

Law firms traditionally hire law students as associates between their second and third years of law school. Most firms also hire "summer associates" as a "try before you buy" program before they make an offer. Firms often budget for a certain number of new associate hires each year. This hiring cycle has gone on for at least the last 40 years. So, what is wrong with it?

Where is it written that the most prominent and successful law firm will assemble a hiring committee yearly to spend precious billable time doing endless law school interviews for potential hires that will remain at your firm on average for two years and four months? The definition of insanity is doing the same thing repeatedly and expecting a different result. Stop the madness!

Before a firm makes its decision to hire its next lawyer, a "why" must be established. Firms must consider if they are hiring because it has always been done this way, or if there is a legitimate reason for bringing someone on board.

Before considering a new hire, firm leadership should examine the following:

- Do we need a new lawyer or lawyers, or do we want a few new associates because everyone else in town is getting new talent?
- Which area or areas need a new hire based on current workload and trends?
- Will the new hire's practice require someone who is law review quality or someone who does decent work and can serve clients well?
- Do we have sufficient work to cover the cost of this hire, including their training, overhead, and associated costs?
- What level of experience do we need? Do we want someone we have to train, or do we need someone with more experience?
- Is there a current lawyer with the capacity to be a good fit for this practice area?

Today's most innovative law firms should consider all these questions.

Design an innovative hiring process

Clearly define the job requirements
Many firms have job descriptions written too broadly. Write a job description that clearly describes the needs and skills required to do the job. Include expected hours, level of experience needed, compensation range, etc. Let your current lawyers, paralegals, and others within the area of need review and refine the descriptions based on real-life experience. If they will be client-facing, include that in the description. If there is an hourly requirement, include it. If community service is involved, include that. If marketing and business development are required to advance, include that in your job description. Do not hide the ball! Candidates need to know the job's good, bad, and ugly.

Utilize assessments to determine the right fit
Innovative firms believe in finding the right lawyers for their firms, not necessarily the candidates who finished in the top ten percent of their class. Why? Depending on the job requirements, a top-tier graduate may not be what you need, and thus, it will be a bad hire. Innovative firms are using many of the following to evaluate potential hires:
- *Situational judgement tests.*[8] These tests assess how a candidate deals with scenarios and challenges that come up in the workplace.
- *Criteria cognitive aptitude tests (CCAT).*[9] The CCAT measures a candi-

date's critical thinking ability, problem-solving skills, and ability to learn new information.

- *Verbal reasoning tests.*[10] This test assesses a person's ability to read and understand written and spoken content.
- *Personality test.* These tests help employers understand a person's strengths and weaknesses and how they will communicate or interact with others. Several personality test types exist, but the Meyers Briggs Test is the most used.[11]

Psychology Today reported in 2022 that about 80 percent of Fortune 500 companies use personality tests to vet candidates for upper-level positions. Other researchers have found that 36 percent of best-in-class organizations use pre-employment candidate assessments, and this percentage rises with each passing year.[12] The tests above are not an indicator of success, but offer employers insight that they may not get with the traditional interview process. Yet, most law firms still hire the candidates with the highest pedigree. These tests help companies learn about candidates through more than just a resume and a brief interview. They help save money and time, increase productivity, decrease turnover, and improve morale. Innovative law firms will utilize these tools in the future.

Overhaul your interview process

Traditional interviews require answers to broad questions, such as "Tell me a bit about your background", or "What are your strengths and weaknesses?". The questions usually cover an applicant's work history, education, interests, and career goals. Many involve multiple individuals and different rounds, but the basics of an interview have remained the same for the last 50 years.

When COVID-19 hit, everything changed. Innovative ideas for interviewing became necessary. Video interviews allow firms to connect with candidates.

Here are some alternative interview techniques to consider:

- *Case interviews.* Case interviews allow firms to evaluate a candidate's analytical and problem-solving skills. In this scenario, employers present candidates with complex business problems before the interview. During the live interview, candidates discuss their proposed solutions, and firms can analyze and assess their ideas.
- *Cultural fit interview.*[13] A cultural fit interview can be a helpful tool to focus on how a candidate will be compatible with and add to the culture at your company. Culture refers to the values, principles, and

behaviors of your firm. A culture interview gives your firm insight into what values are important to the candidate and how they mesh with your firm's values. Culture is vital for today's younger lawyers and should not be forgotten.

- *Reverse interviews put the candidate in the role of the interviewer.* This approach allows candidates to ask questions about the company, culture, and work environment, enabling them to assess whether the firm meets their expectations and career goals. This type of interview allows you to understand their goals better and demonstrates firm transparency.
- *Hold post-interview reviews within four hours of the interview.* If you do not do this, the interviewers will not remember the details of the interview and will be unable to articulate their first impression or any positives or negatives. Include every person involved in the hiring process in the post-interview. Ask questions, including:
  - Why should we hire the candidate?
  - Why shouldn't we hire the candidate?
  - What attributes did you find compelling?
  - Did you notice or hear any negative qualities that caused you to pause?
  - Do you believe this hire would fit our culture well?

State your expectations and hold your lawyers accountable

This topic may seem obvious, and hopefully, most firms do this, but please be honest – are you pulling back the curtain and giving potential hires a clear picture? Job duties, like legal writing, drafting documents, administrative tasks, taking depositions, etc., are included in most generic job descriptions. But duties and expectations are vastly different. Job duties refer to the specific tasks and responsibilities an individual must carry out.

On the other hand, job expectations refer to the level of performance or the standards an individual is to achieve within their role. These may be less explicitly defined and can include things like the quality of work, the speed or efficiency of task completion, or the ability to work well within a team. Job expectations can also refer to a role's broader goals or objectives, such as contributing to company growth or enhancing customer satisfaction.

But lawyers, firm leadership, and hiring managers must go further. They must give young lawyers examples of these duties based on the role and area where the lawyer will work. Here are some ideas for firms that want to "lift the curtain":

- Ask candidates to come to breakfast/lunch with lawyers and legal staff in the same practice. Leadership and the hiring team should not attend. Encourage those who attend to give the candidate an honest assessment of the practice's daily routines and inner workings. Allow them the opportunity to be open and honest about firm politics, rules, and general dos and don'ts.
- Have candidates shadow various lawyers in the same area for up to ten days.
- Have lawyers in the same practice area complete an anonymous survey about their job satisfaction and give comments. Share these results with candidates.
- Give the recruit a project to complete within a time frame, and then have another lawyer in the practice area provide one-on-one feedback.
- Ask leaders to explain the feedback process for work assignments and let the candidates know they are responsible for asking for feedback if they want to receive it.
- Explain the standard for billable hours and the progression path if firm standards are met. Conversely, explain what happens if these standards are not met.
- Detail expectations for community service, business generation, etc., before they are hired and put these in writing.
- Firm leadership should communicate their expectations regarding administrative duties, interactions with staff and peers, time management, organizational skills, and assignment tracking. Do not sugarcoat these topics and explain how failure to meet these expectations will be handled.

To improve retention, you must be upfront and explain that while every day may be different, not all days may be fun. Many first-year associates are still in "law school" or "summer associate" mode regarding their mentality. Laterals may think that, due to their experience level, they can function as they please or at least like they did at their last firm. Explaining what is required and holding hires accountable will improve the entire firm.

Create an extensive onboarding process
Employment rates for lawyers and other legal occupations reached one of the highest levels in the past decade – reflecting renewed strength in the market since the pandemic. From Q2 to Q3, lawyer employment jumped

from 1.13 million to 1.28 million – a 13 percent increase following the two previous quarters of decline – reaching one of the highest levels in the past ten years except for Q4 2019.[14]

The onboarding experience provides the first impression your new lawyers get when they come in for the first day at their new jobs. Are you setting them up for success?[15] Here are a few statistics that demonstrate the power of excellent onboarding – and the dangers of poor onboarding:

- Wonderful team member (lawyers and staff) onboarding can improve retention by 82 percent.
- 88 percent of organizations do not onboard well, and most firms spend less than one month onboarding.
- Only 12 percent of team members believe their firms do a great job of onboarding.
- Firms with a well-structured onboarding process can improve new hire retention by 82 percent while increasing productivity by over 70 percent.
- 33 percent of new hires look for a new job within their first six months if they have a poor onboarding experience – and that number is even higher among millennials.

Successful firms will use an integrated approach to onboard their new lawyers. This approach includes three aspects – organizational, social, and technical.

Organizational onboarding

Organizational onboarding involves teaching your new lawyers how things work and why they work the way they work. This training provides critical information that will allow them to function more effectively. Remember, your new hires do not know your firm's acronyms, organizational structure, or vital processes. Spend time teaching them.

Social onboarding

Social onboarding builds a sense of community. Building relationships during their first year can help new hires feel less isolated and more confident. In partnership with firm leadership, new hires should identify seven to ten people – leaders, peers, legal assistants, technical support, human resources, operations – with whom they will interact regularly. The new hire's manager or firm leader should then craft plans to connect with each identified person one-on-one during their first year. This interaction can be a short meeting over coffee or lunch. Social capital with teammates builds camaraderie and trust. When new lawyers feel welcomed, they are less likely to feel like the new kid on the block, and your entire firm can benefit from that.

Technical onboarding

Technical onboarding involves technology training. New lawyers may be unfamiliar with your firm's technology and systems. This is frustrating and costs the firm valuable productivity time. Even if the new hire has used the same system before, they may need to understand your firm's usage and protocols. Spend time, over time, training them on the essential technology they will need. Do not overlook simple systems like the postage system, the copier/scanner, and even the use of email.

Firms with a standardized onboarding process experience 62 percent greater new hire productivity and 50 percent greater new hire retention.[16] Those that invest time and effort in their new employees reap the benefits. If you want to be a choice for top talent and reduce your turnover costs, increase the time and energy spent on onboarding.

Create meaningful mentor relationships, not just mentoring programs

Formal mentoring programs in law firms have existed for several decades, but their structure has evolved. Even the name *mentor* has been replaced with catchy names to give these programs more panache. Informal mentorship has existed since the inception of law firms, and most lawyers have had the benefit of having an older attorney reach out and help them along the way. The latter half of the 20th century ushered in mentoring programs as a recruitment and retention tool. These structured programs paired junior associates with senior-level partners. The intent was to provide guidance, support, career advice, and establish trusting relationships.

Most successful companies use mentoring programs. Here are a few statistics:[17]

- 84 percent of Fortune 500 and 100 percent of Fortune 50 companies have mentoring programs.
- 76 percent of employees see the importance of mentorship.
- Of those with a mentor, 97 percent say their mentors provide value.
- Only 37 percent of professionals have a mentor.
- 63 percent of women have never had a formal mentor.

- 89 percent of those who have been mentored will also go on to mentor others.
- Since the pandemic, there has been a 30 percent increase in mentoring initiatives at organizations.

These statistics raise many questions, but one thing is for sure – employees want to have mentors and want them to provide value. In doing this, companies almost guarantee a return on their investment.

Law firms lag behind other professional service firms in this area. Many firms have well-defined mentorship initiatives, including training for mentors and mentees, regular check-ins, goal setting, networking, and soft skill development opportunities. Still, many do not see these initiatives as a success.

In the 2019 Millennial Attorney Survey conducted by Major, Lindsey, and Africa and *Above the Law*, which surveyed more than 1,200 attorneys, about 60 percent of respondents reported that an informal mentor had either a significant (40.1 percent) or crucial (20.9 percent) role in their career, while 28.4 percent of respondents indicated that formal mentorship was irrelevant. This correlates with a further finding that most respondents indicated that the level of formal mentorship they received was weak (31.9 percent), while informal mentorship was viewed as strong (53.6 percent).[18]

So, how can law firms improve this dynamic?

Make mentoring an expectation of every lawyer and team member within your firm. Firms do not have to have a formal program. At its core, a mentor is a person who gives a younger or less experienced person help and advice over some time, so every person you hire should be willing to serve in this role.[19] Every member, from the receptionist to the most senior partner, has a responsibility to help newer team members as they integrate into your firm. Each team member should be willing to answer questions or point them in the right direction.

Explain to new hires that helping new hires integrate is an expectation of each team member. Check-in with the new hires monthly to ensure this is happening and, if not, to see who is not providing guidance. Hold your existing team accountable to this standard.

Undertake mentor training

Create mentoring training and make this a required training annually. Once you have set the expectation, it is a disservice not to train everyone to be an effective mentor. The most effective training should include:

- Mentors should clearly understand the purpose and goals of mentorship, including fostering professional development, providing support, and promoting career advancement. For example, mentors should include the mentee in crucial business development activities and events that will allow them to observe essential tasks they will perform.
- Mentor training should emphasize active listening and communication techniques, including providing constructive feedback and asking open-ended questions to facilitate learning and growth.
- Mentors should learn how to establish clear expectations and boundaries. Mentors should set clear goals based on their ongoing conversations with the mentee and work to help the mentee achieve the desired outcomes.
- Mentors should be equipped to provide guidance and advice on career development strategies, firm politics, networking, and professional development.
- Mentor training should include techniques for helping mentees navigate challenges and conflicts in their professional lives. This may involve brainstorming solutions, mediating disputes, or providing perspective from their own experiences.
- Mentors should receive training on diversity and cultural awareness. People from different backgrounds may think and react differently, so it is crucial to ensure mentors and mentees understand this dynamic.
- When it comes to confidentiality, mentors should allow mentees to express their feelings and concerns openly but understand that if a mentee discloses something that will put the firm in danger or if the mentee is a threat to themselves or others, they must disclose this to leadership.
- Mentors will not have all of the answers to a mentee's questions or concerns, so a good mentor should have access to a complete list of resources for the mentee.

The training aims to empower mentors to support mentees throughout their journey. They are not babysitters but should be expected to follow their mentees for at least the first 18 months.

In addition to traditional one-on-one mentoring, firms should consider the following methods:

- *The selection of principal and secondary mentors.* Most firms pair a senior lawyer with a more junior lawyer. However, many firms are now selecting a variety of mentors. A primary mentor may rely on the traditional model. In contrast, the secondary mentor may be a senior paralegal or firm director, from which the mentee can gain valuable practice management knowledge. This allows the mentee to gain helpful knowledge and encourages others to participate in the mentee's development, thus building a team culture.

- *Peer mentors.* Peer mentors are generally around the same age and stage as their mentees. These peers are perfect sounding boards for those who may be too intimidated to talk with a more senior member of your firm. The goal of peer mentoring remains to help a new hire achieve a level of integration and inclusion that might not be achieved otherwise, and this type of mentor can be utilized in addition to a more traditional or senior mentor.
- *Reverse mentoring.* In many cases, a senior attorney can learn a lot from a younger peer. For example, it is almost certain that a 30-year-old knows more about technology than a 70-year-old. Like peer mentoring, this method builds a more cohesive culture and can provide significant benefits over time.
- *Group mentoring.* Group mentoring allows one mentor to help guide two or more mentees. It also provides the added benefit of having mentees learn from each other and their mentors.

Lawyers have limited time, and most law firms focus on billing the most hours possible rather than developing associates into better attorneys. As stated, this strategy leads to continuous turnover and lost profit.

Summary
If firms desire to change the consistent turnover within their organizations, they must undergo a paradigm shift. How firms have traditionally hired, trained, onboarded, and mentored lawyers is not working. Being open to new and tested ideas from other industries should be considered very seriously. Otherwise, the same dynamic will continue for years to come.

I hope this chapter provides you with enough information to begin making the changes you and your firm should make and soon in order to improve the overall performance of your firm and its lawyers.

References
1   www.thomsonreuters.com/en-us/posts/wp-content/uploads/sites/20/2022/01/State-of-Legal-Market-Report_Final.pdf

2   www.thomsonreuters.com/en-us/posts/legal/retaining-associates/

3   https://decipherintel.com/turnover-your-secret-weapon-for-a-better-law-firm/

4   www.mlaglobal.com/en/insights/articles/why-associates-leave-and-how-you-can-get-them-to-stay

5   https://explodingtopics.com/blog/customer-retention-rates#customer-retention-by-industry

6   www.accountingtoday.com/list/paying-competitive-salaries-tops-accounting-firms-retention-issues

7   www.archdaily.com/963026/focus-on-the-fundamentals-10-metrics-of-high-performing-architecture-firms

8   www.lawtests.com/tests/situational-judgement/

9   www.criteriacorp.com/files/Criteria-Overview-CCAT.pdf

10 www.verbalreasoningtest.org/

11 www.mbtionline.com/

12 https://leaders.com/articles/business/personality-tests/

13 https://eddy.com/hr-encyclopedia/culture-interview/

14 https://news.bloomberglaw.com/bloomberg-law-analysis/analysis-lawyer-jobs-up-but-legal-unemployment-is-on-the-rise

15 https://crisp.co/how-to-master-the-art-of-onboarding-for-your-law-firm/#well

16 www.shrm.org/topics-tools/news/talent-acquisition/onboarding-key-to-retaining-engaging-talent

17 https://guider-ai.com/blog/mentoring-statistics-the-research-you-need-to-know/

18 www.mlaglobal.com/en/insights/research/2019-millennial-attorney-survey-new-expectations-evolving-beliefs-and-shifting-career-goals

19 https://dictionary.cambridge.org/dictionary/english/mentor

Chapter 11:
The impact of technology on attracting (and retaining) talent

By Tara Waters, Ashurst LLP

Introduction

Name recognition. Base pay. Bonus. Benefits. Training support. Chargeable hours requirements. Hybrid working policy. Progression opportunities. Directory rankings. Industry specialisms. Client base. Size of team. Size of firm. Locations. Financial performance. PEP. Time to partner track. Strategy. Values. Culture. Innovativeness. Sustainability. Diversity.

Ask any lawyer or other legal professional considering where to apply for and/or accept their first or next role, or why they are considering leaving a role, and these are amongst the most likely responses.

"Technology", however, is probably not a key consideration typically cited – even if it may be part of considerations including "training support", "culture", and "innovativeness".

Why not and is this changing?

The initially gradual and eventually exponential acceleration of adoption of technology-enabled ways of working has had a profound effect on the expectations of both employers and employees alike over the past 70-plus years. The availability of increasingly sophisticated technologies and tools has influenced the redefining of roles and workplaces in all industries.

Law has not been immune to this macrotrend, although it has really been the most recent wave of technological innovation that has pushed it towards a true inflection point when it comes to the role of technology in attracting and retaining talent.

This chapter will explore more fully both the negative and positive impacts that technology has, and will continue to have, on the "war for talent" within the legal industry.

A short history of the evolution of technology in law

First, it is helpful to remind ourselves of the evolution of technology in law, for which we must go back to the mid-20th century.

Technologies such as Dictaphones and word processers were initially aimed at providing efficiency gains for practice support personnel. Over the second half of the 20th century, secretaries, librarians, paralegals, and eventually junior lawyers used technology to prepare documents, send correspondence, and conduct legal research more efficiently for the lawyers they worked with. Lawyers relied on this support so that they could focus on the complexities and the very human and relationship-driven nature of their practices.

Eventually, and particularly with the proliferation of internet-connected computers at the turn of the 21st century, technology became useful (and eventually necessary) also for practicing lawyers. It allowed them to communicate instantaneously with colleagues and clients, stay on top of client matters when on the go, and capture and share their knowledge and expertise more easily. In turn, this gave lawyers independence and self-sufficiency. While new technologies were also created for practice support roles, such as case and practice management software, ultimately the digital empowerment of lawyers created both blurred lines with, and question marks about, practice support roles. In relation to the latter, firms started to grapple with redesigning practice support roles to ensure they added value to legal practices and began outsourcing and offshoring purely administrative roles.

Most recently, and particularly driven by the profound advances in artificial intelligence (AI) of the 2020s, technology has become the great leveler within law. Those without law degrees and practicing certificates can use technology to complete legal tasks as ably as, and more time and cost-efficiently than, most lawyers. It has become the market norm for firms to have multi-disciplinary teams of professionals who contribute fully to the delivery of legal services, including being able to provide lower-cost and more commoditized legal advice. In part, this has created tremendous opportunities for law firms and those people who desire to join firms without needing to be trained and qualified lawyers. However, this also has raised existential questions about the way lawyers learn and are trained, the continued role of the lawyer in business and society at large, and the business models of law firms.

Today and for the foreseeable future, the attractiveness of a law firm, and the perceived strength of its strategy, values, culture, and performance is underpinned by a successful and people-centric approach to technology.

The role of technology in law

Before diving into the specific impacts of technology on legal talent, it is helpful to understand a bit more deeply what types of technology are being used in legal and the benefits they bring.

There have been several attempts at creating a taxonomy for technology used in legal, although none have been adopted widely. For the purpose of this chapter, we propose four principal categories:

- *Core enabling technology.* These are underlying shared enterprise systems and software that form the essential backbone of any legal business, such as servers and other infrastructure, general business software such as the Microsoft Office suite of products, and digital telephony and conferencing tools.
- *Task and workstream improvement technology.* These are individual solutions and digital tools aimed at streamlining, and in many cases automating, the way a particular task or workstream is conducted, such as case management, document drafting, and due diligence. In some cases, these solutions and tools may be practice-specific and so will be targeted at particular audiences.
- *Knowledge delivery technology.* These are individual solutions and digital tools aimed at providing legally correct guidance and information, such as legal resource platforms that are offered by private businesses, law firms, and barrister chambers. Importantly, with very limited exceptions, these solutions do not provide legal advice and cannot be relied upon as such.
- *Client solutions.* These are specific solutions designed and built to be used directly by and/or with law firm clients. They put firms' technology-based capabilities into the hands of the clients and allow them to access digital services and products online and on-demand. Such solutions are typically designed to support and strengthen client relationships, and there is an increasing trend towards commercializing them.

Fundamentally, these technologies enable improved experiences for employees and clients alike, drive efficiencies that in turn can improve profitability, create business and revenue growth opportunities, and can help to reduce and mitigate risk for the firm. When implemented effectively, they can also support a firm's sustainability and inclusivity credentials.

A growing and diverse legal talent base

Just as the role of technology in law has evolved over time, the profile of legal talent has likewise evolved. Today, inter-generational dynamics within law firms is especially acute and presents an added dimension to the technology challenge.

Law firms' most senior cohort of lawyers and legal professionals came of age in the 20th century, meaning they started practicing without the aid of computers or other internet-enabled devices. When they joined the profession, they had no expectation of digital enablement; writing, researching, and analyzing in fully manual ways was not just the way things were done but, in many cases, enjoyed. Over several decades, this cohort has learned to adapt to technological change, in large part through targeted training and a focus on onboarding tools that don't require upheaval of the ways they prefer to work.

Law firms' most junior cohort of lawyers and legal professionals are often referred to as "digital natives". They were born with the whole of the world's information on a small device that fits inside their pocket. They are used to engaging intuitively and haptically with technology that moves with them, rather than following instructions or being provided with formal training on fixed machines. However, much of law firm technology is likely to be unfamiliar and frustrating to them, and so they too require adaptation and training focus.

Thinking about these cohorts, and all of those sitting on the spectrum in between their extremes, it would be easy to surmise that the lawyers and legal professionals of today expect and require modern mobile technology that gives them access to immediate answers and information, more like that they use in their day-to-day lives, and that legal employers who fall short of that expectation are doomed to extinction.

This would be an oversimplification.

Importantly, the types of activities people use technology for in their personal lives are different from the activities they need to undertake in the legal profession. While the gap between these two things may be narrowing with the advent of technologies like generative AI, it will be some time before there is broad commonality between personal and business technologies.

However, it is true that digital natives, as well as the cohorts before them, continue to wonder why the technology used within law firms does not offer better user experiences, work more intuitively and seamlessly, and generate more efficiencies for them so that they can focus on their advisory role rather than on task execution.

How technology impacts talent

As noted above, technology has had and can have a range of impacts on the practice and business of law. These impacts also contribute to a more positive overall perception and experience of the firm by those within and outside of it, and a more positive overall view of the value that the lawyer or legal professional ascribes to themselves.

This is because by investing in technology, a firm is investing in its people.

Having effective systems, software, and tools, as well as the right learning and development support to ensure its people are using technology to its greatest advantage, makes for a better, more supportive, and collaborative workplace.

Moreover, ensuring those technologies are best-in-class and continue to provide greater benefits over time helps to combat the fear of commoditization of legal services, the devaluing of lawyers' training, expertise, and experience, and the reduction of the practice of law to mere digital interactions.

When Ashurst undertook a lawyer-led trial of a new generative AI solution over four weeks in late 2023[1], 88 percent of respondent participants reported that being part of the trial made them feel that the firm was preparing them for the future.

Technology has become an important differentiator for legal talent.

However, and naturally, it is not mere access to technology that creates differentiation, but the approach of the firm in introducing and embedding technology and technology-enabled capability into everything it does.

Technology must be accessible, intuitive, and easy to use, and deliver the intended benefits. Lawyers and other legal professionals must find technology-enabled ways of working better than manual ways. They must have sufficient training and support available, so that challenges and issues can be addressed quickly and easily. But they must also not be required to retrain as a technologist or spend hours learning a new way of doing things. Adopting technology-enabled ways of working and thinking must be incentivized and supported by the firm. There must be both top-down and bottom-up direction.

Done well, people should feel empowered and enabled by technology, and that technology helps them to do their best work.

Done poorly, however, and the legal industry is likely to see "underinvestment in technology" cited ever increasingly as a reason for people leaving either their employer or the industry altogether.

Technology as a positive differentiator for new talent

What can law firms do?

Ultimately, each law firm needs to take the approach and actions that will work best considering its circumstances.

But, regardless of how a firm determines to proceed, progress is likely to require an iterative approach. This may mean starting small, focusing on specific cohorts, practice areas and/or offices, and then replicating successes across the firm. Or it may mean working through common work types or experiences and systematically enhancing them to the benefit of all.

As a result of the most recent generative AI innovations, which has led to widespread speculation about not just whether, but when, AI-based technology will eventually replace the work of lawyers and legal professionals, it has become particularly important for law firms to focus on the impact on attracting and retaining new talent to the industry.

Start with new entrants

Over the past decade, there has been a concerted effort to increase diversity within law firms, starting with new entrants. Proactive steps have been taken to attract new talent from underrepresented genders, ethnicities, and socio-economic backgrounds. Yet how these new entrants – whether apprentices, graduates, or trainees – are onboarded, trained, and progressed has largely remained unchanged. Why might this be a problem? As mentioned above, it is often assumed that new entrants are "digital natives" who are more technologically-savvy than their predecessors. This can lead to complacency and, therefore, deficiency in the provision of essential technology support and training – which, given the growth in technology- enabled ways of working, means they may become ill-equipped to function well in their roles.

It is important to recognize that not all purported "digital natives" will have the same level of digital literacy. Further, they will not all have grown up with access to the latest technologies, or the benefit of technology training in school or otherwise. Universities are only just starting to introduce modules that focus on how lawyers work and the types of technologies that new entrants may be required to use.

It would be a bit naïve to expect that by merely introducing technology into the school or university curriculum, new entrants will be more capable of using the available technology more and to greater effect – and thus be more effective overall in their roles. This is because much of what a lawyer or legal professional must know about working within a firm and being successful in their role is learned by doing.

While most aspiring lawyers and legal professionals recognize that technology will be a more prevalent aspect of their work, their affinity for the industry is still driven by aspirations far greater than becoming adept at using technology.

Ultimately, they want to become leaders and experts in their roles and fields of specialism. They want to do great work and have that work valued by their employers and their clients. They also want to know that there is room for them to grow and develop within or outside the organization, and that they will be equipped with the tools and support to achieve their goals.

Reinforce the importance of expertise and experience

So, what is the best way to prepare new entrants for working in law and what is the role of technology in this?

Most practitioners would agree that there is no greater teacher than experience. This principle has been the foundation on which most law practices have been built. New talent is brought in, learns by observing and doing, builds their technical expertise and knowledge of the market, and progresses. And then the cycle repeats.

But in a post-pandemic world, with the proliferation of technology solutions and tools aimed at automating certain types of legal tasks and work, this premise has started to unravel.

How does a trainee or junior lawyer learn what needs to be in a commercial lease agreement, and how to negotiate it in the best interests of their client, if technology can do the heavy lifting in terms of drafting, reviewing, and analysing its terms?

There are at least two schools of thought on this conundrum.

On the one hand, it can be argued that technology is making the less experienced trainee and lawyer redundant. Any person can use technology to do this work with a few clicks of a mouse, provided they have the right instruction and knowhow to use the technology to faithfully execute that instruction. For example, most reasonably intelligent persons can be trained to follow a playbook to complete a document automation questionnaire or to glean information about the terms of the contract. Therefore, why have a trainee or junior lawyer at all? Why not just have the technology pass that first draft or analysis to the experienced lawyer, or even directly to the client?

On the other hand, it can be argued that although such tasks and work can be done using technology by persons with limited to no specialist legal skill and knowledge, providing legal advice or a legal service is not just an amalgamation of task completions. In the example, at some point a lawyer knowledgeable about commercial leases will need to weigh in, provide quality assurance, and interject practice and market experience points. The ability to do those things is not something learned from following a playbook once. It is learned by performing the task repeatedly (with or without technology) and speaking to colleagues and clients about other relevant considerations that should inform finalization of any outputs.

It is worth noting also that technology does not always get things right. First, many technology tools are automating processes and information created by lawyers. If there is any mistake in those underlying instructions and playbooks, the technology will implement those errors repeatedly. More advanced technologies, such as generative AI, may not simply automate lawyer-created instructions, but they still get things wrong. Getting things wrong sometimes is a key feature of how generative AI works.

Also, there are many practice and market experience points where lawyers and clients can exercise discretion in a way that would otherwise defy a typical instruction. For example, just because a contractual clause is drafted in a certain way 99 percent of the time, the lawyer or client may decide that circumstances exist that mean that clause needs to be drafted a different way. Most technologies simply cannot cater for these exceptional scenarios.

This is exactly the reason why technology should not be seen as a complete replacement for the "human in the loop", and why new entrants to legal must gain their experience through using technology rather than being replaced by it.

Augment talent with technology

The technology-empowered lawyer is the lawyer of the future. The same is true for other legal professionals.

To best understand and augment their talent pool, firms must maintain a deep understanding of the types of work that their people are engaged in. In understanding what their people are trying to accomplish and what helps or hinders their ability to successfully achieve those things, it is possible to identify the full range of needs they have and how to meet them.

Technology can help address those needs, but it's not just about the technology.

Internal innovation and technology specialists who have been tasked with selecting the right technologies for their firms will universally report how great of a challenge adoption has been and continues to be. The reasons for this include the fact that third-party tools are aimed at broad audiences and so may not meet all the needs of individual law firms or lawyers, the technology may require too much training to use well, and/or adoption may require adaptation of behaviors and ways of working that lawyers are simply unable or unwilling to undertake.

Ultimately, there are no silver bullet solutions in technology and any expectation that the introduction of a technology on its own, without the attendant support and mindset and cultural shifts required for law firms and lawyers to understand, appreciate, and extract value from technology, is likely to lead to disappointment.

However, firms that get this mix right will find a welcoming and loyal talent base. If technology helps reduce their workload and the associated stress of managing that workload, improves productivity, creates space in the day to focus, and enables personal and professional growth, then they will not just believe in the benefits of technology augmentation. They will feel invested in and valued.

Conclusion

Over the past few decades new technological innovations have led to the occasional toll of the death knell for lawyers. The advent of ever more advanced technologies, such as generative AI, have heightened those fears. Still the concern is premature.

Yes, technology is becoming ever more relevant and important to the practice and business of law. Yes, apprentices, graduates, trainees, lawyers, and other legal professionals should expect that using technology will become an integral part of their role. And yes, law firms and legal employers will need to adapt and evolve the way they think about, support, and develop their talent as technology embeds itself further. But no, technology has not yet reached the point where people cease to have purpose or value.

Indeed, it can be argued that the rise of technology's prominence has also led to the rise in understanding and appreciation of the value that people continue to have in the legal sector.

In an industry built on relationships, expertise, and experience, how technology is approached, leveraged, and adapted to enable, empower, and augment will play an increasingly important role in the attraction and retention of talent.

References

1   Based on an internal study conducted with 285 lawyers in November 2023. The study findings will be published later in 2024.

Chapter 12:
Beyond the bonus – rethinking the approach to motivating legal talent

By Rebecca Holdredge, director of knowledge management, and Becky Jo Morgan, director of practice operations, Levenfeld Pearlstein, LLC

It is said that the only constant in life is change, and that is certainly true in the legal industry. Due to rapidly evolving technology and shifting client and employee needs, the legal industry is undergoing a fundamental transformation. Although technology is continuously evolving, as are client and employee priorities, the combination of these shifts and the pace of change have accelerated transformations in law firm culture. As a result, law firm operations must shift to keep up with these changes.

Once upon a time, email and then Google revolutionized law firm operations; now, artificial intelligence and other cutting-edge technologies are upending traditional law firm systems. Will the mainstays of law firm life – the billable hour model and partnership hierarchy – soon be obsolete? Only time will tell. But at a minimum, to remain competitive, law firms must lean into more innovative, efficient, and business-like operational structures. To keep up, many firms are embracing specialized departments such as pricing, project management, knowledge management, practice operations, and innovation to remain competitive.

As if technological and operational changes weren't enough, the legal industry is simultaneously navigating shifting expectations of legal professionals. As we see throughout the workforce, employees want more than adequate compensation – they want work–life balance and autonomy. They are seeking personal and professional development opportunities to grow. They want to feel a sense of purpose, doing work that aligns with their values. Law firms can't afford to assume that money will be the magic wand to attract and retain a skilled workforce. And, with these new operational structures emerging, firms need to take a more holistic approach to motivation and ensure they know, *What exactly are we incentivizing our legal talent to do?*

In this transformative era, law firms are invited and challenged to reimagine their approach to motivation by asking, *How can we enhance productivity and client service in a way that emphasizes skills adaptation, continuous learning, and innovative thinking?* To help inspire law firms to ask this question – and help them answer it as well – in this chapter we investigate current legal industry transformations, explore the limitations of traditional financial incentives, and consider various alternative motivational strategies to attract, retain, and empower legal talent.

We begin by identifying the behaviors and outcomes that progressive law firms incentivize as they move away from the traditional billable hour model and incorporate broader goals that serve firm and client interests. We then discuss how motivation strategies should be tailored to individual needs, fostering a culture where personal goals align with firm objectives. We delve into the power of non-financial incentives, revealing how recognition, career growth opportunities, and a supportive work environment can unlock the full potential of legal talent. We also explore ways firms can use the emerging departments they established to help provide operational efficiency, such as knowledge management (KM) and practice operations, to serve as champions for change when crafting and implementing multifaceted motivational strategies. Finally, we share a roadmap for integrating these strategies into law firm operations.

Although change is constant, that doesn't mean it's easy. We will illuminate a path forward for law firms willing to innovate their motivational approaches, ensuring their workforce remains not only competitive but deeply motivated. This chapter will provide you with the inspiration and tools to adopt a comprehensive, forward-thinking approach to motivation – one that promises to attract, engage, and retain the legal talent necessary for success.

The call for change – shifting professional desires

The legal profession is at a crossroads, with firms grappling to balance the allure of substantial salary increases and huge bonuses against the realities of grueling workloads and the fading prospects of partnership. As many legal professionals are fed up with intense work demands and seek genuine job satisfaction, there is an urgent need to reduce the stress and reevaluate what truly motivates them. Fortunately, many firms are heeding the call. The industry is shifting towards a more nuanced motivational approach that emphasizes individual contributions, work–life balance, autonomy, and professional growth. Law firms at the forefront of this shift are implementing unique incentives to create a culture that supports the wellbeing and development of their talent.

Step one: Identify desired behaviors and outcomes

For those firms that have recognized the need for adaptability to cultivate a motivated and engaged talent pool, congratulations. With this awareness comes the work of implementing the changes. The first step in reevaluating motivational strategies is pinpointing the specific behaviors and outcomes most valuable to the firm.

Traditional metrics of productivity, such as billable hours and realization, are no longer the gold standard. Many firms ask themselves if these conventional metrics are an accurate and effective way to measure a lawyer's contribution to a firm's success. Law firms are increasingly rewarding strategic thinking, client satisfaction, profitability, and a commitment to the firm's values and goals. This pivot requires a clear definition of the firm's desired behaviors. Does the firm value proactive client management and effective collaboration with colleagues? How about the strategic use of new technologies, efficient resource management, and robust knowledge-sharing practices?

Successful outcomes are no longer just about winning legal battles or maximizing billable hours. They are about building enduring client relationships, contributing to the firm's reputation, and generating sustainable growth. Recognizing that employee wellbeing is intrinsically linked to these outcomes, law firms are beginning to structure incentives not only to reward the end results but also to encourage the processes and practices that lead to these positive results.

Step two: Tailor motivation strategies to individual needs

True motivation requires more than substantial salaries – it needs a work environment that respects legal professionals' time, values their wellbeing, and promotes personal and professional satisfaction beyond long hours. Intrinsic motivation outperforms extrinsic rewards in the long run, and law firms must embrace a more nuanced motivational approach. Flexibility, professional growth, and individual recognition have become fundamental in attracting and retaining top talent.

In the quest to cultivate an engaged and satisfied workforce, law firms must delve deeper than financial incentives to truly motivate legal professionals. Understanding each legal professional's unique goals and motivations requires a tailored approach beyond the traditional one-size-fits-all reward systems. Firms must determine how to align employees' work with purpose and expertise. Personalization begins with understanding the diverse aspirations and circumstances of each attorney. Junior associates might value mentorship and rapid skill development, while more experienced lawyers might prioritize flexible work arrangements that allow them to balance family commitments with work commitments. The incentives offered must resonate on a personal level, promoting a sense of fulfillment and alignment with the firm's broader vision.

This is no easy task, but the key lies in law firms' willingness to engage in open and ongoing conversation with their attorneys. What are their personal motivators? How can these be aligned with the firm's broader objectives? The goal is to create an environment where lawyers feel their individual goals are actively supported so the workforce is more engaged, productive, and satisfied.

This tailored approach extends to the practicalities of day-to-day work. By providing clear and accessible performance metrics through dashboards and regular feedback, firms empower their lawyers to take ownership of their career trajectories. The modern legal professional thrives on transparency and the ability to track progress towards both personal benchmarks and the firm's strategic goals.

Incentivizing individual needs also means recognizing accomplishments beyond billable hours, such as contributions to firm culture, knowledge sharing, and pro bono work. These actions, often intangible and overlooked in traditional models, should be celebrated as integral to the firm's identity and success. For instance, at Levenfeld Pearlstein, LLC (LP), such contributions are prioritized as a part of the firm's culture – a part of our ecosystem. This assures young attorneys and laterals alike that we take these contributions seriously.

Unlocking potential – the power of non-financial incentives

As mentioned above, in the competitive legal industry, non-financial incentives are becoming increasingly important. While things like recognition and career growth opportunities might seem like "cherry on top" extras compared to cold hard cash, these things matter – quite a bit actually. Non-financial rewards validate a legal professional's value and achievements, while also encouraging continued growth and improvement. Firms that recognize individual efforts and offer transparent career advancement opportunities, where success is measured not just in outcomes but in personal and professional fulfillment, are more likely to create a motivated workforce.

How to empower through recognition and career growth
In the high-stakes and sophisticated legal industry, recognition means more than a simple pat on the back or passing acknowledgment. It means intentionally and consistently affirming an individual's contributions. Law firms are increasingly designing formal recognition programs, personalized accolades, and peer recognition initiatives to foster a culture of appreciation. But one caveat – these programs cannot be one-size-fits-all. They must be tailored to an individual's preferences to be meaningful and effective. While some individuals prefer quiet recognition, others relish their moment to shine. Law firms need to pay attention to these differences when crafting and implementing recognition programs.

Alongside an authentic recognition program, firms can offer – and *support* – career growth opportunities as a path for achieving personal goals while also honoring the firm's vision. Law firms can do so by providing clear advancement paths, diverse professional development resources, and lateral options within the firm. Attorneys can feel more in charge of their own career, and because growth begets growth, this holistic approach to career development creates a mutually beneficial cycle of growth and advancement for both the attorney and the firm.

Career development opportunities – like recognition programs – should include bespoke options. Whether it is mentorship, training programs, or clear routes to partnership, when personalized, these programs are a testament to the firm's investment in each individual's potential. For instance, LP has both formal and informal mentorship programs and customized leadership programs. Junior attorneys can participate in the formal mentor program, where they are matched with an experienced attorney outside their own practice group. Our leadership programs are offered to aspiring leaders at several levels and align in their message and terminology, although the specific scope may vary depending on the participants' specific roles.

The synergy between recognition and career growth is the "special recipe" for creating a dynamic law firm culture. The strategy applauds what has been accomplished and equips professionals with the tools and opportunities needed to innovate and excel as their career progresses. As legal professionals receive validation and see tangible options for professional fulfillment, their motivation expands beyond financial incentives to a deeper sense of achievement and belonging within the firm.

Motivation mirrors the work environment and firm culture

We can't talk about motivating legal talent without also looking at the role of work environment and organizational culture. It's no secret that a positive, inclusive, and supportive workplace enhances job satisfaction, and a collaborative spirit drives engagement and performance. But this is about more than interpersonal relationships. Everything from the physical workspace to an inclusive culture impacts motivation.

Does the firm's office space promote productivity and provide ergonomic comfort? Does the firm's culture emphasize open communication, diversity, and respect? Does the firm actively promote work–life balance through flexible schedules and wellness initiatives that recognize the holistic needs of their employees? Does the firm encourage continuous learning and innovation? These are not easy questions, but firms need to undertake these challenging issues if they want to succeed in developing motivated and engaged professionals who feel their diverse needs are acknowledged and valued.

Encouraging active participation in decision-making and celebrating innovative solutions to complex challenges invites legal professionals to shape the firm's future. Flexible work arrangements, including remote work options, enable employees to balance their personal life and professional obligations. A firm culture that prioritizes inclusivity and open dialogue nurtures a sense of shared mission and loyalty. All of these cultural attributes are steppingstones for facilitating motivation.

What is at the core of all these components? People. When long-time LP team members are asked why they have worked at LP for so many years, they often respond, *"It's the people. The people I work with day in and day out make my work meaningful and enjoyable. I look forward to being with them. We are a family."* The LP culture champions inclusivity and ethical practice, while also prioritizing comfortable ergonomic designs and collaborative spaces. Law firms that similarly prioritize this kind of people-first culture will be several steps ahead in the quest to inspire and motivate their workforce. This culture shows employees that they are more than just a cog in the machine – they are valued members of a community with a common purpose.

How emerging departments can energize talent

Operational and technological changes in the legal industry have ushered in a wave of specialized departments, such as KM, practice operations, and learning and development (L&D). These teams enhance operational efficiency, bolster workforce wellbeing, and provide new avenues for professional growth and fulfillment. They address the diverse needs of legal professionals by implementing innovative strategies, playing a critical role in creating a supportive, engaging, and forward-thinking work environment.

KM – using information empowerment to motivate talent

In the legal industry, information is power. KM has emerged as a vital tool for driving innovation and empowering legal professionals. Many firms have created KM departments to harness the firm's collective intelligence. The individual and collective knowledge in law firms is substantial, but to date, firms have struggled with ways to efficiently access this information. Through KM departments, firms can ensure that legal professionals have immediate access to the resources and information they need to better serve their clients. Not only can KM departments boost productivity, but they also improve job satisfaction by minimizing the time and stress of digging for information.

KM encourages legal professionals to share insights and best practices with colleagues. Innovative KM tools such as AI-driven legal research platforms, intranets, and collaborative databases can enhance the accessibility and relevance of information. Because these tools facilitate immediate problem- solving and encourage legal professionals to contribute their insights, they can foster a sense of ownership and pride in the collective knowledge pool. Armed with additional information, legal professionals who value teamwork and collective success often feel more empowered and motivated.

What's more, because information is more accessible throughout the firm, KM contributes to a more inclusive, collaborative, and efficient work environment. KM departments are instrumental in capturing tacit knowledge – valuable insights and experiences often unrecorded but inherent within seasoned professionals. KM tools can preserve the firm's intellectual capital, while also fostering a cycle of continuous learning and development when used to mentor and train junior associates.

Practice operations – resource management and work–life balance initiatives

Practice operations energizes talent by enhancing efficiency, productivity, and overall performance, which, in turn, addresses resource management and promotes work–life balance initiatives. While this can be structured in various ways, at LP, practice operations encompasses resource allocation, technology integration, workflow optimization, training, and professional development.

Practice operations bolsters motivation in several ways. First, assigning legal professionals to tasks that align with their strengths and interests is not only efficient for the firm, but also ensures that each team member is appropriately utilized, allowing law firms to enhance overall productivity and job satisfaction.

Second, assessing the need for and implementing advanced legal technologies such as automation tools, case management systems, and other software solutions adds value for the law firm. These solutions can streamline repetitive tasks, allowing legal professionals to focus on higher-value work. Integrating technology (or other) solutions to identified problems contributes to a more efficient and less stressful work environment. When employees understand that the firm cares enough about them to invest resources in problem-solving, they become motivated to help find solutions.

Third, by identifying bottlenecks and implementing streamlined procedures, a practice operations team can significantly reduce the time and effort required to complete tasks. This contributes to a more manageable workload for legal professionals, reducing stress and improving overall job satisfaction.

At LP, practice operations works closely with the technology and learning and development teams to ensure that legal professionals on all levels have opportunities to continuously develop and improve their skills. Employees have repeatedly indicated that they highly value professional development and growth opportunities, so practice operations is on the frontline working to identify where these opportunities are needed.

As we've noted, legal professionals express different preferences for recognizing and rewarding outstanding performance. At LP, practice operations helps firm leaders to identify these preferences and implement different styles of recognition and reward, and employees consistently say that recognition for a job well done is highly motivating.

Cultivating professional growth and collaboration

As discussed above, attorneys increasingly identify professional development opportunities as key motivators and differentiators when determining where to grow their practice. They also want to do meaningful work and develop strong relationships with their colleagues. At LP, we view these motivators as being interdependent. Accordingly, we design and implement personalized development strategies that connect to our values to drive behavior and change. Our KM, practice operations, and learning and development departments work hand-in-hand to identify opportunities for growth, coaching, training, and development strategies.

Success stories – non-financial incentives in action

Contrary to common misconceptions, non-financial incentives do not need to be costly or time-consuming. At LP, we have a tradition of acknowledging employee anniversaries via a personalized email from their manager or the practice operations team. This email is sent to the employee's entire practice group, the CEO, and the managing partner. The email often results in a flurry of congratulatory emails. Employees feel recognized and appreciated – a free employee goodwill program, so to speak.

On the other hand, significant investments in technology solutions are sometimes necessary. For instance, LP has recently invested in software leveraging AI to assist with a variety of routine tasks, such as due diligence organization and review. Drawing on our resources in practice operations, KM, IT, and learning and development, we designed and implemented the integration plan for the software. This kind of change takes time and effort, but it is now paying off through committed use by our attorneys. They can work more efficiently and effectively, freeing them up for more meaningful work they desire.

Looking ahead – the future of motivation in a law firm

With shifting cultural norms and changing workforce expectations, law firms will continue to reconsider how they are fostering motivation among their legal professionals. Many firms are recalibrating the traditional models of employee motivation, which heavily relied on financial incentives, to incorporate a more nuanced understanding of what drives legal talent. As we look ahead, we expect firms to increasingly shift towards creating more holistic, employee-centric environments that prioritize wellbeing, professional development, and work–life integration.

One emerging trend is the recognition of the importance of mental health and wellbeing. Law firms are beginning to implement comprehensive wellness programs that go beyond the standard health benefits and include mental health resources, stress management workshops, and initiatives aimed at fostering a healthier work–life balance. This "whole-person" approach to employee wellbeing recognizes that a motivated workforce is one that feels supported in all aspects of their lives.

We also expect technology's impact on motivation strategies to expand. The use of artificial intelligence and data analytics can assist with personalizing recognition and career development plans for each employee. This personalization ensures that motivation strategies resonate with the individual, fostering a deeper sense of engagement and alignment with the firm's goals.

Career development opportunities will also continue to shift, moving towards more flexible and diverse career pathways. Gone are the days of the traditional linear progression to partnership as the sole career path for legal professionals. Instead, there will be an emphasis on lateral movements, skill diversification, and alternative leadership roles that allow for a broader range of career trajectories within the legal field. This flexibility acknowledges that not every person with a law degree wants to make partner and honors legal talent's diverse professional aspirations.

Another trend is the increasing importance of purpose and values in motivating employees. Legal professionals, especially those from younger generations, want more than a paycheck – they want to work for firms that align with their personal values and contribute to the greater good. Law firms that demonstrate a commitment to social responsibility, DEIB (diversity, equity, inclusion, and belonging), and ethical practices will have a competitive edge in attracting and retaining talent.

Lastly, the future of motivation in law firms will likely involve a greater emphasis on flexibility and autonomy. The pandemic accelerated the acceptance of remote work, flexible schedules, and alternative work arrangements, and we expect these to remain key components of the work environment. Providing legal professionals with greater control over where and when they work increases job satisfaction and motivation because it allows them to better manage their personal and professional responsibilities.

Integrating new motivational approaches

Motivational approaches within the legal industry are undergoing exciting and revolutionary changes. The trends reflect a broader shift in the industry as firms try to better understand and address the complex needs of their workforce and leverage evolving technologies. To stay competitive, law firms will need to think creatively about what motivates their workforce and adapt personalized motivational strategies that incorporate both financial and non-financial incentives. Law firms that embrace these changes and implement more innovative motivational strategies will be more attractive employers and produce more engaged, satisfied, and productive employees.

To do this, firms need to tailor their motivational approaches to the individual employee, understanding what makes them feel empowered and appreciated. A paycheck is the motivational baseline. Legal professionals crave professional development, work–life balance, and a sense of purpose. By prioritizing recognition, career progression, and a supportive culture, law firms can harness powerful non-financial incentives to enhance morale, promote excellence, and foster loyalty. In other words, they will successfully motivate their workforce.

As shown throughout this chapter, firms that are already moving towards more business-like structures to meet evolving client needs should leverage emerging departments such as knowledge management, practice operations, and learning and development to help spearhead these motivational initiatives. As LP has found, these teams of business professionals are well-positioned to gather insights and offer valuable suggestions regarding how best to encourage legal professionals to incorporate new technologies into their day-to-day work, optimize available firm resources, and maintain a culture that values continuous learning and growth. As we look ahead, it is clear that firms that want to stay competitive in the legal industry will need to think creatively about what motivates their workforce and adapt personalized motivational strategies that incorporate both financial and non-financial incentives.

Chapter 13:
Developing talent in the exponential age

By Dr Catherine Mcgregor, director of professional development at Chief Legal Executive, and executive coach

We are now living in The Exponential Age. This is phrase that has been coined to describe the increased pace of change human society deals with because of increasing technological advancement. However, our minds are not yet prepared for the reality of an exponential change. What is going to be central to coping with this is education focused on changing our minds and behaviors to cope with this. In my professional development and executive coaching practice, working with legal departments and law firms, my partner, Lloyd M Johnson Jr and I have been using The Exponential Age as a framework for our programs based on interactive learning and group coaching to help lawyers develop mindsets and behaviors to be able to keep up with the pace of change.

In The Exponential Age, talent development will need to be a fundamental area of focus for all businesses. The Exponential Age is characterized by increasing use of technology and much faster pace of change. Legal departments and law firms will not be immune to these changes. The shift coming with the digital age reveals a greater focus on skills rather than traditional markers of attainment such as degrees, and on lifelong learning rather than higher education attainment. This will only intensify as change and acceleration become the new normal. By analysing the results of 200 large-scale digital and AI transformations, McKinsey[1] has found that long-term success only comes when the C-suite fundamentally changes their talent, operating model, technology, and data capabilities, in that order.

However, if we look at legal through this lens, change is still a long time coming. Many law firms recruit from a smaller amount of law schools than ever before, and legal education does not seem to be relevant to many aspects of legal work now, let alone in the increasingly digitized age of the future. By most metrics, talent development has been less of a focus in the legal profession than many others. What we have found through our education programs is that talent development is still not the priority it needs to be in the legal profession.

What will be needed to truly maximize workforce potential in law is to imagine how different the legal workplace can look like, what success is, and how that can be achieved.

A significant part of how we imagine differently will be focused on what success looks like and therefore processes for advancement and judging these. I will go into more detail later about the benefits of coaching and a coaching mindset in the workplace, but part of this is an understanding of the different techniques via which ends can be achieved. There is no one blueprint for success, and individuals need to unlock their own vision of success and therefore the paths to achieve this. Too often in law, this insight can be lost.

In law firms, the path to success is clear cut and defined. For many lawyers and clients, this notion of success is built upon only certain skills – not all of which will be increasingly useful in The Exponential Age. During 2023, we conducted some research with in-house lawyers in major legal departments who were primarily responsible for instruction and management of outside counsel. We found that there was still a striking mismatch between what clients wanted and what law firm lawyers were giving them. These missteps were firmly rooted in human-centered skills, not technical legal aptitude.

The research showed five major areas of client service where in-house lawyers are focused and where frequently their outside counsel come up short:

1. Understanding the client.
2. Taking meaningful steps to strengthen the client relationship.
3. Being positioned as a business partner, not simply a legal advisor.
4. Understanding the client's risk appetite.
5. Making pitches that persuade and win.

To drill into these for understanding the client, in essence, clients want their outside firms to:

- Ask questions;
- See the big picture; and
- Know their audience.

Too often, outside counsel fail to take the time to think and prepare "three very crisp questions" in advance of a meeting. Further, outside counsel should not hesitate to ask questions to clarify exactly what the client needs, so that a 20-page memo is not delivered if what the client wants or needs for a specific matter is a seven-bullet email.

Client relationships shouldn't be so hard, yet many outside counsel often fail to take basic, common-sense steps that in-house counsel say would go a long way to building a much stronger connection. These basic steps include applying general principles that are relevant in all relationships. Some fundamentals to relationship building are straightforward but are too often overlooked. Clients are more comfortable when their outside counsel gets to know them personally, by making the effort to interact in person when possible.

This relationship and the understanding that builds it is also about understanding the specific hard realities for clients. That often means taking discussions about costs seriously. Too often, firms are indifferent to the pressures their in-house clients are under. Managing costs is paramount, and when a firm demonstrates flexibility and creativity, it goes a long way to being a preferred firm.

"Being a business partner" is a phrase many law firms use, but it seems that for clients it is lacking in practice. Being able to see the bigger picture is fundamental. Senior in-house counsel believe that what distinguishes valuable outside lawyers and firms is their ability to have a wider lens. In-house lawyers want firms to help them benchmark where they are relative to competitors and share market intelligence. Too often firms fail to bring this value-add. Thinking like a business colleague is also fundamental. Companies value when their outside counsel anticipates what they need and can speak the language of their business. Business executives want information so they can make business decisions. They don't need to see every legal issue that an attorney can conjure.

Too often, clients feel that lawyers over-index on legal risk without understanding the other areas of business risk that interplay with legal risk and how these can modify the entire risk landscape. Associated with this is the trait of overemphasizing even esoteric risks. As one client in a large consumer goods company defined it, this is the "Chicken Licken" mindset where the sky is constantly falling in. The danger of this is that clients become immune to all mentions of risk and may ignore the risk warnings they really need to heed. Firms are more successful when they caution about risks but discuss these risks in context of things to watch out for and what the firm has seen before, without overstating and cramming in every conceivable risk ever possible (and some others you might not have even considered!).

When clients think about law firm pitches, they want the firm to demonstrate all the other themes – understanding of the client, a strong relationship, a true business perspective and partnership, and a sophisticated view of risk. They also want to see diversity as an essential element of client service, not as an add-on. Unfortunately, it seems "diversity eye-candy", as one client defined it, is still alive and well.

Future readiness

The mismatch that our research uncovered between law firms and their client's expectation is going to be even more pronounced if legal education and training does not change substantially. We conducted this research as part of preparation for the training program we ran for URG senior associates in leading US law firms throughout 2023. The program, called *Think Like A GC*, was focused on practical interactive tasks run with our in-house legal faculty to get senior associates more comfortable with competencies that we discovered were critical to developing more enhanced client service. These are also competencies that we find are central to our leadership development training with in-house lawyers – self-awareness, strategic mindset, and executive communication. What was transformational for many of the senior associates who were working in small groups with the in-house faculty was understanding how central human-centered skills which are not technical legal aptitude can be the defining factor in building a lasting relationship with outside lawyers. Too often, associates told us that this was completely missing from the focus of their training, yet is going to be a crucial component of the skill set needed to meet the current criteria of success in most law firms – working successfully with corporate legal departments.

What is clear is that as the business landscape changes, so too will its definition of career success. The advent of generative AI makes the divide between what human and machine can do even smaller so that human-centric skills, particularly those of creativity and collaboration, will be what is needed going forward. What this might mean is a re-imagining of what success looks like in law firms and the ability to be agile when defining and redefining success as client needs change more quickly. The current hierarchical vision of promotion with a fixed notion of success based only on billable hours will need to adapt.

The legal department talent landscape

In legal departments the challenges are ultimately similar but operate within a different structure. Most US legal teams suffer from a flat structure with little opportunity for regular advancement. Rather than a clearly defined path of success, often it is too opaque. Multiple in-house counsel I work with speak of the culture of the "tap on the shoulder" regarding advancement still being alive and well in legal departments. Too often, promotion opportunities are not advertised, and many are clueless about why these happen, even if they are the lucky individual who has been successful.

In 2022, with the Black In-House Counsel Network, I conducted a research study of diversity, equity, and inclusion (DEI) in nearly 40 in-house legal departments in the US.[2] One of our major topics was retention and promotion. Whilst this study was refracted through the lens of DEI, many of the findings are relevant more broadly to speak to a crisis of talent development in most in-house legal departments.

Common themes included:

* Lack of transparency around opportunities for advancement.
* Opportunities are not widely promoted.
* Lack of investment in professional development.
* Dearth of regular open discussion by mangers with direct reports on their talent aspirations.
* Little or no effort in understanding attrition.

Reframing development

What drives success in my experience are leaders who are intentional about their approach to development and who look at this much more broadly. This intentionality can result in a leader as coach mindset, discussed later, which I feel will be fundamental in the Exponential Age.

There are several key ideas here. First is having a clear definition of success at different stages and the competencies beyond just legal aptitude needed to achieve this. Some large global legal departments are developing descriptions of what each level in the department can identify as success so that advancement and promotion can be much more transparent and objective.

In legal departments, what is also fundamental is understanding the "building block" opportunities that lead to promotions. These are often high visibility projects or stretch assignments that put individuals in the line of sight of leaders who will have input in promotions. Too often, these are left to the discretion of managers who may default to the person who did it well last time. In Intuit's legal team, an analysis of promotion decisions led to the insight that it was the allocation of these high visibility opportunities that had a striking correlation with success in formal promotions. When such opportunities were audited via a DEI lens, it was found overwhelmingly that URGs were being overlooked.

Intuit introduced an audit of all the high visibility projects that could lead to advancement on an annual basis and legal leaders came together to discuss these and consider who was given these in a much more process driven way. This led to more equality of opportunity and therefore a larger pool of candidates who were perceived to be ready for promotion.

Impact of remote working

One of the most seismic impacts on all work in recent years was the wholescale shift to remote working by many professions during the COVID-19 pandemic. This was sudden. Interestingly, many professions that had previously resisted the shift to flexible work, such as law firms and investment banks, found that working was not impacted at all. In many cases, productivity went up. The shift to a remote model has continued for many and for some corporate legal departments, remote working long predated the pandemic. Due to space concerns, many corporate offices have been operating a hot desk or partial model. This is generally driven by space constraints. At one legal department I worked with, I lauded the flexible working model, which was driving great dividends in terms of diverse hiring and retention. They noted that this had been driven by downsizing to a smaller campus, where it was impossible to fit everyone all the time! Nevertheless, for many in-house lawyers, this was less of a shift in mindset than for many in private practice, particularly for those in the associate ranks for whom long hours in the office are seen as a necessary rite of passage. If this is no longer necessary, what other tenets of legal training might be up for grabs?

For many legal departments, the shift to remote working opened a great deal of hiring potential. In the US, where I live and work now, legal departments located in states and cities not known for diverse communities, and/or who found it hard to woo candidates to relocate, had a myriad of new hiring possibilities via offering fully remote roles.

For women and historically underrepresented groups, this represented an opportunity. A 2022 survey by Slack's research arm, Future Forum showed that amongst knowledge workers Black and Latinx workers much preferred remote work, as did working mothers.[3]

Law firms were not immune from this, moving surprisingly easily to fully remote when needed during the pandemic, despite assertions for many years prior that this would not be viable. For associates whose norm was working remotely at least a percentage of the time, the encroaching demand to get them back into the office is not universally popular. Most associates I speak with favor three days a week in the office, but four is increasingly becoming the norm with a move back to full-time in the office imminent for many.

There can be a difference between what you want and what you need. Many law firms queried whether younger lawyers would get the osmosis of learning provided by working side-by-side with more experienced lawyers. However, law firm DWF in the UK came up with an ingenious solution to this during the lockdown of 2020 by offering employees the ability to work in hubs with others via Teams, replicating the notion of a shared office where you could initiate conversation or ask a question virtually as it came up.

It's clear that from a work–life balance and personal preference point of view, many lawyers feel there is no going back from some type of hybrid working arrangement. However, where this seems to hit challenges is where it comes to development and promotion in a hybrid environment.

As an executive coach and management consultant, I have spoken to several legal teams who have hybrid policies and are happy to continue to embrace these but feel uneasy about the potential impact of development and advancement on those who are fully or partially remote.

For many large law firms, the impact is starker. To be remote or hybrid now may mean an impacted professional development track that will not lead to equity partnership.

The challenge at the heart of the questions I am asked by legal teams, and the potential lack of flexibility amongst traditional law firms, comes down to what could best be described as a lack of imagination regarding advancement considering office politics. What lurks beneath this is the unkillable zombie of presenteeism. It's not just about being seen to be doing the work and putting the hours in – although that's a substantial factor in law firms – it's also being there in the room with the right people and part of the right conversations. That is the aspect of hybrid work and talent development that also impacts legal departments, particularly those where some employees remain fully or partially remote.

Too often, those with the ability to promote will have a proximity bias to those that they regularly see and for whom the evidence that they are achieving is right in front of their faces. Proximity bias refers to the phenomenon that managers tend to treat those who are closer to them physically more favorably. It's also linked to the (refuted) idea that remote workers are less productive than those in the workplace.

Gleb Tsipursky, writing in *Harvard Business Review* in 2022, quotes a 2021 survey from the Society for Human Resource Management (SHRM) of over 800 supervisors:

"SHRM reported two-thirds (67 percent) of supervisors overseeing remote workers admitted to believing remote workers are more replaceable than onsite workers. Forty-two percent said they sometimes forget about remote workers when assigning tasks. This may explain why remote workers are promoted less often than their peers, despite being 15 percent more productive on average."[4]

This is inevitably going to put remote and even hybrid workers at a disadvantage. Long-term, this is likely to be more of an issue in-house where remote and hybrid working was the norm for many legal teams even pre-COVID. But it will also affect law firms as some lawyers take advantage of hybrid policies. Lawyers themselves need to be mindful of the effects of proximity bias in advancement and allocating opportunities that will lead to advancement.

Intentionality is once again the keyword here. Those leading legal departments and law firms need to acknowledge proximity bias and consistently reinforce what Tsipursky calls a "culture of excellence from anywhere". Central to this is regular scheduled check-ins with remote workers where performance goals can be set and checked. Setting performance goals and accountability regularly is a best practice that should not only be confined to remote workers. Agreeing on goals and building in accountability is a hallmark of a coaching style of leadership that is fundamental to success in managing hybrid teams or, indeed, any team in The Exponential Age. What underlies this is leadership that is not being as fully intentional as it could be about its talent development strategies. A key part of this is coaching and a coaching mindset for leaders.

Benefits of coaching on professional development in the legal profession

What is coaching? Coaching is a relationship between a coach and a coachee, where the coach asks questions, challenges, leads exercises and visualizations, which will act as a catalyst for the coachee to recognize mindsets and behaviors they have that might hold them back and then develop the tools and behaviors to change these. Coaching is not telling others what to do – that is consulting. It is not sharing experiences – that is mentoring. Coaching has grown in popularity in professional settings, particularly in the executive suite. Increasingly, many large companies will provide coaching for employees once they reach executive level. However, coaching is useful for employees no matter what level they are at. For employees at the start of their career, coaching can be incredibly beneficial. Unfortunately, coaching remains unregulated. This means that literally anyone can call themselves a coach, whether they have training or not. It is advisable to select a coach who has undergone a training program that is accredited by the professional body for coaches – in the US this is the International Coaching Federation. This means that the program will have the required depth and rigor. Many corporations now will not hire coaches unless they have an ICF accredited qualification. An interesting point for lawyers is that the ICF accreditations focus heavily on the ethical obligations of the coach in the professional relationship.

As mentioned above, I see coaching being used mostly when lawyers, whether in-house or in law firms, reach a certain level in their professional journey. Coaching is often used as lawyers approach leadership or attain a leadership role.

The use of executive coaching is still much more in use in corporate legal departments than in law firms. Often, this is dependent on size and budgets available. Smaller companies and start-ups may be much less likely to invest in coaching for their employees. Arguably, the intensity in an early-stage company could make investing in coaching an incredibly valuable investment for professionals working in this arena due to the way interpersonal dynamics can become more heightened and the way in which the needs of early-stage companies mean all employees must move out of their professional comfort zone.

During the coaching relationship, the coachees and the coach will start by setting a focus for the engagement. This could range from becoming more comfortable with public speaking, feeling more like a leader, becoming more comfortable with difficult conversations, and developing more empathy in their professional role. The coach will usually conduct a discovery session with the coachees to understand the totality of their current situation and explore what will be most resonant to focus the coaching relationship on. Generally, the coaching relationship will be defined for a particular time frame – in my practice this is six or 12 months but can obviously be extended as desired. During the agreed time frame, the coach will check in with the client to see if progress is being made and the original goal is still being served. In coaching, the focus is on letting the client speak and providing feedback, but also using exercises, which might include visualization, embodiment, and challenging.

These will all provide ways to allow the client to be more in touch with the emotions that are driving their mindset and therefore their behaviors and then to find ways to change these. I coach many lawyers and it is interesting that some are more open to coaching than others. A challenge for many lawyers is moving outside of their head. A way I have found to solve this is not allowing my coachees to use their head or their mind as a focus for feeling or emotion – this can flummox many!

There's an interesting link here with the ways in which lawyers are trained and define success as residing primarily in knowledge and being right. As lawyers move into leadership positions, whether in law firms or in-house, they will find there are many instances, particularly in managing or dealing with people, where there is no obvious right or wrong. This opens the possibility of not knowing the right answers, not being prepared, and the potential for failure, which can be hard for those who have spent their life until now feeling that they have all the answers.

Leader as coach

Increasingly, coaching is a skill that all leaders will need to develop. A coaching style of feedback will focus much more on exploration than pronouncement. The leader works with the report as an ally to be with the report as they develop. But for a coaching leader, as opposed to an external professional coach, what is fundamental is understanding when to coach and when to lead. There may be times that leading from the front and making decisions is appropriate. Certainly in the sphere of talent development, leading from the back or leading from the side style of coaching is appropriate. Supporting, challenging, stimulating greater creativity, and getting beyond professional discomfort are the key manifestations of a coaching leader.

I coach legal leaders on how to coach direct reports and one of the key starting points must be a sense of curiosity and openness. In Co-Active, the coaching methodology I predominantly trained in one of our cornerstones is "Everyone is naturally creative, resourceful, and whole". People can achieve change – the potential simply has to be unlocked, rather than something being wrong or lacking. How this might look in practice is a much more enquiring starting point and asking questions of the direct report, rather than telling them what they could do.

For example, if you think a lawyer (either in-house or in a law firm) needed to take a much bigger picture, rather than a risk averse view, a starting point from a coaching leader might be to explore what the individual's relationship is to risk. What's there for them emotionally in connection to this topic? Is it a discomfort with uncertainty? Is it a fear of failure? By questioning and getting the employee to reflect on their own responses, we can help them own the initial response, which may not have been ideal, and then help them see the path to a new response. This then sets them up to do this on their own.

To make coaching truly impactful, setting actionable steps and development plans to put feedback into action is what is needed.

For example, I often encourage coachees to try a new way of responding to an issue or to take baby steps towards a developmental step. If you have a fear of public speaking but know this is something you need to do to develop in your role, as a leader/coach the first stage might be a request for your report to commit to making a comment in every meeting they attend.

Accountability for such requests must be positive and inquiry focused. If the report does this, the first step is to celebrate the achievement via positive feedback. If they are unable to complete this, the first step is to inquire what was there in that failure. By exploring that gently and supportively, it helps them take control of the issue with the coach/leader supporting them and metaphorically going with them into the topic.

Differences in feedback given to women and minority ethnic individuals and how to correct biases

Honest, constructive feedback facilitates professional advancement, because there is always room for improvement, no matter what level you train in your career. Quality feedback enables you to see how others perceive you. It may alert you to blind spots you have about your own behavior or reactions. Feedback is to your career as water is to a plant. It can be a challenge to recognize feedback for the gift it is, which can be hard since most people focus on the negative aspects of feedback. Learning to process feedback is a skill, often benefiting from work with an executive coach who can help provide perspective and develop a plan to move forward.

The coach will often be alert to feelings and topics that the client finds difficult to be with. It can be useful to be alert to this in your reaction to feedback. Why might reaction to certain feedback be so heightened? Could it resonate in a way that is uncomfortable for you to admit?

Feedback is not a level playing field. A range of research shows that underrepresented groups, particularly women and minority ethnic individuals, find it much more difficult to get constructive and actionable feedback from majority managers. For minority ethnic employees, particularly black employees, this became more heightened after the 2020 murder of George Floyd. Racism became a major topic in society and at work and majority managers who were already more sensitive to being considered racist became even more unwilling to give open and constructive feedback to minority ethnic employees.

The result is that black executives state that their white counterparts receive more frequent and better-quality feedback. This in turn can make it harder for black professionals to gain promotions. The same is true of other minority ethnic groups and for women but this phenomenon is most pronounced for black professionals.

What can professionals and managers do to overcome this feedback bias? Introducing a culture of informal and frequent feedback in the moment can be helpful for everyone, not just underrepresented employees. Rather than waiting for formal performance reviews, giving feedback as it occurs can be beneficial for both sides. The manager is not overthinking the response and the employee will know exactly what behavior is being referred to. This opens the possibility for ongoing dialogue, which will provide a much more constructive feedback loop.

At times, underrepresented professionals are seemingly expected to make their uncomfortable manager feel comfortable to give feedback. This underscores the need for psychological safety on both sides of the equation – the giver and the receiver. Some successful tools to create psychological safety include active listening and direct solicitation of constructive feedback. This requires becoming comfortable asking for feedback as the employee. If you're an underrepresented employee in a predominantly white environment, actively seeking out feedback may be what you need to get comfortable with. If your direct manager continues to not provide meaningful feedback, you need to seek out feedback from others in the organization.

A tip is to cultivate a "personal board" for meaningful feedback. Successful leaders often rely on trustworthy peers outside of their organization, which can be other successful professionals who may share similar experiences. These advisers can give honest, candid, unvarnished responses.

References

1 McKinsey, Rewired and running ahead: Digital and AI leaders are leaving the rest behind, 12 January 2024. www.mckinsey.com/capabilities/mckinsey-digital/our-insights/rewired-and-running-ahead-digital-and-ai-leaders-are-leaving-the-rest-behind

2 Black In-House Counsel Network, *Roadmap to Inclusion*, August 2022. https://22382928.hs-sites.com/roadmap-2022

3 Future Forum by Slack, "Levelling the playing field in the hybrid workplace", January 2022. https://futureforum.com/research/leveling-the-playing-field-in-the-hybrid-workplace/

4 Gleb Tsipursky, "What is Proximity Bias and How Can Managers Prevent It", *Harvard Business Review*, October 2022. https://hbr.org/2022/10/what-is-proximity-bias-and-how-can-managers-prevent-it

Chapter 14:
A little HELP – rewarding and nurturing talent

By Molly Peckman, founder, Molly Peckman Training & Development

Introduction

Law firm associates want and need to be nurtured. Nurtured associates stay longer at their firms, do better work, and become better lawyers. This chapter offers suggestions for how individual partners can better nurture and positively impact associate development, retention, and morale. We encourage you to share it with those partners who need to read it.

Skeptical partners might not be inclined to invest the extra time and effort to help associates. Perhaps as associates they never needed anybody's help in any way. Maybe they tried helping before and think they no longer possess the patience for it. Or they are not natural nurturers and relegate the care of associates to professional development consultants at firms wise enough to employ them, or to the handful of "nicer" partners, the caretakers. Every firm has caretakers – "super mentors" who take the time to train, coach, teach, develop, and nurture associates. These caretakers are accessible and approachable; they welcome and integrate lawyers and they help others leave the firm gently.

The partners who nurture associates understand the cost of a lost associate is more than recruiters' fees and related costs, including the lost time replacing departed associates. Caretaking partners understand the priceless cost of turnover on morale, firm reputation, and client service. They also realize departed associates can end up as informal spokespeople and even potential clients of the firm. This is why associate development is the responsibility of every partner.

So, how do individual partners know what associates want and need? We ask associates often... and they tell us. There are surveys for every season from the major legal publications, lawyer rating services, and recruiting agencies, and they report feedback from thousands of associates. Many firms supplement this feedback by conducting internal surveys, focus groups, and external assessments. Conducting stay interviews is a recent trend, with firms utilizing consultants to interview lawyers, synthesize the feedback, and provide recommendations to improve the associate experience.

Over the past few years, I have interviewed hundreds of associates about their experiences at their firms and asked what kept them at their firms and what would tempt them to leave. While individual associate experiences varied, the stay interview results shared common themes with survey responses. While compensation is important to many, the associates also wanted to talk about other rewards and how their interactions with individual partners impacted their experiences. Most associates attribute their satisfaction, or lack thereof, to their work teams and work streams, much of which is managed, or should be, by law firm partners.

When I ask associates what they would miss most if they left their firms, almost all respond that it is "the people". The most satisfied associates tell me personal connections, especially with partners, keep them from replying to recruiters' outreach. The unhappy ones tell me they do not feel connected or cared about. Individual partners can make significant impacts on the associate experience. The associates have told us they want partners' HELP – honesty, empathy, listening, and professional development.

H = Honesty

Associates deserve honesty. Honesty breeds trust and individual partners need to develop that trust by being true to their words and following through on their commitments. Associates need trustworthy information. This starts before associates arrive at the firm with candor during recruiting about firm culture and the expectations for associates and continues through their careers with information about the path to and requirements of partnership. Throughout their careers, associates need information about their performance and advice on how to develop their skills. Associates expect and deserve honest feedback.

Many partners I work with admit to needing help when it comes to delivering feedback. And it is not just law firm partners who struggle with that "F" word. In the introduction to her bestselling book Dare to Lead, Brene Brown discusses her team's interviews of hundreds of individuals, trying to identify the "secret sauce" for what made great leaders. Instead, they repeatedly heard what derailed leaders – an inability to give honest feedback. Brown explained:

"We avoid tough conversations including giving honest, productive feed-back. Some leaders attribute this to a lack of courage – others to a lack of

skills. And shockingly, more than half talked about a cultural norm of 'nice and polite' that's leveraged as an excuse to avoid tough conversations."[1]

Associates expect and need feedback. They deserve it. Whether it is because of a perceived lack of time, courage, or skills or because the partners are too "nice and polite", many associates do not get timely and candid feedback. When associates do not get effective and sufficient feedback, the consequences include a lack of trust and engagement, passive-aggressiveness, gossip, and other "back-channel" communications. This results in a lack of clarity for the associates and a resulting delay in their development, all of which impact client service, all of which impacts morale.

That is where the "H" in HELP comes in – honesty. In my training and coaching work, I remind partners to reflect on their own experiences receiving feedback – or not – as associates and I share best practices. I remind them feedback is not just a once-a-year exercise for annual evaluations. In fact, those annual reviews should merely confirm what the associates already know – because the associates received feedback throughout the year.

Like all important communications, delivering successful feedback requires preparation, including deciding what you want to say and the best way to do it. Considering the associate's likely reaction forces partners to think about how to be most helpful, since the ultimate purpose of feedback is to help someone get better. Thinking through messaging also forces partners to prioritize feedback and to be mindful of its delivery. That delivery should be in person when possible and partners should remember it is not just what they say, but how they say it, including tone, eye contact, and body language.

Feedback is more than making a sandwich of constructive feedback wrapped in compliments. More effective methods include putting the feedback into context, explaining its impact, and offering guidance and advice for the next time. Associates need to know there will be a next time. They need to know where they stand and what they specifically need to do to advance. They need an honest assessment of their skills. They need advice.

Taking time to prepare to deliver feedback allows for any necessary cooling-off period so feedback is not delivered in the heat of the moment, and it also allows time for reflection. That reflection gives partners the chance to make sure they are in the right state of mind with the requisite time and attention for a candid conversation.

That self-check before delivering feedback includes identifying and eliminating bias and assumptions and making sure the feedback is not influenced by the associate's reputation, how they present themselves, their prior performance, or how similar (or not) the partner and associate are to each other. Partners should calibrate their feedback and not hold associates to the partner's personal values and standards.

When delivered well, feedback is a gift. When feedback is ineffectively delivered or delayed, it can result in great injustices. Throughout my career, I watched too many hard-working associates learn on the eve of partnership that they needed further development or worse, "did not have what it takes" to make partner. Associates should not need to guess if they are on track and what they need to do to advance, and partners should provide timely and honest developmental feedback.

E = Empathy

Empathetic partners motivate associates and engender loyalty. Empathy is an important but often underutilized management tool of law firm partners. The surveys reporting on associate satisfaction focus on partner–associate relations and how the associates feel they are treated. The most satisfied associates across the globe reference partners who take the time to train and coach, listen, and care. The most disgruntled associates attribute their dissatisfaction to feeling unappreciated, dispensable, and, for some, abused, neglected, or disrespected. These unhappy associates talk about unmanageable workloads and unresponsive partners and feel undervalued.

Why care? Empathetic partners engender loyalty and motivate associates to want to do their best work. Isn't that what we want, for all associates to reach their full potential and provide the best service to clients? I remind partners to think about which partners they wanted to work for when they were associates, the ones they did not, and why. I ask if they had cheerleaders and champions and if they received praise and how it made them feel.

A practice group leader I know actively manages his individual associates' workloads and encourages them to reach out to him directly if they start to feel overwhelmed. His best practice is to place a moratorium on associates at risk of burnout from taking on more work or getting any more assignments without his approval and he reassigns work when necessary. He is loved by his associates for how much he cares. He is especially in tune when his associates are experiencing something in their personal lives.

For many, the associate years coincide with important life events, such as marriages and other unions, babies and parenthood, major purchases like new homes and cars, and experiences with family sickness or death. Partners should know it is okay and still professional to show compassion during challenging times and recognize when associates need support.

Being empathetic means respecting privacy but offering support, understanding, and resources. This could be sending a congratulatory birth note, cutting someone slack during bereavement leaves, or reminding someone of employee assistance coaching or counseling services. Empathy requires partners to exercise their emotional intelligence muscles – their people smarts. Partners ought to be aware of their associates' feelings, and care about them. I am not promoting mollycoddling. To the contrary, I am all about directness (see "honesty", above) and am advocating for tough caring, but caring all the same.

Being empathetic means being understanding when associates try and giving them the benefit of the doubt. It means not writing off associates early but giving second and even third chances and remembering what it was like to not be so self-assured. Several of the most successful law firm leaders I know admit to slow starts or early stumbles and mistakes as associates. My favorite former associates who are now general counsel also have good memories and remember the partners who gave them the most chances and cared about their careers.

Partners who care adapt their management styles to recognize individual associates who may need more hand holding and direction, or more client contact or responsibility. They also say thank you. Being an associate should not be a thankless job. Empathetic partners show appreciation often, especially for extra efforts, and give praise when deserved.

In addition to sharing honest feedback regularly, empathetic partners think about what else individual associates need to succeed – and they provide it. This could be by direction for a specific assignment or career goal, exposure to clients, or more autonomy. Partners should ask what associates need to succeed and remember that small acts of kindness and caring, including praise when deserved, can be impactful. Caring relationships matter as much or more than compensation for the most satisfied associates.

L = Listening

Associates want to be heard. Successful relationships require effective communication, especially a genuine willingness to listen. I hear from partners I coach that their associates need to ask more questions and I usually suggest the partners could be better listeners. Associates need partners who listen, who are approachable, encourage questions, and even anticipate and answer the unasked questions. Associates also need partners who are available and responsive, in their office with their doors open or otherwise accessible; who read and promptly reply to associate emails; and do not act like every question is the dumbest one ever asked. This can be a blind spot for the busiest partners who might think they are approachable but are not.

A veteran US Supreme Court litigator I know credits his success, in part, to listening, and not just to the questions and body language of the justices. Often called in to brief and argue prominent appeals, he usually works with teams consisting of lawyers at all stages of their careers. His best practice is to have a listening meeting early on with the team, encouraging all members to share ideas, questions, and concerns. He starts with the most junior members of the team, often trainees, summer or first-year associates, and ensures no one is interrupted and everyone is heard. He acknowledges that several of his most successful arguments were first suggested by the most junior members of the team in those listening sessions. The associates who work for that partner praise him for soliciting their ideas and giving them voice. They feel included, involved, valued, and heard.

Other listening best practices include finding teaching moments like asking associates to explain their thought process, reviewing strategy decisions, and conducting after action review meetings to solicit suggestions from associates to improve client service and team management.

Ineffective listening impacts delegation, especially for partners who delegate on the fly without confirming a mutual understanding of the assignment. Delegation best practices include taking that extra five minutes to put assignments in context, to offer suggested approaches, examples, and resources, to set expectations about communications, such as asking for check ins and updates, and to confirm deliverables and deadlines. The deadlines should be reasonable and include a realistic estimate of how much time it should take, recognizing it will take the associates longer than partners (see "empathy", above).

Effective listening during delegation includes anticipating and asking questions and really listening to the associates' responses as well as encouraging associate questions and responding to those questions. Listening includes "hearing" and reading and reacting to nonverbal communications too, such as eye contact, body language, or emotional responses. This is why partners should try for more in person conversations and not communicate only by email. Developing a rapport makes associates more comfortable to report concerns, offer suggestions, and ask questions. Partners who listen and are responsive are helpful partners indeed.

P = Professional development

Individual partners play an important role in associate development. While associates need to take ownership for their own development and careers, they need help and direction. It is the responsibility of all partners to help associates develop and refine their skills and advance in their careers. Professional development includes every stage of an associate's career, including orientation and integration, formal and informal training, mentoring, sponsorship, and coaching, as well as evaluations and advancement.

Orientation is not just a welcome lunch and training sessions to learn how to bill time and navigate the firm's systems. Proper onboarding involves partners and includes making sure associates feel like they made the right choice in joining the firm. Partners also play important roles in successful associate integration, including guiding associates as they figure out the firm, practice area, and office cultures, processes, and politics. A successful rainmaker of one of the largest law firms in the world told me integration is making new associates "feel the firm flag wrapped around them so they become part of the fabric of the firm". Individual partners can make all the difference in making associates feel like they belong.

Training is another key area of professional development that needs partners' support. Formal training at law firms has evolved from partners reading from scripted slide decks to cultivated curriculums of on-demand libraries and interactive learning experiences. Even if not involved in delivering training programs, all partners should care about content and offer input into curriculum and course design. In addition, partners should recognize that most associates want on-the-job training and look for informal teaching opportunities within assignments, such as offering to moot an oral argument, explaining the reasoning behind edits to a draft, sharing a lesson learned, and giving timely, candid feedback (see "honesty", above).

Partners can perhaps make the most positive impact on associate development by being good mentors. Ida Abbott, one of the pioneers of lawyer professional development and author of *The Lawyer's Guide to Mentoring*, explains how "powerful" mentoring can be for associates:

"A mentor cares about you, supports you and is committed to your success. At its best, mentoring can be transformative, both personally and professionally. Even limited mentoring relationships can produce important benefits for individuals, employers, and the legal profession."[2]

Mentoring is not only an investment in individual associates, it is also an important contribution to the firm's future success. Mentoring helps develop associates so they provide excellent client service and go on to train and develop other, more junior, associates. Mentoring also helps the mentors refine their skills.

Every partner has the capacity to mentor. Some partners focus on training and teaching associates, transferring knowledge, and helping refine the associates' skills. Other partner mentors serve as role models, guidance counsellors, or career coaches to their associates, helping associates achieve professional development goals, and navigate career paths. These partners explain the rules of engagement and expectations for associates. They share the unwritten rules, clarify the firm's policies and office politics, and help associates better understand the path to partnership. Some mentors take that extra step and sponsor their associates. Sponsors are super mentors who open the doors for success by promoting associates in and outside of the firm. Sponsors make key introductions and advocate for their associates' advancement. I challenge partners to strive to be better mentors and sponsors and to help advance their associates' and firms' professional development efforts.

Next steps for partners who want to HELP
Partners should reflect on their experiences as associates. If they did not feel valued, respected, nurtured, and cared for as associates, partners should break the cycle and strive to be more helpful to their associates. Breaking the cycle also means partners must speak up if they see other partners bullying, abusing, shaming, holding grudges, ghosting, or otherwise treating associates poorly. This includes interrupting biases and microaggressions, making sure work and opportunities are fairly and evenly distributed, and that no associate is written off before getting honest feedback and the resources to address it.

An important initial step for partners is to assess their skills as managers, motivators, nurturers, listeners, and mentors. In addition to that self-awareness, partners should consider next steps to further develop their associate management skillset, which could mean getting training or coaching.

Below are specific action items for consideration for partners who want to help their associates more:

- Think about the individual associates who do the most work for you and what more you could do to help make each successful. Find the time to meet and discuss with them.
- Ask about their professional development goals, including asking open-ended questions and listen.
- Think about how to delegate earlier and more effectively, and commit to do so.
- Identify and eliminate bias in how you assign and evaluate work.
- Be more inclusive. Do not just round up the usual associates but give others opportunities.
- Look for shadowing opportunities to let associates watch, listen, and learn.
- Deliver more – and more honest – feedback.
- Think about how to be a more effective mentor and schedule a mentoring meeting.
- Consider sponsorship.
- Push back on unreasonable and disrespectful clients.
- Remember to say thank you and give praise and recognition.
- Be a resource and identify other resources for associates such as internal or external career counseling, coaching, and training resources.
- Use those resources, including participating in training or coaching.

Individual partners can make all the difference in individual associates' experiences with honesty, empathy, listening, and professional development support. Won't you please, please HELP them?

References

1   Brown, Brene, *Dare to Lead*, Random House, 2018.
2   Abbott, Ida, *The Lawyer's Guide to Mentoring, 2nd Edition*, NALP, 2018.

Chapter 15:
Keep your talent engaged – how to cultivate a skill-building discipline

By Patrick McKenna, author, lecturer, strategist, and advisor to the leaders of premier law firms

Whenever I ask leaders, *"What is most important to the partners working within your firm?"* I elicit four responses. The most important is always, *"Being able to continually learn and grow my skills in order to be better recognized and deliver greater value".*

As a general rule, firm leadership needs to help partners understand that they are in competition will millions of other professionals all over the world, often capable of doing the same work that they can do, and the sad news is that nobody owes you a career. To continue to be successful you must continually dedicate yourself to *retraining* your individual competitive advantage.

In his 1982 book, *Critical Path*, futurist and inventor R. Buckminster Fuller estimated that up until 1900, human knowledge doubled approximately every century, but by 1945 it was doubling every 25 years, and by 1982 it was doubling every 12-13 months. Today, IBM estimates that human knowledge is doubling every 12 hours![1] How precise is IBM's estimate? Hard to tell. But I suspect you would certainly agree that data and knowledge are increasing at an exponential rate, which will only be accelerated by further development of Generative Artificial Intelligence (AI).

This enhanced growth of knowledge is not all we have to contend with. Compounding the challenge is how long that knowledge remains useful – or how long it takes for your knowledge to become outdated, inaccurate, or irrelevant. One measure of this is known as the "half-life" of knowledge – the amount of time it takes for our knowledge to lose half its value. For those in almost any profession, from medical and engineering to law and consulting, the half-life of our knowledge is shrinking such that what may have been valuable to know a few years ago may have very limited value today.

What all this obviously means is that the systematic development of legal knowledge and skills, over time, depreciates in value – especially as your competitors acquire and offer similar or equivalent expertise; and technology makes it easier to access information. With each passing year, the fees that clients willingly pay for any legal expertise diminishes, such that even your most loyal clients will not value as highly what you or I do for them the second or third time as they did the first.

Therefore, I strongly believe that firm and group leaders need to pose a few very serious questions to each of their partners in one-on-one (virtual) coaching discussions:

- Do you believe you are adding real value or simply passing along legal information to our clients? In other words, what is it that you can specifically do for clients today that you could *not* do for them at this same time last year?

- What do you need to do, in the time that you have available right now, to build your skills, enhance your knowledge, and reinforce any market opportunities so that you can have an even more successful practice going forward?

- Are you plugged into what is happening around you and inside your client's industry, such that you can interpret whatever new trends and developments may be transpiring and be the source of proactive counsel – before the client even has to ask?

- Are you trying out any new ideas, new techniques, new technologies? And I mean personally trying them, not just reading about them? Or, are you waiting for others to figure out how to innovate and re-engineer your practice (and re-engineer you right out of that practice)?

I would suggest that provoking a negative response to any of these four important questions is indicative of a condition some astute observers label as *"human capital obsolescence"* – a poorly understood phenomenon that has crept into many firms trending toward the LOSER end of the spectrum. Human capital obsolescence can be interpreted to mean that there may be some partners who are not performing in accordance with what clients would accept as high value. In other words, they are merely a commodity provider and these individuals' economic contribution to your firm is no longer in keeping with what one might expect from an equity partner. While being labelled an "underperformer" may be a symptom of the issue, I would submit that simply having more "junk" work to occupy their billable time does not solve this problem.

Therefore, going forward, the most successful firms – i.e., those that have *no problem retaining their valuable talent and attracting other high-*

performers – will be those that rethink the concept of where they encourage and perhaps incentivize partners to invest some portion of their non-billable time. To succeed in today's environment of rapid change requires continually building your knowledge base, your skills, and learning how to do entirely new things. If our lawyers don't dedicate sufficient time to building their skills, we end up solving yesterday's (commoditized) client problems (usually at a hugely discounted fee) instead of tackling tomorrow's burning issues, before someone else does.

To do that and execute it effectively requires working with all of your lawyers and following some sequential steps.

Step 1: Begin to develop a learning culture

Since law firms sell professional skill, talent, knowledge, and ability, rather than time, it makes sense that one should think of those as valuable firm assets and have some kind of program to manage rather than squander those assets. The culture you work to develop plays a critical role in helping everyone build skills for the future. Industry and practice groups that build a shared value for continuous learning and make it a key ingredient in their overall group strategy, which all partners willingly invest in, can gain a competitive advantage.

If it might help, encourage one member of your group who has the appropriate interest to serve as your group's director of skills-building. Consider assigning some duties to a support staff person who could help coordinate and assist your team. Being a non-billable activity, skill building can become infinitely postponed, such that any time devoted to capturing and sharing knowledge becomes a "backburner" priority. Therefore, it is important to remember that, in increasingly competitive times, the issue of continually building marketable skills requires a long-term focus. Small bites are better than no bites at all.

Step 2: Encourage partners to debrief on their most recent client matters

The accumulation of most new knowledge and skills usually occurs while you are working on some client matter. Recognizing the potential in these learning opportunities requires that you employ a systematic effort to debrief upon conclusion of a client's assignment and attempt to capture, "What I learned from this one...". As trite as it sounds, the essence of some learning and skill development comes by way of forcing yourself to examine your client assignments, and taking the time at the end of each matter to ask yourself a couple of basic questions. Each team leader needs to work with their partners to have them answer:

- What went well and why did it go well?
- What did not go as well as expected with this client matter, and why not?
- What sort of things came up that I did not have time to give attention to but noticed that the client seemed to be interested in?

In essence, professionals have to debrief. Help your colleagues force themselves to slow down long enough to think things through instead of simply charging off to the next client file. They will usually come up with something that will help them going into the future. Then if you have them commit those lessons to writing, either in a physical journal or electronic one, they are far more likely to remember and apply those lessons to their next projects.

Another way to debrief is to have those colleagues that worked with any particular partner on the same client transaction come together to share learnings. Now admittedly, this takes time, but the substantive learning that can take place if you get together (virtually) over coffee and simply ask of everyone – "If we had to do it over again, what would we do differently?" – is amazing.

I will never forget an incident while I was working with a European law firm, when I had the opportunity to hear a general counsel say to the group members at the end of one particular litigation matter:

> *"You idiots! You completed the litigation and you go back to your offices. I gather together my entire team to review what happened, why the crap hit the fan, what we might have learned from this experience, and whether there is anything we need to do differently. If you did that for us at no fee, I would have you presenting to all of our unit presidents and make you famous throughout our company."*

Step 3: Have groups debrief together on engagements

One of the competitive advantages that *should* accrue to well managed firms is the value that each professional can bring to clients as a result of the accumulated knowledge, wisdom, systems, methodologies, and experiences of the colleagues in their practice or industry groups. It is trivial to observe that most new learning happens while professionals are engaged in their client matters. What is not trivial to point out is that many firms (and their groups) fail to capture and disseminate much of that knowledge, such that it never gets leveraged and used to the benefit of outperforming competitors.

Dream, create, explore, invent, pioneer, imagine. Do these words describe what it is that you do as a professional? And if not, why not? You should be identifying how your combination of personal assets (skills, strengths, competencies) and aspirations (dreams, values, interests) can create a unique and valued offering in your competitive marketplace.

At least once every month, have each partner pull out the list of client work and assignments that you have been working on and examine each. Allow sufficient time for each member to make a presentation. Because everyone knows this is coming, each is subtly forced to reflect on his or her experiences and is more likely to convert the knowledge gained from those experiences into a shared resource.

Invite discussion to provide critical feedback and to examine whether the activities described benefit others in the group. Try some of the questions below.

Please identify and explain to our group, any particular client matter that:

- *Exposed you to an entirely new type of client / industry / geography / transaction?*
  (For example, this involved work undertaken on behalf of an "unusual" client as defined by the nature of this client's business, geography or matter size.)
- *Allowed you to successfully deal with a relatively unique client problem?*
  (The particular client matter that you were handling was completely novel and involved you having to take an unprecedented approach to resolving the client's issue.)
- *Allowed you to develop new knowledge or refine a skill that you can now market to other clients?*
  (For example, amid an unprecedented run with sky-high valuations and competition, M&A deal teams are being asked to close transactions in a compressed period of time, and with your latest deal you developed a methodology to dramatically speed up the due diligence process.)
- *Provoked you to document some new checklist, tool, template or process?*
  (For example, where some client work was becoming somewhat repetitive, you developed a diagnostic checklist to streamline the process and make it more cost efficient.)

- *Introduced you to an important new market niche?*
  (For example, you did some work with one of your manufacturing clients that exposed you to the cutting-edge designs that they were doing in 3D printing and some challenges that they were facing.)
- *Allowed you to work at a more senior C-level within the client's organization?*
  (For example, your work with the client culminated in their asking you to do a formal presentation for their entire executive committee on what was learned from this particular litigation matter and how it could be avoided in the future.)
- *Exposed you to previously unexplored areas within the client's organization?*
  (For example, your work with your in-house legal contact introduced you to the executives within the company's risk assessment department and some of the new issues that the entire industry was having to address.)
- *Exposed you to technology being used that could be emulated within your firm?*
  (For example, your legal department client had AI-driven internal knowledge-sharing programs and video systems to promote collaborative internal experiences that could be copied and utilized.)
- *Allowed you to conduct some research or identify some new industry trends?*
  (For example, your work with the client involved you in conducting some research with other industry players/regulatory authorities, etc. and identify findings that proffer new trends impacting the industry.)
- *Provided some insight that can allow you to build your professional thought leadership?*
  (For example, your work with a client exposed you to fresh knowledge that could be leveraged into an important article and/or seminar presentation on a subject that was both valuable and innovative.)
- *Enabled you to collaborate with some other multi-discipline specialist to provide a total business solution?*
  (For example, your work with a client had you working hand-in-hand with a specialist in predictive analytics such that you learned how the combination of your two disciplines delivered enhanced value for the client.)

Skill development comes in little bits and we need to capture those little bits, especially where some bit might portend an entirely new area of possibility, lucrative micro-niche, or emerging practice opportunity.

Simply sharing these client experiences and what was learned while working with particular clients can be a powerful influence on our skill development. It often forces us to relive and re-examine the entire situation and better understand what actually transpired as we were engaged in helping our client deal with their issue. We build confidence in what we accomplished and how we did it, which furthers our perception of what we learned from the experience. Our colleagues may often raise insightful questions than can then shift or refine how we might approach these same kinds of client situations in the future.

Step 4: Capture and codify each group's knowhow database

Work with your group members to develop shared tools and methodologies and to compile procedural "knowhow", much of which may arise as a result of the higher quality client matters that have been handled within the group.

This knowhow resides primarily in each lawyer's head and among rough assignment notes. It may include standard forms, checklists, undocumented procedures, research notes, details on alternative ways to structure deals, methods of approaching certain projects, and the work product itself (briefs, memos, and documents) – in written form or electronic. I have seen a couple of occasions where the group's knowhow got converted into a new computer software program for everyone to utilize. Keep in mind that these materials can form the basis of your group's own shared tools, data banks, specialized correspondence libraries, methodologies, and a host of other practice aids. This knowhow represents the intellectual property of your group and may make it far easier to serve clients, avoid the need to reinvent the wheel, but most importantly build your group's competitive skills and comradery – by having colleagues learning from each other and collaborating together.

As part of this knowhow database, give some attention to compiling your own industry-specific archive. Work together to collect industry materials – subscriptions, books, training materials, industry trend reports – that can be maintained in a centralized resource library for everyone in the group to contribute to and utilize. Compiling research on specific targeted industries enables you to share important and timely information with clients and to respond to clients in a way that reassures them that you are on top of "what is going on in their kind of business".

Finally, consider initiating a cross-collaboration initiative for reciprocal benefit. Approach an academic institution, government department, financial services firm, research agency, or some other non-competing professional firms known to have a level of expertise for serving a similar client base and propose to collaborate on conducting substantive training for each other's colleagues. Also, as much as possible, participate in joint projects with professionals from other disciplines. We learn and develop from our client work experiences and if you have the opportunity to be on the same assignment as a top professional from another area you will likely learn in a way that no amount of reading or 'offline' conversations with that professional could ever provide.

Step 5: Have each partner identify their personal skill gaps

"If you take two people, one of them is a learn-it-all and the other is a know-it-all, the learn-it-all will always outperform the know-it-all in the long run, even if they start with less innate capability."
Satya Nadella, CEO of Microsoft

As a practice or industry team leader, you need to help each group member identify and understand their particular strengths, their weaknesses, and the skill gaps that may exist wherein they could become a go-to lawyer and expert in some selected area, if they were prepared to invest the time. Perhaps you might ask each, *"What do you want to be able to do by this time next year, that you cannot do today?"* or *"What kind of special expertise do you want to develop that will make you the go-to expert in our market footprint?"* Then have each member identify the specific skill, experience, or knowledge that they would like to personally enhance.

To help them think about skill gaps you might also ask each:

- What area of emerging client need do you think there will be an increasing market demand for lawyers to provide meaningful assistance in?
- How much work would it take to become a recognized expert in helping clients solve this business need?
- Are you ready to take it on and how much time are you prepared to invest in developing your substantive knowledge and skills over the next three months?

Use the answers you elicit to help each partner conduct a brutal self-assessment. If you both discover that the knowledge gap is fairly small and the opportunity fairly lucrative, that should provide the confidence to set out some initial action steps. If you both determine that the knowledge gap is really large (your partner has had very limited experience to build on) you will need to collectively determine whether the partner has the courage and resolve to bridge it, what specific support and resources (e.g., some sort of credit for non-billable time) are they going to need, and what milestones will need to be set and monitored on the path to progress.

Step 6: Ensure the creation of personalized skill-building plans

Each partner should be encouraged to develop a formal, personal career plan for making themselves continually more valuable in the marketplace. They should constantly be seeking out new things to become involved in and eagerly seeking ways to delegate the more familiar parts of their client work. Once any partner has a good sense of what skills they might want to focus on, they can create a personalized learning or skill plan based on self-knowledge and their career aspirations.

To ensure that your group provides skill-building opportunities to partners and non-partners alike, you must manage your practice development activities carefully. It is hard to be effective at building your skills if a high percentage of your work is repetitive, commoditized, and routine. One of the essential ingredients in realizing any skill-building effort is the active pursuit of frontier, higher-value client engagements. Accordingly, your group requires a well-organized, constant push to upgrade the caliber of the work brought in. Your group members must become disciplined in avoiding, if at all possible, the trap of pursuing too much work for volume reasons only. Personal growth is not about bringing in more work, it's about bringing in "better" work.

When your partner sets goals around their learning, they focus on what they should be spending some non-billable time on. For example, when Rita decides that she would like to focus on learning more about women-owned start-ups within the firm's market footprint, she could then set out an action plan for how she might acquire more knowledge (books, podcasts, mentoring, etc.) and build her skills (becoming an active member in an appropriate organization).

It is critical to provide the necessary support that allows for both failure and success when taking on any new challenge. This means encouraging your partner to take on stretch client assignments so that the individual can enhance their learning while serving the client, as well as giving the partner the time they might need to refine the skills they have identified and are working on. You need to remember that it may not always be comfortable for any partner, especially overachievers, to jump into areas where they do not feel completely competent, but with your and other partners' support and encouragement, these opportunities can help shape their career achievements.

Step 7: Ensure that each partner "owns" their career development
As one firm leader expressed it to me:

"We need to let partners clearly understand it's all on you. If you have developed your skills to the point where the client wants only you, we will want you. If you have not achieved that notoriety, then you should ask yourself why you think we should want you."

While firms and practice/industry groups can assemble the tools, process and guidelines to help their professionals develop their expertise, it is then up to the individual to do whatever it takes to get what they need. In other words, partners need to understand that while practice leaders may guide them and even mentor their efforts, they are the ones in the driver's seat and responsible for furthering their career.

Step 8: Include skill development in goal setting, evaluation, and reward
Most compensation schemes focus on short-term achievements – client originations, billable production, collections and so forth. To develop a competitive advantage, it becomes important to also give attention to the longer-term achievements of professional knowledge and skill-building. Therefore, those firms that strive for the longer-term strategic gains ask that each of their partners report in specific detail on:
- What are you doing to enhance your skills and make yourself the go-to professional in the future?
- In what ways are you now personally more valuable on the marketplace than you were last year?

Step 9: Have an investment fund available to finance projects

How do we give people credit for investing their non-billable time in developing some tool that all of the lawyers can use?

Lawyers discover vital new things during the course of their transactions – an important new way to negotiate a client deal, a potential client problem that they could prevent, an innovative technological tool that could benefit and perhaps even be sold to clients – but because no one is ever reimbursed for their non-billable (investment) time, the individual lawyers involved don't ever take the time to transform their knowledge into something that everyone could utilize or benefit from. The critical strategic question becomes, how do you encourage entrepreneurial behavior?

One solution – have your firm set up an investment fund, an internal review committee, and invite anyone in your firm to come forward with proposals. In other words, if someone comes up with a new revenue-producing, or client effectiveness, or cost reduction, or innovative legal delivery system idea and believes that if they devoted 40 or 50 hours of time into converting that idea into a template, computer program, or tangible tool that others could use, then their time should be compensated. They are then invited to apply to the firm's review committee to have their idea funded.

Here is the clever twist that one (unnamed) firm does. If your project is approved by the review committee, the firm buys your time at 125 percent your standard hourly rate. In other words, your personal productivity numbers can look even better if you had a project approved and delivered on your proposal. The individual proposing the idea realizes a premium in credit, assuming that they actually deliver on what it is that they promised they would do (and this firm does provide some billing safeguards so that if the undertaking doesn't quite meet expectations, our entrepreneurial partner will not suffer great hardship).

Step 10: Communicate success stories

Have your partners spend some time at your group's regular meetings to relate learning experiences, client wins, and specific success stories related to the particular skill quest that they have been working on pursuing.

Please do recognize that it is more than just sharing successes. When any professional is around high performers, they feel the subtle but compelling peer pressure to keep up with their colleagues – which then leads to an environment where colleagues themselves are raising the bar on what is expected within their group and engaged in the group and the firm's progress.

"Before you are a leader, success is all about growing yourself. When you become a leader, success is all about growing others."
Jack Welch, former CEO of General Electric 1981-2001.

Being a non-billable activity, skill building can become infinitely postponed, such that any time devoted to capturing and sharing knowledge becomes a "backburner" priority. Therefore, it is important to remember that, in these increasingly competitive times, the issue of continually building marketable skills requires a longer-term, highly disciplined focus. But it is well worth the effort.

References

1   https://www.industrytap.com/knowledge-doubling-every-12-months-soon-to-be-every-12-hours/3950

Chapter 16:
Succession – transition strategies for lawyers, law firms, and clients

By Heather Suttie, legal market strategy and management consultant, Suttie.

Introduction

It's not how you start; it's how you finish.

While succession can be the ultimate exit strategy, it does not necessarily signal a dramatic end. In the best circumstances, and with care and consideration, it enables an expected and non-turbulent handoff.

A smooth succession is the pinnacle of client service because it cements client retention and ensures stability for all parties concerned.

Like so many other changes in life, succession is reliant upon three key factors – forethought, planning, and grace. A graceful succession is preferrable to clinging like a barnacle to what was. Barnacle-like behavior can happen when someone prevents change to protect themselves due to being fearful of what change may bring.

Look at the word "succession". What do you see? Success. That's what succession is all about. However, succession pertaining to aging demographics is an increasing cause for concern.

According to the 2023 American Bar Association's *Profile of the Legal Profession*,[1] nearly 14 percent of all lawyers in the US are 65 years of age or older. That is in stark contrast to about seven percent of all US workers being 65 or older.

In 2021, the American and Canadian Bar Association[2] said that 30 percent to 40 percent of lawyers in private practice were beginning to retire or consider phasing down. Findings also indicate that most law firms have actively practicing lawyers in their late 60s and 70s, many of whom are rainmakers, and that partners aged 60 or older control at least one-half of firm revenue in 63 percent of law firms.

According to American Lawyer publications, most lawyers retire at the age of 65 with 40 percent of law firms having requirements for lawyers to retire before they are 70 years old. But here is the most worrisome number. Only 17 percent of law firms have formal succession programs.

This chapter will discuss succession – culture, planning, and techniques – as well as alumni programs that help retain ties and nurture goodwill with all levels of former law firm members, and that result in enormous gains for law firms that have the vision, fortitude, and management skills to institute them.

Prepare for a wave of retiring partners

Throughout the next decade, succession in the legal services industry will be impacted by the retirement of senior law firm partners who are members of a hard-charging demographic bubble as well as a bumper crop of young partners and senior associates seeking new or different work styles.

In the executive ranks populated primarily by individuals in their 60s or older, there has already been a marked change in the c-suites of many major Canadian law firms. In a wave that began in 2015, blue chip law firms such as Osler, Hoskin & Harcourt, Stikeman Elliott, Torys, McMillan, Blake, Cassels and Graydon, Bennett Jones, Borden Ladner Gervais, Norton Rose Fulbright Canada, and Gowling WLG, to name only a handful, began changing out their top-ranking, long-time senior executives and have new chairs, CEOs, or managing partners. US-based law firms, including Reed Smith, Goodwin Proctor, Holland & Knight, WilmerHale, Cooley, Fried Frank, and Troutman Pepper, to name another handful, announced in 2023 that their chairs, CEOs, or managing partners will step down or plan to early in 2024.

As Baby Boomer lawyers born between 1946 and 1964 shift out – willingly or not – their replacements (Generation X born between 1965 and 1980, and Millennials born between 1981 and 1996) will be expected to service clients conditioned to high expectations for speed and results.

This is the same class of clients who – already well-aware of the hollowing out of private practice legal talent that began before and accelerated during the pandemic and is now somewhat unstable due to burnout and life–work re-evaluation – have been compensating by adding to their in-house legal departments over the last few years. These clients will also continue to be proactive in sending outbound work elsewhere and getting it done by other means.

Law firms are businesses – run them that way

Contracts are part-and-parcel of legal services. Yet it is amazing how many law firms do not include exit clauses when negotiating legal talent entry agreements.

Smart law firms are crystal-clear on how a lawyer will enter and exit a firm. An explicit clause pertaining to retirement and succession – when it will happen, why, and how – helps everyone involved to understand boundaries, timing, and expectations. While this is an excellent strategy for lateral hires, it also provides a guide for a law firm's organic talent roster who are on a partnership track and acts as a reminder that there is a process in place for those who will eventually step back from active practice.

Smooth succession is reliant on culture

"Culture eats strategy for breakfast" is a well-known and well-worn quote from famed management consultant Peter Drucker. It means that no matter how clear and concise your strategy, it will fail if the culture does not or will not support it. In other words, culture trumps strategy every time.

Culture is about people – in particular, their behaviors and beliefs. So, this is where we will start the core features of this discussion.

Succession in its most robust form is reliant on a culture that institutes, supports, and embraces it. Consistent and successful succession outcomes are the hallmarks of a law firm culture built upon these qualities.

A law firm with a robust succession culture is attractive to both its client base and talent roster because this cultural trait aids in retaining and engaging top talent due to valuing and instituting progression. Whether that progression pertains to "up or out" mechanics is immaterial because succession-bound leadership talent will prevail. This is because a culture of succession signals that a firm rewards talent primarily on merit rather than tenure or longevity, and that change management is recognized as a key feature of the firm's DNA.

Succession, flexibility, and change management have become critical factors for law firms wanting to rank head-and-shoulders above their competition as a destination for top-tier talent at all levels and of all disciplines.

There was a time when a lawyer joined a firm as a student, graduated to becoming an associate, and if they had the "right stuff" and could afford to finance an investment of capital, would be added to the partnership ranks. And this is where they would stay until, in the best situations, they stepped back from practice and retired gracefully or, in the worst circumstances, died at their desk and went out on a board.

Retiring gracefully has always happened and still does, as does dying at one's desk. However, in the last ten years, another phenomenon has been on the rise – lawyers, many of them at the partner level, changing firms.

Clients of the firm versus clients of the individual

Are clients "clients of the firm" or "clients of the individual"? The difference enables varying degrees of ease and success of succession.

A culture based on "clients of the firm" will have an easier time and greater success when transitioning clients prior to the departure of a lawyer. That is because a shared-clients culture and the corporate structure that accompanies it enables more than one lawyer – ideally a partner – to be tied to and provide legal services to a client.

In a large firm, the ideal number of partners tied to a key or institutional client is seven. Obviously, the number of partners to clients is scalable depending on the size of the firm and the depth and breadth of a client's needs. Regardless of scale, connecting partners to a key client is not difficult to accomplish, particularly if the client is business-oriented.

Not only do numerous ties to a key client help retain that client, but this technique also protects and may help to retain the firm's relationship with that client if or when any one partner who works with that client leaves the firm.

Clients that are "clients of the individual" are more at risk since there is a perception – which is often not reality – that an individual lawyer with a handsome book of business will take clients with him or her upon their departure to join another firm. In some cases, the lawyer with the handsome book of business and client roster will believe and state this sentiment (usually loudly), but reality and its results often have the opposite effect.

In this instance, the firm is smart to proactively and speedily address the issue pertaining to a lawyer's departure with his or her clients to ascertain how these clients may react and, if need be, provide incentives to stay tied to the firm. Most often, a client will choose to remain with the firm rather than deal with the upheaval and harangue of following a lawyer to a new law firm and transferring their business elsewhere.

This very effective client retention strategy is another reason why – in addition to being attractive to new recruits and those advancing within the firm – a "clients of the firm" culture trumps "clients of the individual".

Succession plans must be transparent

The global legal services market, which has undergone explosive change over the last 20 years, is evolving and accelerating at a ferocious pace. This is primarily due to boomer lawyers retiring now or soon, fallout from the pandemic, an unstable legal job market, and acceleration of technology within legal practice, in particular, artificial intelligence.

As a result, lawyers at all stages of their careers are reimagining how their working lives will unfold. Moreover, they are acting on it and, in many cases, are loving the results.

While this may be good news for lawyers, it is not good news for clients. Clients do not want or welcome surprises of any kind. Neither does law firm management. In both cases, predictability wins.

This is why succession, as part of business strategy, is best planned in detail two to five years before a lawyer begins to scale back or enters full-on retirement. As a result, the succession process has a stronger likelihood of being managed smoothly and in conjunction with colleagues and, most importantly, the lawyer's clients.

It is vital that management and the lawyer share succession plans in full transparency with other lawyers in the firm, practice groups, and industry teams, as well as with clients and the client's other professional service providers.

There are four essential steps to ensure smooth succession while empha-sizing transparency:

1. Selection, training and mentoring of appropriate successor lawyers and their support teams to ensure they have the qualifications as well as the right temperaments to serve specific clients.

2. Position successor partners for a smooth handoff by enabling them to dovetail with the retiring partner on client engagements with the client's approval.

3. Encourage and support the retiring partner to gradually step back from the client–successor relationship to allow for deeper familiarity to develop without continuing influence.

4. Transfer increasing parts of the origination credit from the retiring partner to successors as they take on increasing responsibility for the client relationship and work.

Once a client handoff is complete and as need be, the retiring partner may continue to coach her or his successor discretely for an agreed length of time without attending client meetings, appearing on calls, or rendering or billing any services.

It goes without saying that law firms also need to have contingencies and emergency plans in place should there be a need for early or unanticipated succession execution of any kind.

This is simply smart business since while there are law firms that have mandatory retirement at a specific age, others do not. Most law societies and governing guilds have rules in place for succession and transferring clients upon a lawyer's retirement, diminishing health, death, or a firm's dissolution. That said, it is astonishing how often this does not happen or fails to be executed smoothly. The upshot is chaos for clients as well as the firm when the unforeseen happens.

Not to beat a dead horse – or in this case, a dead lawyer – but this is yet another reason why "clients of the firm" is a smart business strategy due to providing a safety net for a firm's culture, structure, finances, and brand as well as its clientele.

Voice of the client is key to smooth succession

Change doesn't happen in a vacuum. The ripple effect that accompanies any change means that clients must be involved in the succession plans of those who serve them. After all, without clients, any succession planning is a moot point.

Having conducted many client feedback interviews, I can tell you from experience that even though a lawyer or their firm may not have succession on their minds, clients most certainly do. I have been asked many times what an aging or sometimes, in the worst case, ailing partner's plans are around bringing in supports that will enable a smooth transition for a client and their work.

In many of these instances, a client will positively support a partner wishing to scale back their workload or retire. In other cases, a client will breathe a sigh of relief and ask, "How soon will this happen?" Without regularly interviewing clients it may never be known that they have been suffering in silence – sometimes for years – and counting the days to their lawyer's departure. There have been instances when a client's perspective is communicated directly, such as, "You got here in the nick of time; we've been thinking of leaving", to "We've needed to hear this, are happy to hear it now, and insist on being heavily involved in the selection of new counsel".

These are real-life examples of conversations I have had with a law firm's clients, but no one would have ever known had I or someone who is a third-party ombudsperson or firm-neutral, and not the servicing lawyer or partner responsible, had a service-oriented conversation with these clients.

A client who will be affected in any way, shape, or form by a lawyer's departure will welcome a succession plan and formal proposal. This hallmark of professional service and consideration helps both the client and firm avoid service disruption and is the ultimate grace note for a departing professional.

For law firms and legal service providers with deep bench strength and talent rosters, there are various strategies and tactics that can be considered in addition to a traditional successor handoff.

The four best solutions are:

1. Permanent embedding.
2. Term secondments.
3. Cohort laddering.
4. Cross-service teams.

While these solutions are most easily implemented within a large law firm environment with breadth and depth, they can often be scaled for mid-size and sometimes smaller size firms and can work especially well within firms offering boutique or specialized legal services.

The value of embedding, secondments, cohort laddering, and cross-service teams

Law firms and legal service providers with sterling client rosters often subscribe to building their organizations through organic talent growth.

As a result, these law firms and legal service providers often invest in and protect relationships with institutional, blue-chip clients by permanently embedding one of their own "organically grown" lawyers as in-house counsel. Even though it may be painful in the short-term for a law firm to transfer a solid, highly regarded, and firm-polished lawyer to a sterling client's in-house legal department, in the long-term that embedded lawyer may be elevated to general counsel or a c-suite role, which helps cement the client-firm/provider relationship.

Secondments are another highly valued firm-client connector. Providing legal talent to a key client on a term arrangement of six to 12 months (or even longer) enables deeper knowledge and solidification of trust between a firm/provider and a key client. Rolling secondments where lawyers cycle in and out of a key client's legal department on short terms of between three and six months also affords continuous opportunities to lend talent while enabling mutual learning and deepening trust.

It is no secret that clients love embedding and secondment arrangements, and handsomely reward law firms and legal service providers who engage with clients in this manner.

Cohort laddering is another strategy that enables collaboration. This technique involves the pairing and the continuous graduation of sets of cohort-colleagues often matched by seniority. Like how a ladder or elevator works, the paired firm/client lawyer cohorts gain seniority within their organizations and, most vitally, familiarity with each other over many years. As the paired cohorts graduate into higher levels of seniority and the most senior firm-client cohort eventually retire, matched firm-client pairs on the rungs or steps below rise together in equal ranks. Laddering in this manner can provide natural steps to solidifying relationships and helps smooth the succession path while enabling better traction and talent retention for both the firm/provider and the client's in-house legal department.

Creation of a cross-service multidisciplinary team around key clients is often a graceful way of both enabling succession while transitioning a client from being a "client of the individual" to a "client of the firm". This classic client retention strategy enables cross-servicing and growth of clients identified as key accounts while enabling an individual lawyer to experience a smooth succession and make the transition with dignity.

While embedding, secondments, cohort laddering, and cross-servicing are often more easily accomplished within law firms of large size and wide scope, firms and providers with shallower bench strength or that have fewer areas of practice or offerings can either scale these processes accordingly or combine with other law firms or legal service providers that offer complimentary services. Even though this level of collaboration requires deep trust, crisp boundaries, clear communication, and constant management, it bolsters business and enables all ranks in all entities to rise through mutual expansion.

These types of collaborative combinations may also be effective as test cases or precursors to formal mergers and acquisitions. In turn and ironically, the upshot of a formal tie-up between groups of professionals such as these may trigger a rebalancing of a combined talent roster, which could result in succession planning for some individuals of the combined entity.

Coming to terms with succession

While succession often means concluding lawyer–client relationships, it does not necessarily mean the end of a lawyer's involvements. In fact, it can be the start of a different relationship between a lawyer and their firm.

There is a plethora of statesperson roles that are enjoyed by lawyers who continue to have the drive to thrive in the legal services environment. Such roles can include law firm ambassadors who represent the firm in outside professional arenas such as corporate board work, or who offer senior counsel pro bono service to firm-supporting philanthropic efforts or provide connections between current and prospective clients as well as introductions to the firm. Oftentimes, these new roles can also extend to acting as advisors or counsel to the firm or mentoring the next generation of lawyers.

Roles such as these and more can be created to suit the individual. This enables a retired partner to continue to provide value to the firm, its clients, stakeholders, and the community without having to deal with politics around voting or being encumbered by management responsibilities.

Regardless of ongoing involvement, lawyers in many jurisdictions are mandated by regulators to have contingency arrangements, so it behooves them, their firms, clients, and colleagues to discuss succession and possible next roles in full transparency and plan for it openly.

One of the easiest ways to begin the process is by conducting a set of lawyer/firm/client succession interviews. Often this happens in steps, such as a one-on-one with the lawyer that expands to include the law firm, the lawyer's successors, and then clients. Law firms say that with the aid of a neutral third party, succession can often be more easily broached, discussed, planned, and acted upon.

Strategic management of a client, lawyer, and firm's ongoing interests are paramount to the success of any succession plan. Therefore, solutions, consensus, and most importantly, continuation of trust can be gained with respect and grace while providing a seamless and smooth transition that retains professionalism and respect while instilling peace of mind for all parties.

Alumni programs keep talent engaged and connected

Gone are the days when talent of all descriptions would stay put at a law firm. Enforced loyalty – an attitude and behavior supporting a notion of "the firm before all" – that at one time was a point of pride in some law firms is finished.

Prior to the pandemic and, much worse since, law firm partners, associates and legal service professionals of all stripes have been sloshing in a volatile job market. They have been trading one firm for another, setting up their own shops, going in-house, and changing industries to the point where one now needs a program to tell the players.

The pandemic taught many people that they alone are responsible for their happiness, health, and career. These people also learned that change can happen, regardless of whether it is a job-seekers' market or not.

Now, and in years to come, law firms and legal service providers that buck that reality will lose dearly in terms of attracting and retaining strong talent.

They will also erode their brand in the legal market along with goodwill.

However, law firms and legal service providers that embrace our changed world of work, find a give-and-take balance, and build upon it in "people-first" fashion will be winners.

Alumni programs are a winning business strategy

Alumni programs, along with embedding, secondments, cohort laddering, and cross-service teams are investments in people that pay enormous returns to law firms that have the vision, fortitude, and management skills to institute them.

Below is an outline of just some of the benefits of an alumni program for a law firm or legal service provider and its alumni, as well as notes pertaining to people data capture.

Benefits for the firm/provider:

- *Business development and referrals.* Emphasis on lawyers who have moved to in-house roles or law firms that can provide referrals and/or in-bound work.
- *Industry knowledge.* Alliances to former law firm members who have moved to industries outside of legal services and may be able to share industry-specific insights and perspectives.
- *Strategic partnerships.* Helpful in cross-service teaming where the firm seeks to partner with familiar and like-minded outside talent on work that is best done when shared with external resources.
- *Sources for outbound work.* Alums can be trusted to handle outbound work.
- *Networking.* Staying in touch provides an opportunity to broaden connections and deepen relationships.
- *Direct hiring.* Recruiting costs are diminished due to alerting alumni to opportunities within the firm. Alums often return – they are often referred to as "boomerangs", which cuts recruiting expenses and onboarding/training time. If alums don't return, they can recommend other strong talent.
- *Recruiting tool.* Prospective recruits are attracted to firms that value

and maintain mutually beneficial relationships over the course of a career regardless of position and/or tenure.

- *Feedback.* Former employees at all levels may provide constructive feedback to improve client services, internal procedures, and workplace satisfaction within the firm.
- *Goodwill.* Those who depart a firm are more apt to have a positive impression, while current members will have advance knowledge that the end of their tenure is not necessarily the end of a professional relationship.

Benefits for alumni:

- *CPD.* Free continuing professional development (CPD).
- *Resource access.* Free access to information sources, databases, and tools that may not be readily available in their next role.
- *Networking.* Invitations to firm-initiated webinars, events, job board, alumni directory, etc.
- *Privilege extension.* Continuation of appropriate firm-sponsored corporate discounts.

People data capture:

- *Incoming.* Determination of information gleaned during the recruiting and onboarding phases as well information to be kept and updated.
- *Outgoing.* Exit interviews for lawyers and staff to plumb for positive, neutral, and negative lessons as well as probe for nuance.
- *Database.* Gathering, updating, and housing this information in a robust client relationship management (CRM) database is critical to retaining clean data and achieving program success.

A strong network is the backbone of a robust alumni program

No one knows your law firm like the people who have worked there. Valued former employees are your firm's best ambassadors. Providing a forum for alumni in all roles and at all levels and enabling them to remain connected to a firm and each other signals that nurturing relationships with all employees is of value even when they are working elsewhere.

An alumni program based on a strong network is a smart business strategy to deploy from early recruiting to onboarding stages, and through to departure. People who leave to work or live elsewhere often continue to be assets for a firm. This level of investment in people provides huge returns when their former firm receives the first call that a business opportunity has arisen.

A strong network is an even smarter business asset when a professional expresses interest in exploring opportunities not readily available within their law firm. This is especially relevant when considering that a 2017 NALP Update on Associate Attrition[3] suggested that the cost to replace an associate could range from $200,000 to $500,000. Costs aside, and to preserve a relationship, this is when astute management looks to its clients, alumni, and connections to ask if there is a need or role that could be a suitable fit and makes a match in a manner much like that of embedding law firm talent within a key client organization.

Inherently, and because humans are social beings, we know the value of connections and strong networks. And this is why a continuous sense of belonging – even when people have moved on to other ventures and adventures – creates enormous goodwill along with opportunities and mechanisms to sustain relationships and further nurture mutual growth.

Conclusion

There is absolute and irrefutable truth behind "It's not how you start; it's how you finish", and those words bring us full circle to where we began this discussion on succession.

While there will always be lawyers and other legal services practitioners who look forward to bringing their legal service career to a close and upon retirement jump the gate with abandon, there are many others who fret about who they will become and what they will do after cycling out of active service.

Providing time, space, and planning as well as a graceful and soft landing goes a long way to easing the succession transition. This is equally important when, intellectually, an individual knows that retirement is on the horizon as well as coming to terms with this change physically, emotionally, and spiritually.

Succession planning done well with two to five years of lead time will help prepare the lawyer, their workmates, family members, and clients to transition to a new work–life-relationship balance that is considerate and kind to the individual, and smart business for all concerned.

References

1   2023 American Bar Association's Profile of the Legal Profession,
    www.abajournal.com/files/POLP.pdf
2   https://abovethelaw.com/2021/08/aba-report-lawyers-and-technology-trends-in-
    2021/
3   The Cost of Law Firm Associate Turnover, https://abovethelaw.com/2022/05/the-
    cost-of-law-firm-associate-turnover/

About Globe Law and Business

Globe Law and Business was established in 2005. From the very beginning, we set out to create legal books that are sufficiently high level to be of real use to the experienced professional, yet still accessible and easy to navigate. Most of our authors are drawn from Magic Circle and other top commercial firms, both in the United Kingdom and internationally.

Our titles are carefully produced, with the utmost attention paid to editorial, design and production processes. We hope this results in high-quality publications that are easy to read and a pleasure to own.

In 2021, we were very pleased to announce the start of a new chapter for Globe Law and Business following the acquisition of law books under the imprint Ark Publishing. Our law firm management list is now significantly expanded with many well-known and loved Ark Publishing titles.

We are also pleased to announce the launch of our online content platform, Globe Law Online. This allows for easy search and networked access across firms. Key collections include the Law Firm Management Collection and a brand new AI and New Law collection. Details of all titles included can be found at www.globelawonline.com. Email glo@globelawandbusiness.com for further details and to arrange a free trial for you or your firm.

We'd very much like to hear from you with your thoughts and ideas for improving what we offer. Please do feel free to email me at sian@globelawandbusiness.com. Happy reading and thank you for your time.

Sian O'Neill
Managing director
Globe Law and Business
www.globelawandbusiness.com